WORLDVIEWS

worldviews

A **Christian Response**
to **Religious Pluralism**

ANTHONY J. STEINBRONN

CONCORDIA PUBLISHING HOUSE · SAINT LOUIS

Published 2007 by Concordia Publishing House
3558 S. Jefferson Ave., St. Louis, MO 63118-3968
1-800-325-3040 • www.cph.org

Text © 2007 Anthony J. Steinbronn

Cover photography: Shutterstock®

Manufactured in the United States of America

Library of Congress Cataloging-in-Publication Data

Steinbronn, Anthony J.
Worldviews : a Christian response to religious pluralism / Anthony J. Steinbronn.
    p. cm.
ISBN 0-7586-0598-6
1. Christianity—Philosophy. 2. Religious pluralism. 3. Christianity and other religions.
I. Title. II. Title: World views.
BR100.S756 2006
261.2—dc22

2006019591

2 3 4 5 6 7 8 9 10   16 15 14 13 12 11 10 09 08 07

Contents

Abbreviations   7

Preface   9

1. Major Worldviews on Ultimate Reality and History   17

    Buddhism __ 17
    Confucianism __ 20
    Hinduism __ 22
    Islam __ 24
    Tribalism __ 25
    Modernity __ 27
    A Biblical View of the Nature and Orientation of God __ 36

2. Major Worldviews on External Reality   45

    Buddhism __ 45
    Confucianism __ 47
    Hinduism __ 48
    Islam __ 51
    Tribalism __ 53
    Modernity __ 55
    A Biblical View of External Reality __ 59

3. Major Worldviews on the Nature and Orientation of Man   71

    Buddhism __ 71
    Confucianism __ 73
    Hinduism __ 75
    Islam __ 78
    Tribalism __ 80
    Modernity __ 84
    A Biblical View of the Nature and Orientation of Humankind __ 90

4. Major Worldviews Concerning Truth and Ethics   99

    Buddhism __ 99
    Confucianism __ 103
    Hinduism __ 105
    Islam __ 108
    Tribalism __ 112

Modernity __ 114
Ethics __ 117
A Biblical View of the Basis and Nature of Truth __ 120
A Biblical View of Ethics __ 124

5. Major Worldviews Concerning the Social Location of Religion   129
Buddhism __ 129
Confucianism __ 131
Hinduism __ 133
Islam __ 134
Tribalism __ 138
Modernity __ 139
A Biblical View of the Social Location of Religion __ 142

6. The Orders and Root Metaphors of the Modern
and Postmodern Condition   155
The Synchronic, Cultural Order of Modernity __ 157
The Diachronic, Cultural Order of Modernity __ 163
The Cultural Order of Postmodernity __ 167
The Synchronic, Cultural Order of Postmodernity __ 176

7. Observations and Strategies   181
A Post-Christian World __ 181
Biblical Examples toward Worldview Understanding __ 183
Biblical Insights toward Worldview Construction and Change __ 185
Historical Insights toward Worldview Construction and Change __ 186
Modern, Evangelical Insights toward Worldview
Construction and Change __ 188

8. The True and False Church   201

Conclusion: Saving Formulas of World Religions
and the True Saving Formula   219
Moralism __ 220
Mysticism __ 220
Speculation __ 221
The Saving Formulas of the Major World Religions __ 221
The Saving Formula of the Christian Faith __ 223

Bibliography   229

Acknowledgments   233

Notes   235

Abbreviations

AC	Augsburg Confession
FC	Formula of Concord
LC	Large Catechism
LW	Luther, Martin. *Luther's Works*. American Edition. General editors Jaroslav Pelikan and Helmut T. Lehmann. 56 vols. St. Louis: Concordia, and Philadelphia: Muhlenberg and Fortress, 1955–1986.
Tappert	Tappert, Theodore G. ed. *The Book of Concord*. Philadelphia: Fortress, 1959.

Preface

THE BIG PICTURE

"Come on, Steinbronn, don't you understand the big picture yet?" That was the frustrated question of my eighth-grade football coach during one late summer afternoon. I was trying to figure out what to do as a defensive end. The coach was wondering whether or not I understood the reason for my presence on the football field.

"Containment and tackling is the big picture, Steinbronn. I need a defensive end who can *contain* the surging offensive line and one who can *tackle* the opposing offensive back. *Now* do you understand the big picture?"

The Big Picture of Human Existence

Humans have never been content to simply exist without a rationale for life. Historically, people have turned to their religion for an explanation and a validation for existence. Through religion, believers can have an explanation of *why* things are the way they are and a prescription of *how* things should be done.

Religions have been characteristically monolithic throughout history—they established the worldview of society and had a monopoly over the ultimate authority of individual and collective life. However, in our current era of modernity and postmodernity, where many worldviews coexist and compete as plausible alternatives to one another, the pluralistic situation deprives the competing worldviews of their taken-for-granted status. As a result, no single view has such uncontested legitimacy that a person expressing it authoritatively could be certain of being taken seriously.

Why This Book on Worldviews?

During the Reformation Era there was confusion and debate on three main issues:

1. **Ultimate reality**—who is God and what is God like?

2. **The basis and nature of truth**—Scripture, tradition, and papal decrees versus Scripture alone; truth as uncertain versus certain truth as revealed in the Scriptures

3. **Ethics**—searching for and performing good works that are meritorious in the sight of God versus faith active in love

Similarly, our current situation is, at its root, religious because it deals with our concern with the ultimate meaning of our existence. As a result of the cultural and scientific revolutions of the past three centuries, we have experienced a significantly reinterpreted Western worldview in which everything is questioned and the old formulas that have defined our moral and epistemic boundaries are breaking away, thereby allowing a new *Zeitgeist* (spirit of the times) and *Weltanschauung* (worldview) to take its place. Because of this change in thinking, many people feel that the Christian Church is only one of the many brands in the ideological supermarket without a statement of ultimate belief. Carl Henry laments the meteoric rise of secular humanism and deconstructionist thought in the late twentieth century and identifies it as a "new barbarianism," one born "out of a thoroughgoing humanistic rejection of God and the Judeo-Christian foundation of Western culture . . . [that] claims there is no fixed truth, no final good, no ultimate meaning and purpose, and that the living God is a primitive illusion."[1]

Yet God's people have the opportunity, as they have had in every historical age, to engage in the hermeneutical task of communicating God's truth and authoritative meaning systems concerning the main categories of human existence—truth concerning the nature and orientation of God, the nature of the world around us, the nature and orientation of humankind, the basis and nature of truth, how a person is to live before God and before others, and the role of religion in society.

The Present Shift in Worldviews

Every historical age manifests "the spirit of the times" in its own way. The basic attitude of rebellion and lawlessness toward God remains the same, yet its particular manifestation in each generation must be sought out and understood. The *Zeitgeist* of our current generation is the feeling that we live in a universe that is ultimately silent, one in which "the spirit of the age is autonomous freedom."[2]

Therefore, the real battle Christians must confront with the world spirit of our age is our worldviews. It is a conflict concerning (1) the way we think and (2) the way we live and act. It is a conflict "between two fundamentally opposed views of truth and reality."[3] As a result, we are witnessing a shift in worldviews; a fundamental change in the overall way that people think and view the world and life as a whole.

Cultural Accommodation

In response to this shift in worldview within our culture, author Francis Schaeffer observes that Christians have failed to stand for truth as truth. The Christian community has accommodated to the world spirit of the age by permitting the culture to bend the Bible instead of the Bible bending and convicting culture. Schaeffer remarks that this "accommodation has been costly, first in destroying the power of the Scriptures to confront the spirit of the age; second, in allowing the further slide of culture."[4]

Thus the more the Church becomes one with the modern and postmodern world, the more she is compromised in her message and life. If the Church is to be God's salt and light in this world, she must be faithful in her witness as instruments of His Spirit. The Church must convict the world of its sin and proclaim God's truth in a comprehensive way to a lost world to allow people to "make sense" of God's nature and orientation, of history, of the universe and the world around us, of the nature and orientation of humankind, of truth and ethics, and of the place of religion within culture.

The Desire to Be a Good Soldier

Martin Luther declared that we must stand firm on God's truth:

[I]f I profess with the loudest voice and clearest exposition every portion of the truth of God except precisely that little point which the world and the devil are at that moment attacking, I am not confessing Christ, however boldly I may be professing Christ. Where the battle rages, there the loyalty of the soldier is proved, and to be steady on all the battlefields besides, is mere flight and disgrace if he flinches at that point.[5]

In order to engage in the present battle of the shift in worldviews, a proper understanding of today's cultural context should be essential for *the Church militant*. When Jesus encountered the different belief systems of His day, He was fully aware of what the scribes, Pharisees, Sadducees, and the Samaritans believed about God, man, and the world.

In the same way, in order to engage in the battle where it presently must be fought, a proper understanding of today's cultural context should be essential for *Christians*. We need to seek answers to the following questions: What are the views of the people who live in our age? What is in their minds and what is in their hearts? How can we communicate the truth of God's Word with meaningful application so that minds and hearts are touched?

The Desire to Be a Dangerous Christian

If one is to be a good soldier, one must also become a dangerous Christian. Os Guinness defines a dangerous Christian as one who seeks "to secure and send back information" and to work "from the situation as it is, not from what they would like it to be."[6] A dangerous Christian wants to know where the battle is being fought, what kind of weapons the enemy is using, and how the Word of God can be communicated so His kingdom can come and His will be done through the missionary endeavors of His Spirit-led and Spirit-filled people.

The Desire to Be a Bridge-builder

In his book *Between Two Worlds* John Stott defines the proclamation and missionary endeavors of God's people through the metaphor of bridge-building. A bridge is a structure linking two places together that would otherwise be cut off from each other. Like a collapsed bridge, the unbelieving world has been cut off from God because of its sin and blindness. How can God's people communicate the Word so that all nations might know not only of His judgment but also of His mercy and grace?

In the construction of these missiological bridges, God's people, as instruments of *Missio Dei*,[7] have been called and enlightened by the Holy Spirit to relate the biblical message to their particular culture and to relate God's unchanging Word to our ever-changing world. In order to accomplish this, we need to understand not only our own worldview "but also that of other people, so we can first understand and then genuinely communicate with others in a pluralistic society."[8]

According to Stott, the missionary task is "faithfully to translate the Word of God into modern language and thought-categories, and to make it present in our day."[9] However,

> if we are to build bridges into the real world, and seek to relate the Word of God to the major themes of life and the major issues of the day, then we have to take seriously both the biblical text and the contemporary scene . . . Only then shall we discern the connections between them and be able to speak the divine Word to the human situation with any degree of sensitivity and accuracy.[10]

At the heart of this bridge-building activity is a threefold commitment by those who are serious about making disciples of all nations: (1) studying God's Word; (2) studying one's target culture; and (3) discerning and constructing missiological bridges that communicate the apostolic message into the hearts and minds of the hearer because "faith comes from hearing, and hearing through the word of Christ" (Romans 10:17).

The Highest Missiological Priority

Modern Western culture has been described as "the most widespread, powerful, and persuasive among all contemporary cultures." It is also proving to be the most resistant culture to the Gospel. Therefore, there is no higher priority for the work of God's people than to ask, and keep asking, "What would be involved in a genuinely missionary encounter" between God's Word and this modern Western culture?[11]

FUNDAMENTAL PRINCIPLES OF A MISSIOLOGICAL ENGAGEMENT

There are several missiological and hermeneutical principles that are fundamental to our understanding of engaging modern and postmodern Western culture with the Word of God.

Missiological Principles

In his opening chapter on the *Missio Dei*, Georg Vicedom lays the biblical foundation for the Church's missionary labors by asserting that God would have all people to be saved and come to the knowledge of the truth about Jesus Christ as the world's only Savior. God "is the Protagonist in the mission" and the work belongs to him.[12] God is the one who sends His people into their evangelism labors. God is always present as His people go out into the world, and He builds the bridge and "woos [them] through

His revelation, through His Word."[13] Through His gracious drawing, faith comes from hearing and hearing through the preaching of Christ.

Vicedom explains that God sends His people so humankind can be "placed before the only living God." As the Law and Gospel are proclaimed, former gods and ways of salvation are declared false, for God "alone is Salvation and He alone brings salvation."[14] For believers, the Gospel "becomes a proclamation of rescue, and for those who refuse it a proclamation of damnation."[15]

The scope of God's sending is that His Law and Gospel be proclaimed in the entire "living space of the nations."[16] Every nation presents a unique environment for the proclamation of God's Word; as a result, God's people "will always wear a local costume."[17] In order to accomplish the mission of proclamation, God's people are sent out as pilgrims, "going from people to people, from continent to continent, and thereby ushers in the day of salvation for the nations."[18]

Hermeneutical Principles

The hermeneutic basics of any missionary work are the authoritative position of the Scriptures as the sole source and norm for faith and life, and the justification of sinful people by God's grace in Jesus Christ as the heart of the scriptural message. This justification is received solely by grace through faith in the person and atoning work of Jesus Christ and is communicated to people by God's appointed means of grace, His Word, and the sacraments of Baptism and the Lord's Supper.

WHAT IS A WORLDVIEW?

A worldview is the lens through which we make sense of the world. It is the set of universals through which we make sense of the particulars of life. It is the model of reality that governs a peoples' perception of reality. Each culture has its own worldview or fundamental way of looking at things. Consequently, peoples and nations perceive the world differently because they make different assumptions about reality.

• A worldview includes beliefs about God:

Does God exist? What is the nature of God? Is there only one God or are there many gods? Is God a personal being who can be known, loved, and related to, or is God an impersonal force or power? What is the relationship between God and the universe? Did an eternal, personal, omnipotent God create the world? Are God and the world coeternal and interdependent?

• A worldview includes beliefs about the world:

Is the universe eternal? Was the universe created or has it always existed? Is the world best understood in a mechanistic way or is there purpose in the universe? Are there invisible beings who inhabit the universe?

• A worldview includes beliefs about truth and ethics:

Is knowledge about the world, and the things of the world, possible? Can we trust our senses to give us knowledge concerning the nature of things? What are the proper roles of reason and sense experience in knowledge? Is truth relative to each person or is truth the same for all people? Is knowledge of God possible? If so, how? Can God reveal Himself to human beings?

Are there moral laws that govern human conduct? Are there moral laws that are the same for all human beings? Is morality relative to individuals, to culture, or to historical periods, or does morality transcend these boundaries?

• A worldview includes beliefs about humankind:

Are human beings free or are they pawns of deterministic forces? Are human beings only bodies or is there a human soul? If so, how is the soul related to the human body? Does physical death end the existence of the human being or is there a conscious, personal survival after death? Are there rewards and punishments after death?

Formal Definition of a Worldview

Paul Hiebert, in his book *Anthropological Insights for Missionaries*, provides one of the most comprehensive definitions of a worldview. According to Hiebert, a person's worldview consists of cognitive,[19] affective,[20] and evaluative[21] assumptions. Taken together, these assumptions "provide people with a way of looking at the world that makes sense out of it, that gives them a feeling of being at home, and that reassures them that they are right. This world view serves as the foundation on which they construct their explicit belief and value systems, and the social institutions within which they live their daily lives."[22]

Functions of a Worldview

A person's worldview serves a number of important functions. Foremost, it explains why things are the way they are and how things should be. The worldview adherent, therefore, has emotional security knowing that his or her beliefs are true and certain, and a reliable guide for behavior.[23]

AN INVITATION

The material in this book provides a cursory introduction to the way that billions of people view reality—their worldviews. It is my hope that this introduction will help you be fruitful in your ministry of making disciples of all nations and becoming all things to all people so that you might bring some to a saving knowledge of Jesus Christ. I also hope this material will help you to not be tossed about by all the false teachings that Satan has ignited in this world, but that you may remain built upon Christ, the only true light of the world.

1

MAJOR WORLDVIEWS
on Ultimate Reality and History

Buddhism

Introduction

Buddhism began with a man, Siddhartha Gautama. When asked, "Are you a god?", Gautama said no. "Are you an angel?" "No." "Are you a saint?" "No." "Then what are you?" Gautama answered, "I am awake." While the rest of the world was asleep, one man woke up and became "the Awakened One."

The Four Passing Sights

According to fortune-tellers, Siddhartha Gautama, or Buddha, could take one of two paths. He could either become the greatest ruler in human history or, if Gautama were to see four things—sickness, old age, death, and a monk who had renounced the world—he would give up his earthly rule and discover a way of enlightened liberation for all of humankind.

Gautama's father rigorously secluded Gautama from the life of society from the time of his birth. He gave orders that neither the sick, the old, a dead body, nor a monk could be allowed near the palace. But the gods had other plans for Gautama. One of them would be sent down to earth to assume the shapes that would awaken the young prince to the common fate of all people and to his true destiny as the Buddha.

One day, as Gautama was being driven around the royal park that surrounded his palace, a god took on the disguise of a man who was broken-toothed, gray-haired, and bowed down with age, and positioned himself where Gautama could not avoid seeing him. Gautama asked his charioteer who this stranger was, and, on being told that all men must grow old, he was greatly distressed. On a second journey, Gautama encountered a man racked with disease, covered with sores, and shivering with fever lying by the road. For the first time in his life he came to know how physical illness and misery may be part of man's existence. On a third journey, Gautama encountered a corpse being carried to the burning ground to be cremated and came to know the dreadful fact of death. These three passing sights robbed Gautama of all peace of mind.

Alarmed at Gautama's depressed spirit, his father unsuccessfully sought to cheer him with varied entertainment. The prince remained distraught until he beheld the fourth passing sight, that of a shaven-headed holy man who had dedicated himself to the pursuit of the ascetic life in order to find a release from the apparent futility of life. Gautama thus turned to the life of the shramanas, the life of a wandering ascetic, hoping to find a solution to the problems of human existence. That is, to discover the source of suffering, learn how to eliminate it, and know the freedom from the chain of births and rebirths. Late that same night he took a last look at his sleeping wife and child, then left the palace forever. Putting on simple clothing, he went into the world with nothing but questions.

The Six-year Quest

It is common in Indian spirituality to seek a teacher, and Gautama's first act upon leaving the palace was to seek out two of the foremost Hindu masters of the day in order to discover wisdom from their vast tradition. He learned a great deal, but became convinced that the technique and substance of Brahmanism (Hinduism) would not bring him to the true way of enlightenment.

His next step was to test the extreme bodily asceticism of Jainism. Was his body preventing him from experiencing enlightenment? For five years Gautama underwent severe and strenuous self-discipline in the belief that his mind would become clearer as his body became more disciplined, but this way of life left him skin and bones and without enlightenment.

The Great Enlightenment

Six years of searching along the two most widely recognized roads to salvation known to India, philosophic meditation and bodily asceticism, had yielded no results. Could there be another path to enlightenment? Gautama's quest ended in the solitude of a quiet grove of trees. He sought no help from deities nor did he receive any. He found the answer to his quest from within himself.

Gautama left the ascetics and went on his way until he came to a place on a riverbank where, beneath a bo tree, he began to meditate earnestly after the manner of Indian holy men and resolved that he would remain in meditation until he reached the enlightenment he was seeking. As he meditated, Gautama discovered that his inability to experience release from suffering was due to desire (*tanha*). To eliminate this desire, he had to determine its causes and find a way to overcome it. Legend says that he saw his past lives, fathomed the laws of karma that govern everyone, and finally achieved insight into release from suffering and rebirth.

As he reflected on these things, tradition tells us that Mara, the evil one, tempted him to give up his quest by sending desire in the form of three goddesses and death. Mara assailed Gautama with wind and rain, flaming rocks, and boiling mud, but the missiles became blossom petals as they entered his consciousness. After a night of intense spiritual struggle, all the evil factors that tie men to this imperfect, mortal existence were overcome, and he ended these temptations of Mara by touching the fingers of his right hand to the ground, causing a great thundering roar to arise from the earth so that the evil one had to flee. Shortly thereafter, full enlightenment came to Gautama and he experienced the earthly foretaste of Nibbana. From then on he became the Buddha, the Awakened One.

The Mission

Mara immediately confronted Buddha with one last temptation: He should leave this earthly world and enter Nibbana forever. Who could be expected to understand the truth that he had now discovered? In response, Buddha confidently answered that there would be some who will understand and, with that, Mara was forced to leave Buddha's life forever. Thus, out of compassion for the mass of humankind, Buddha devoted the rest of his mortal life to proclaim the Dhamma, the central truth into which he had "awakened."

Buddha rose from his meditation and went back into the world to communicate his saving truth to others. At the Deer Park in Benares, India, Buddha proclaimed the Middle Path to five ascetics; that is, by avoiding the two extremes of life (pleasure and mortification) the Middle Path grants insight, which leads to wisdom, knowledge, enlightenment, and finally, to nirvana. He challenged them to believe his testimony and to admit that he was an arahat, a monk who had experienced enlightenment, and to try the Middle Path he now advocated. The five ascetics were converted and the Sangha, the Buddhist order of monks, came into being. For forty-five years Buddha traveled the dusty paths of India and preached his message. Each year he spent nine months in the world and three months, during the rainy season, with his monks.

God and History

Buddhism believes that god is ultimately impersonal, for Buddha replaced the Hindu understanding of god, the Brahman, with nirvana—a state where all desire, with its attendant suffering, is extinguished. Negatively, nirvana is the state in which desire has been completely consumed and everything that restricts the boundless life has ended. Positively, nirvana is that boundless life itself—imperishable, immovable, ageless, deathless, a secure refuge and a place of unassailable safety.

For adherents of Theravada Buddhism, god is nirvana, an abstract void. For adherents of Mahayana Buddhism, god is nirvana, but also an undifferentiated Buddha essence.

The Buddhist view of history is cyclic. The wheel of history revolves continuously, without beginning or end, and human fortunes ebb and flow. Each kalpa, or revolution of the wheel, is divided into four quarters, the first of which is decline; the second, stillness; the third, advance; and the fourth, realization. Then the cycle begins again and the wheel commences another revolution.

Confucianism

Introduction

The Confucian view of reality has been the orthodox belief system in China since the Han dynasty (207 BC–AD 220) and has exerted great influence upon Chinese thought and life. Confucianism is not limited to China; it is practiced in Korea, Japan, and other areas in southeast Asia.

Shang Ti

In the earliest Chinese history, the Creator God was called Shang Ti, meaning "the emperor above." He is self-existent and his years are without end. He existed before the heavens and the earth and the sun. He made heaven, earth, man, and all things with their reproducing power. All things are indebted to his goodness.

For forty centuries the reigning emperors of China traveled annually to the border of the country and there, on an outdoor altar, they sacrificed and burned young, unblemished bullocks to Shang Ti, the Heavenly Ruler.[1] During the summer solstice "the emperor took part in ceremonies to the earth on the northern border of the country, while at the winter solstice he offered a sacrifice to heaven on the southern border."[2]

During the first three dynasties of Hsia, Shang, and Chou, from 2205 to 255 BC, the Supreme Heavenly Father, Shang Ti, was venerated. The earliest account of religious worship, found in the Shu Ching, records Emperor Shun in 2230 BC offering sacrifice to Shang Ti. It was during the Han dynasty, however, that polytheistic services began to supplant the original worship of Shang Ti. With the introduction of Taoist and Buddhist concepts, all original meaning of the Shang Ti rituals were lost and these same rituals were used to worship various spirit deities.

Gods

Traditionally, the gods of the Chinese people were, at the local level, gods of the land. Each piece of land had its own god and it was his task to care for the inhabitants of that land. Thus each family, each town or village, each larger division of land, and each state had its own god. There was also a hierarchy in which the gods of the larger units of land were superior to those who ruled over smaller areas of land. These gods were worshiped at earth altars in the open air. In addition to the gods of the land, there were also gods of grain, of rivers and mountains, and of wind and rain.

The Place of God, and of History, within Confucianism

Confucius did not deny the existence of God or gods, but he was agnostic, believing that man cannot know things beyond this world. Moreover, he believed that he did not know enough about God or the spirits to discuss them intelligently. An ideal man, Confucius decided that he could not speak about a god whom he did not know enough to speak about; therefore, in order to be truthful, he remained silent.

As a result, Confucianism is not a theological system because it does not engage in the "study of God." It is a humanist moral system with a focus upon man and his relationship to other human beings. Confucius was concerned with helping men to be better individuals here on earth in relation to others.

History does not seem to be cyclical for Confucianism as it is for other Asian philosophies. Instead, it is linear. Confucianism looks back to the glorious past for wisdom with which to build a glorious future, yet the focus is on the here and now.

Hinduism

Introduction

Hinduism is not so much a religious system as it is a vast complex of belief systems, not all of which are consistent with one another. The earliest strands of Hinduism date back to the year 2000 BC with a mysterious civilization that developed in northwest India near the Indus River. As with many agricultural societies, the religion focused on fertility.

Vedic Gods

The early portions of the Hindu scriptures, known as the Vedas, describe a number of deities who, for the most part, are personifications[3] of natural phenomena, such as storms and fire.[4] Prayers and sacrifices were offered to these gods and an extensive system of priestly rituals and sacrifices were eventually developed that served as a means of obtaining blessings from these gods.

The later writings of the Vedas, called the Upanishads, reflect a significant development in the Hindu conception of the divine. The Upanishads expound the idea that behind the many gods stands one reality that is called Brahman. Along with this idea of a single divine reality, the Upanishads teach that at the core of every person's being (atman) we are identical with Brahman—atman is Brahman. In fact, all living things are Brahman at their innermost core.

Though this monistic (Brahman) or pantheistic (Vedic gods) philosophy provided a comprehensive intellectual understanding of the divine reality, it lacked a strong appeal to the heart. As a result, just before the dawn of the Christian era, a great transformation in Hindu thought occurred with the writing of the Bhagavad Gita. The Gita records a conversation between the warrior-prince Arjuna and his charioteer Krishna (an incarnation of the god Vishnu) in which personal devotion to a deity is endorsed as a way to salvation for all classes of people.

From this time forward, these two major streams of Hindu thought and practice grew and developed—the more intellectual and philosophical stream that emphasized the oneness of all things, and the stream that emphasized personal devotion to a god. The latter stream has predominated among the common people of India to this present day. Chief among the gods so venerated are Brahma, Vishnu, and Shiva.

Brahman

In the Upanishads, Brahman is no longer the magic power of the sacrifice that can move gods and the universe to do what the worshiper desires, but it is a supreme, infinite, impersonal Reality that is present throughout the universe and which constitutes the true identity of every being. Brahman is pure being, pure consciousness, pure bliss. Brahman is ultimate reality and is the single, self-subsisting reality underlying all things. It is "that One Thing" and it is said to be imperishable.

The true Brahman is Nirguna Brahman, Brahman without attributes or predicates. Although we may speak of Brahman in terms of being, consciousness, or bliss, in truth Brahman transcends all our concepts and all our understanding of the divine essence. In the later Upanishads, Brahman becomes more personal. Brahman is no longer "It" but "the Lord." He is Saguna Brahman, Brahman with attributes. This personified form of Brahman is called Ishvara and became known to humanity through three manifestations: Brahma, the creator;[5] Vishnu, the preserver;[6] and Shiva, the destroyer.[7] Beyond these three principal deities, it is estimated that there are 330 million gods in Hinduism.

History

History, for the Hindu, is cyclical as the world goes through endless cycles of creation, growth, decline, and destruction but has no real beginning or end. There are four yugas (each yuga is 4,320,000 years) of increasing creation and destruction. The present world is in its fourth cycle. At the end of this age, Vishnu will descend on earth and will usher in a new yuga, an age of peace and harmony.

Islam

Religious Belief before the Advent of Muhammad

In the days before Islam arose, the religions of the Arabian Peninsula were Judaism, Christianity, Zoroastrianism, and traditional religious practices; a great majority of Arabs during the days of Muhammad worshiped local gods and goddesses. Some of these deities were strictly tribal while others presided over certain geographical areas. It was also a widespread religious practice to venerate certain nature and astral deities, goddesses who were the daughters of Allah and who were related to nature, the moon, and fertility: Al-Lat, Al-Manat, and Al-'Uzza. Allah was the creator, a far-away god who was venerated by Muhammad's tribe—the Quraysh.[8]

There were also lesser spirits, angels, and various sorts of jinn, some of whom were friendly, but many were viewed as hostile and evil. Particularly among the Bedouin, animism existed. Consequently, many places in nature were held with great respect—pillar-like stones and noteworthy rock formations, caves, springs, and wells.

Of special interest in the city of Mecca was a meteor, a black stone believed to have fallen during the days of Adam. From far and near, year after year, people of Arabia would come on a pilgrimage (hajj) to offer sacrifices of sheep and camels near the stone and to circle it seven times, following the direction of the sun around the earth; and hopefully, even kiss the stone in order to receive heaven's blessing. As the years passed, a cube-shaped Ka'ba[9] was erected in honor of the stone and images of local and distant deities were placed inside it. Chief among the idols of the deities placed in the Ka'ba were Hubal and the three goddesses: Al-Lat, Al-Manat, and Al-'Uzza.

Allah Is One

The Muslim understanding of god is that god is one. Muhammad's call to become a prophet was a call to restore monotheism to the descendants of Ishmael who had fallen into the worship of many idols. The central teaching of Islamic theology is tawhid, the unity and singularity of god.

The greatest sin in Islam is shirk, which is the offense of associating partners or companions with god. To suggest that anyone is equal to Allah is the unpardonable sin.

Allah Is the Creator and Preserver of All Things

Allah is the creator and preserver of all things. Everything within creation is dependent upon him for its existence. Yet because of Allah's transcendence, and even though "god is nearer to man than his jugular vein" (Surah 50:16), he remains very distant from man. Allah is never addressed as "Father" or as one with whom one has a close, personal relationship but is addressed, instead, as "Master" as his people are his slaves.

Unlike Christianity, which knows that God the Father has revealed Himself in the person and work of Jesus Christ, the Qur'an speaks only of Allah's many names and of his will for humankind. Allah himself is utterly unknowable and man is not capable of possessing a proper and intimate knowledge of him.

History Is Linear

Muslims see history as moving forward from the day of creation to a day of judgment. The course of history is not free but is predestined with all things being determined by the will of Allah.

Tribalism

Introduction

As we begin the third millennium after Christ, a tribalist worldview may still be understood to be the dominant worldview for a large percentage of the world's population. Stephen Neill estimated that the effective religion of 40 percent of the world's population is animistic, even while they may be identified as adherents of such major world religions as Hinduism, Buddhism, Islam,[10] and Christianity.[11]

Ultimate Reality

First and foremost in Tribalism the Supreme God is said to be the Creator of all things. This belief is common everywhere among tribalist peoples and is reflected in the many names that describe him as Creator, Begetter, Maker, Potter, Fashioner. There are also hundreds of stories that tell about the creation of the world. Some creation stories say that god created the universe out of nothing, but other creation stories indicate that he created things in a certain order, then used their substance to create more things.

God continues to sustain and uphold what he has created so that it does not fall apart, and he is often referred to as Keeper, Upholder, Protector, Preserver, Guardian, and Caretaker. As the caretaker of his creation, god provides life, sunshine, rain, water, and food, and he ensures the ongoing fertility of people, animals, and plants.

There are many images that are used to describe god and his activity among humankind. He is the King who rules the universe and there is no place that is not under his control. He is the Father who has begotten a people whom he protects, provides for, and from whom he hears their prayers and responds to their needs.

In terms of his attributes, god is spirit. He is merciful and kind. He is holy and pure and is the one who receives the sacrifices of people who revere, respect, and honor him. He is all-powerful and can do all things. God never changes and he is not subject to the natural processes of growth, old age, decay, and death. God knows all things and there is nothing that is hidden from him because he is present everywhere. Yet god cannot be explained and he cannot be fully known.

However, while god is acknowledged as the Supreme Being and Creator, man lives out his life amidst a plethora of spiritual beings who intimately impinge upon his daily existence. It is these spiritual beings and spiritual forces about which the average tribalist is most concerned about, and to which attention is given.

History

History is very important in tribes because it is the history that gives definition, meaning, and guidance to the group and to every individual. History is the repository of all that has happened, including the stories, the ancient ancestors, and the customs and laws of society. One of the primary roles of the tribal elders is to tell the tribal histories and to apply their knowledge of the past to current issues. This is one of the reasons why elders are so highly respected and valued; they, having lived longer, have greater access to the wisdom of the past.

Western societies regard time as a commodity that can be wasted if one so chooses, that is always moving forward and that waits for no man. For the tribalist, time is "made" as things happen and it has two dimensions: a past and a present, but virtually no future. Actual time moves backward, rather than forward, and people focus on what has taken place, rather than on the future, because individuals accept that they will join the ancestors of the past when they die.

Finally, much of what occurs in time is repetitive in nature such as sunrise, sunset, and the four seasons. Even man repeats his life cycle as he is born, grows, ages, dies, lives as an ancestral spirit, and then again is born, grows, ages, dies, and lives as an ancestral spirit. Thus historical events come and go in the form of minor and major rhythms. The minor rhythms are found in the lives of people, animals, and plants as they are born, grow, procreate, and die. The major rhythms are events like day and night, the lunar months, the seasons of rain and of dry weather, the flowering of certain plants, the migration of certain birds and insects, and the movement of the heavenly bodies.

Modernity

Origin of the Modern Worldview

In the Western world, up to the end of the seventeenth century, the theistic worldview was clearly dominant.[12] Moreover, "Christianity had so penetrated the Western world that, whether people believed in Christ or acted as Christians should, they all lived in a context of ideas influenced and informed by the Christian faith."[13] This biblical doctrine was preached not as *a* truth but as *the* truth. The Scriptures gave expression to God's will for the world and told the Western conscience how it was to think and live. These truth-claims, derived from the Bible and reflected in the ecumenical creeds, not only formed the religious base of society but its cultural, legal, and governmental bases as well.

Willis Glover, in his research into the origin of modern secular culture, suggests that

> A major turning point in the history of Western consciousness was experienced in the single generation between 1680 and 1715. In this period, for the first time in the history of Christian Europe, a sizable number of sensitive and educated people repudiated Christianity as having any unique and superior truth and took their stand on other ground.[14]

What happened during this period was that man achieved, at least in his own self-consciousness, emancipation from the transcendent God. "The enlightened, with a handful of exceptions, still believed in a God who had created the world, but creation was restricted to a past event, and God was no longer sovereign over it in any active sense. The world, once created, was capable of existing and operating on its own."[15]

The thinkers of the Enlightenment spoke of their age as the Age of Reason. It "was a movement in the intellectual history of Western man in which traditional perspectives and loyalties were abandoned in favor of man-centered alternatives," that is, human beings were made the determiners of reality.[16]

The modern world, in its continuation of this act of emancipation, has cast itself loose from all external authorities, especially the authority of the church, and centered its authority in man himself. Thus in our time secular humanism has replaced Christianity as the consensus of the West and has provided the modern man's view of God and of himself.

What Is Humanism?

There are three basic humanistic principles that provide the core assumptions of humanism: naturalism,[17] anthropocentrism,[18] and scientism.[19]

Humanism is a system whereby man, beginning absolutely by himself, tries rationally to build out of himself, having only man as his integration point, to find all knowledge, meaning, and value. It is "the effort of modern man to find the meaning of his life in his own purposes or in his own communities and historical causes."[20] In a thoroughly anthropocentric world, there is no room left for God.

The world spirit of our age, observed Francis Schaeffer, is autonomous man setting himself up as God in defiance of the knowledge and moral and spiritual truth that God has given. It is freedom from "any restraint, and especially from God's truth and moral absolutes."[21] Humanism, in its most fundamental expression, is man putting himself at the center of everything.

A Modern, Intellectual View of God

There was a time when hardly anyone doubted the existence of God. Or, at least, an atheist was well advised not to display his convictions in public. However, for over a century now, the notion of God has been under attack from various atheistic sources. He may once have been regarded as the source of meaning for all human activities, but today God has been relegated to the attics of history. People still refer to Him from time to time, possibly at Christmas and Easter, and during the "big moments" of life, such as at a baptism, confirmation, marriage, or funeral. But they call Him to mind less frequently as they go through their days or make their decisions. It is a fact that increasing numbers of people live as if God does not exist.

Beginning in the eighteenth century, religion began to lose ground, especially among intellectuals. In the nineteenth and twentieth centuries, religion came to be completely stripped of any meaning and even rejected as harmful to society by the leading intellectual thinkers. The reason that Feuerbach, Marx, Nietzsche, Freud, along with Jean-Paul Sartre and Albert Camus, succeeded in their attack upon God was because they were able to clearly express a state of affairs that many people experienced. What, then, was the thinking of these men in regards to the nature and orientation of God?

LUDWIG FEUERBACH (1804–1872)[22]

For Ludwig Feuerbach, "theology is anthropology."[23] God is merely a product of man's creation and is the mirror of man. God is an imaginary superhuman being, objectifying the higher characteristics of man himself. God is the book where man registers his highest feelings and thoughts, the volume in which he has recorded the best part of himself. Thus this projection we call god tells us very little about god himself, but it tells us a great deal about human beings, their desires, their aspirations, and their hopes. In his god, a man brings forth everything that he is not, but longs to be. Man desires to be supernatural, independent, infinite, and immortal, so he ascribes these attributes to his god.

Also, because the earthly part of man's existence is hard, filled with pain, frustration, and anxiety, and always moving toward death, man longs for a place of unlimited fulfillment, perfect happiness, and everlasting life, so he constructs a god who will grant these human hopes in a world to come. For Feuerbach, man is the beginning, middle, and end of religion.

KARL MARX (1818–1883)[24]

Why is there a God? Why have human beings invented God for themselves? Why do they want him to continue existing? They keep him because they need him to help them cope with an unbearable life of suffering and oppression.

Karl Marx accepted Feuerbach's view that God is nothing other than the objectification of human traits in a very, very big way. Marcel Neusch summarizes the thinking of Marx in his treatise *Contribution to the Critique of Hegel's Philosophy of the Right*, by noting that "God is the 'reflection' of man, but a magnified reflection that images forth man as completed and fulfilled."[25] But Marx added a new twist by suggesting that belief in God springs from man's situation of being frustrated and oppressed at the hands of the ruling economic class.

Religion, then, is "the sigh of the oppressed creature, the heart of a heartless world."[26] Religion expresses the great longing of its adherents for another world in which this world's evils are overcome. The task for those who are enlightened is to help human beings get rid of the false images of themselves that religion offers them, images of weakness and dependency, and become people of this earth and ready to seek the fulfillment of their lives here in an earthly hope and a revolutionary consciousness. Human emancipation requires the rejection of every form of transcendence, and it is the role of the modern state to help people build their own futures without God and without religion.

FRIEDRICH NIETZSCHE (1844–1900)[27]

Nietzsche, with his famous and startling statement, "God is dead," announced that the God of Christianity had lost his power to impart meaning to human life. God came into existence when men were bewildered by the forces surging up in nature and looked for an explanation somewhere outside of nature and of man. But it is the lot of all gods to die, and the Christian god is no exception. What caused his death? Nietzsche claims that God must have died of old age or people just got tired of putting up with him.

Man must, instead of listening for the voice of an imaginary god, experience his freedom, affirm his powers and potentialities, develop fully all his capacities, and assert his will to power without any arbitrary restrictions. "I beseech you, my brothers," writes Zarathustra,[28] "remain faithful to the earth and do not believe those who speak to you of otherworldly hopes!"[29]

It was the view of Nietzsche that Christian morality is slave morality that sucks all the love and hope out of life. The Christian man is like a camel-spirit that devotes all its courage and life to accepting, in an uncritical way, whatever absolutes are set before it. It accepts the heaviest of moral burdens; thus the Christian man is a reverent animal! In its place, Nietzsche advocated the overman, the individual who purposefully disregards traditional values and who is a creator of values; for those who would create must first destroy. Only then can man be open to a new world, writing his own tablets and defining good and evil as he pleases.

With the light of God gone from the world, man's only light is to be shed by the lanterns that he himself sets aglow. There are no enduring principles and no binding norms. Man has nowhere to turn but to himself, for the lion-spirit refuses to be led. The lion-spirit, in contrast to the camel-spirit, wants to be its own teacher and to live in its own space, but he is like a wild beast who can only roar, destroy, and tear to pieces everything that is conventional and lawful. The lion-spirit can only sit amidst the ruins that he has made; a creator must come.

Yet in order for a creator to come, the lion must undergo a metamorphosis and be changed into a child. This child is the person who is open to a new world, who has torn himself from the old values, and has decided to no longer live a life tied to any pre-existing world. He can define good and evil as he pleases.

SIGMUND FREUD (1856–1939)[30]

Freud's understanding of god is based upon a primeval event in which several sons, resenting their father's prohibitions regarding sexual relations with his females, unite to kill and eat their father. However, once the murder has been performed, their love and admiration for their father causes them to become overcome by guilt and remorse. Thus in the Oedipus conflict[31] Freud sees the source of religion. The murder of the father made civilization possible, but the trauma of killing the father inflicted guilt upon humankind as the father took up residence in their consciences.

For Freud, then, a man's personal relationship to his god is based upon his relationship to his physical father. God is nothing else but an exalted and magnified father. Just as a child remains helpless while he is growing up and is in constant care of a protective father, so man invents an all-powerful father who fulfills his needs for safety, protection, love, and comfort. But there is more: religions are man's way to counteract his sense of guilt as all religions are attempts to resolve the guilt caused by the primal murder.

Jean-Paul Sartre (1905–1980)[32]

The existential ideas and writings for Jean-Paul Sartre dominated the intellectual circles of continental Europe after World War II. They struck a responsive and powerful cord in the soul of a period that was marked by a sense of existential emptiness.[33] As one representative of his generation, he thought and lived human life without God. In Sartre's view, God is simply a ridiculous answer to the questions: "Why am I here? Why do I exist?" If God is anything at all, he is the shameless onlooker, the indecent fellow who violates consciences.

According to Sartre, all thought about reality is grounded in the fact that man exists. Thrust into existence, all alone, man begins with no fixed or given human nature; rather, he makes himself what he becomes by his free decisions and actions, from moment to moment, and he is nothing other than the choices that he makes. It is up to the individual to give life meaning because it certainly does not come from any supernatural source. Yet this is an awesome responsibility for man because he exists in relation to other men and his choices affect their lives. Man, conscious of the seriousness of his responsibility, experiences dread realizing that he might make some bad choices in life. Thus man is condemned to be free and he must use his freedom to make choices, some choices that are good and some choices that are bad. It is a long, cruel affair to live this freedom to the full without God and in complete responsibility for one's decisions.

The apparent absurdity of this kind of life is illustrated by Sartre in his play *The Wall*. Pablo, a captured freedom fighter, is given the choice between being executed or having his life spared on condition that he reveal the whereabouts of Ramon, another freedom fighter. Pablo feels there is no reason to protect Ramon because his life has no more value than his own and, even though he knows where Ramon is, he chooses to die rather than reveal the location of Ramon. Pablo's sole concern is that he die respectably, so, as a joke, he informs his captors that Ramon is hiding in the cemetery and awaits death as soon as his lie has been discovered. In the meantime, however, Ramon quarrels with his cousin and flees to the cemetery where he is promptly taken captive. When Pablo learns why he had not been shot, his head spins and he laughs until tears come; first, at his own relief at escaping death and, then, at the bizarre meaningless-ness and absurdity of man's ethical choices.[34]

ALBERT CAMUS (1913–1960)[35]

The senselessness of man's life is also the dominant motif of the writings of Albert Camus. His novel *The Plague* is not only a terrifying day-to-day account of the effects of the bubonic plague upon the life of a North African city, it is a portrayal of Camus's conception of human existence and of God. As the order of this world is shaped by death, the best course in life is to refuse to believe in a God who permits children to suffer and die and to struggle with all our might against death, without raising our eyes toward heaven where God, if He does exist, sits in silence and indif-ference toward the needs of humankind.

THREE MAJOR REASONS FOR MODERN UNBELIEF

First, some reject God because He is merely the projection of man's high-est qualities. He is viewed as the One who provides another world in the life to come, a place where all will be overcome. Some people feel the harsh reality is that there is no loving God and there is no imaginary world to come.

Second, people argue that the notion of an active and present God is judged inconsistent with a scientific understanding of reality. As more and more of the universe has been explained by natural science, God has been rendered increasingly unnecessary and useless as a source of expla-nation. Also, there is no objective evidence for the metaphysical assertion that there is a God who has created and continues to sustain this world and its inhabitants.

Third, the notion of a compassionate and caring God is incompatible to many in a world where two World Wars and an Auschwitz have taken place. Additionally, it is hard for some people to believe in a caring God when a carload of people die at the hands of a drunk driver, children die of cancer even after months of intense chemotherapy, infants die sud-denly in their cribs, and terrorists take down immense skyscrapers filled with people while a nation watches in grief-filled agony.

Modern Interpretations and Understandings of History

The Cyclical View

The cyclical view of history is that the historical process is like a revolving wheel. The pattern of growth, from birth to maturity to death, is projected upon the historical process, or that the yearly rhythm of the seasons has played itself out in the world of men.

For example, for Chinese historiography, "people turned to history to discover examples of how to live upright lives" according to the "mandate of heaven" and "of warnings of what errors to avoid."[36] For the Indian, history was measured by four yugas, and each yuga marked a decrease in human longevity, morality, and happiness. After the whole cycle is completed, the universe dissolves into chaos and a new cycle begins. Since all things take place exactly as they did before, what matters is not great deeds but escape from history.

The Christian View

The Christian view of history has three traditional aspects: (1) that God intervenes in history to accomplish His purpose of judgment or mercy, (2) that God guides history in a straight line with the entire historical process under His guidance and activity as He works out His divine plan, and (3) that God will bring history to a conclusion when Jesus comes to judge humankind. On that day, humankind will be divided into those receiving eternal punishment and those receiving eternal life.[37]

History is the drama of fall and salvation, a history of non-recurring actions accomplishing the purposes of God for humankind. History can be properly understood by seeing that God and Satan have been engaged in a great conflict over the will of each person since the Garden of Eden. In the one kingdom, Satan reigns and holds captive to his will all those who have not been wrested from him by the Spirit of Christ. In the other kingdom, Christ reigns and people are translated in His kingdom by the grace of God. As a result of this conflict, there are only two kinds of people: those who belong to and follow Satan and those who belong to and follow Christ.

The Marxist View

The Marxist view of history is based upon the understanding that the historical process is created by man as he labors to satisfy his basic needs. All history represents a struggle to improve the human condition. Despite progress in this regard, various social institutions continue to perpetuate exploitation; this is the price humanity pays for progress in an unjust society. The history of society[38] is a history of struggles between the ruling class and the oppressed masses, between those who exploit and those who are exploited. The end result is that the whole content of history is a history of economic antagonisms moving toward a final world revolution and world renovation.

History as the Record of Man's Improvement in His Human Condition

From Augustine until the eighteenth century, a providential[39] knowledge of history was the key to understanding historical events. World history, as well as every local history, was written from this perspective.

However, the Enlightenment was responsible for the emergence of a new school of thought regarding the historical process; that of human progress.[40] As history progresses, it moves through three stages that govern all human and social development: a theological[41] or fictitious stage, a metaphysical[42] or abstract stage, and a scientific[43] or positive stage. This final stage would be led by an elite group of individuals who would use scientific methods to solve human problems and improve social conditions.

Human history is, therefore, the account of the improvement of the human condition[44] from barbarism to civilization and the record of man's evolution[45] as he moves upward to higher and higher forms. It is the firm conviction that it is the very nature of reality that progress must take place. Enlightened humankind, with their immense powers that science and technology have given to them, will create the new heavenly city on earth.

The View of Historicism

Historicism is a reaction against the idea of progress. Instead, its central idea is that each nation lives out a distinctive culture and that it is the historian's task to understand and record the customs and beliefs of a nation through its historical process. Historicism is the conviction "that nations are the chief actors on the historical stage."[46]

A Biblical View of the Nature and Orientation of God[47]

What Does It Mean to Have a God?

Martin Luther's concise answer to this question is that God is the one to whom I look to for every good thing in this life, and the one who provides for me in times of urgent need. Simply stated, a god is whatever your heart cleaves and on what it relies.[48]

The Living God Is the Triune God

There is one divine essence who is called God and who is truly God. Yet there are three Persons in this one divine essence, equal in power and eternal: God the Father, God the Son, God the Holy Spirit.[49] The Christian faith can be summarized in this confession: "I believe in God the Father, who created me; I believe in God the Son, who redeemed me; I believe in the Holy Spirit, who sanctifies me." [50]

The First Article of the Apostles' Creed deals with God the Father and explains how He made all things. The Second Article explains how the Son set us free. In order to accomplish our rescue, the Son became a human being, was conceived by the Holy Spirit and born without any sin of the Virgin Mary, suffered, died, and was buried to make amends for the sins of all people—not with money, but with His own precious blood. Afterward, He rose from the grave, put an end to death, and swallowed it up, and finally ascended into heaven, taking command at the Father's side. As a result, the devil and all other powers have been made to submit to Him and are under His control. Finally, on the last day, He will separate those who believe in Him from the devil and all who reject Him. The Third Article of the Apostles' Creed deals with the Holy Spirit and explains how He makes us holy. This Good News of humankind's rescue takes place as the Holy Spirit uses the Word and Sacraments to bestow God's grace to His people. His baptized people are the Church with Christ as their Savior. The Spirit then uses the pastor and the people of God to be His spokesmen to spread the Word among the peoples of the earth.

It is these three articles of faith that distinguish and separate us Christians from all other peoples on the earth. Although many other religions believe in and worship one god, they do not know what their god thinks of them. Such revealed knowledge of the Triune God is given to us through the Son "who is a mirror of the Father's heart. Apart from him we see nothing but an angry and terrible Judge."[51]

Why is it so difficult for us to possess revealed knowledge of God? To help us understand this fundamental human condition, Martin Luther uses an analogy from a childhood game—"Blindman's Bluff." Man's unregenerate reason[52] plays this game with God, calling God what *is not* God and not calling God what *is* God. For reason seeks God and roams through countless errors in its own endeavors in an effort to find Him, but all these are undertaken in vain. "We shall be safe from these dangers if we follow that visible form or those signs which God Himself has set before us. In the New Testament we have as a visible form the Son of God on the lap of His mother Mary. He suffered and died for us, as the Creed teaches."[53]

In Christ's incarnation, God Himself would be present yet hidden and concealed. He became manifest in this way so that He could be seen, touched, and apprehended without the beholder being consumed by His majesty. For "God does not deal with us in accordance with His majesty but assumes human form."[54] Yet this flesh is "flesh permeated with God. Whoever encounters this flesh encounters God."[55]

In Christ, God is found, and outside of the person born of Mary He is not to be found. His incarnation is the only view of the divinity permitted and possible in this life. Therefore, if you want to encounter God, you must first seek Him under a mask, that is, the incarnation of the Son.

Jacob's Ladder: the Mystery of the Incarnation

According to Luther, the dream of Jacob, whereby he sees a ladder set upon the earth with its top reaching into heaven with angels descending and ascending, reveals the mystery of the incarnation in which the same Person is both true God and true man. As the angels descend, they adore the Child at His mother's breasts and on the cross.[56] As they ascend, they behold the Son of God from all eternity. If they look down, they see God and the Divine Majesty subject to demons and to every creature.

Thus, the ladder is the wonderful union of His divinity with our flesh. His flesh must be true flesh born from a flesh outstandingly sinful and contaminated by sin.[57] In support of this assertion, Luther recalls the story of Tamar becoming pregnant by Judah through the shameful act of incest.[58] Yet, if He is to be the Savior of the world and not just of the Jewish people, Gentile seed must be mixed with that of Abraham so that He would be born of and for all people. Therefore, His father's side was Israelite, but His mother's side included "Gentiles, Moabites, Assyrians, Egyptians, Canaanites."[59]

The Savior of the world must be descended from the accursed, lost, and condemned seed and flesh of a fallen humankind. According to nature, Christ has the same flesh that we have; but in His conception the Holy Spirit came and overshadowed and purified the mass that He receives from the Virgin so that He might be united with the divine nature and be without sin and corruption.[60]

In summary, this Promised Seed would be a human being whom people could see, touch, hear, and feel. This Jesus is indeed the "right Man"[61] who was set plainly before our eyes. At the same time, He must be true God because only the Son of God is able to reveal God.[62] This Blessed Seed and Promised Savior does all of this so that all of humankind might be saved and know the way to heaven. "It is most certainly true," writes Luther, that

> no one enters heaven but the Son of God and of Mary. He is the only one who knows the way. But He does not keep this knowledge to Himself; otherwise He would have remained in heaven. No, He shows us the way by means of His dear Gospel, so that we will be born anew of water and of the Holy Spirit, adhere to His testimony, and believe in Him. And then we, too, will ascend into heaven, not by virtue of our own person but by nestling up and pressing close to Him who alone ascends into heaven.[63]

Finally, this dream was given to Jacob that he might understand that His incarnation would take place in a definite place. This very place of Jacob's dream would become the place of Christ's earthly ministry as He preached, healed, and taught. Luther even went so far as to maintain that He was crucified at this very place, slept in the sepulchre, and rose again where the angels ascended and descended.

Later in Jacob's life, the Lord came to him and wrestled with him until daybreak. He came in this way, suggests Luther, so that Jacob and his descendants would know that one day He would dwell among them in human flesh and that only by faith can anyone accept the revelation that He is true God and true man.

38

God Is an Omnipotent, Omnipresent, Active God

God is the Lord—a zealous and mighty one. "He alone is powerful, is all-sufficient of Himself, has power over everything, needs no one's help, and is able to give all things to all."[64] God's omnipotence is the power at work in everything, and without Him nothing would exist and nothing would happen. God is always active everywhere, energizing each created thing to act according to its nature. He would be a ridiculous God "if he could not and did not do everything, or if anything took place without him . . . [for] we have not been made by ourselves, nor do we live or perform any action by ourselves, but by his omnipotence."[65]

Thus all things depend upon the will of God alone who works all things by His own eternal Word. For He alone moves, makes to act, and impels by the motion of His omnipotence all those things which He alone created; they can neither void or alter this movement, but necessarily follow and obey it, each thing according to the measure of its God-given power.

This being true, all human works and endeavors have a certain and definite time of accomplishment that lies beyond human election. "God determines when and how an act will occur, and unless the time, the God-fulfilled moment is present, man affects nothing."[66] All things take place by necessity, which even pagan authors acknowledge: "The wise men of those days were well aware of what fact and experience prove, namely, that no man's plans have ever been straightforwardly realized, but for everyone things have turned out differently from what he thought they would."[67]

Luther, in *The Bondage of the Will*, outlines his understanding of the foreknowledge of God and of the importance of knowing that God necessitates all things. What man thinks is done contingently is actually done immutably and necessarily according to the will of God, who knows what He wills and wills what He knows. For if He wills what He foreknows, His will is eternal and changeless because His nature is so. "From this it follows irrefutably that everything we do, everything that happens, even if it seems to us to happen mutably and contingently, happens in fact nonetheless necessarily and immutably, if you have regard to the will of God."[68]

And yet, as He works all things, He "wants to govern the world through angels and through human beings, His creatures, as through His servants, just as He gives light through the sun, the moon, and even through fire and candles."[69]

God no longer wants to act in accordance with His extraordinary or . . . absolute power but wants to act through His creatures, whom He does not want to be idle. Thus He gives food, not as He did to the Jews in the desert, when He gave manna from heaven, but through labor, when we diligently perform the work of our calling.[70]

Because God works all in all, He moves and works of necessity even in Satan and the ungodly. Yet He works in them as He finds them, according to what they are by nature. That is, because they are inclined away from God and are evil, and since they are mightily moved by the activity of God's omnipotence, they do only what is evil and opposed to God. The righteous, however, are moved by the Spirit of God and co-operate with God because through them He lets the fruit of the Spirit grow: the putting to death of the flesh, love to others, and humility before God.

History Depicts Two Kingdoms at War with Each Other

Since the Garden of Eden, God and Satan have been engaged in a great conflict over man's will for the soul of every individual. God wants man to be saved from the power of sin, and the devil wants man kept in it. The world and its god cannot and will not bear the Word of the true God, and the true God cannot and will not keep silent. Out of that invisible combat come all the agony and anxiety that enter into human life. There is no middle ground between the kingdom of God and the kingdom of Satan.

In the one kingdom, Satan reigns and holds captive to his will all those who have not been wrested from him by the Spirit of Christ; nor does the devil "allow them to be snatched away by any powers other than the Spirit of God, as Christ testifies in the parable of the strong man guarding his palace in peace [Luke 11:21]. In the other Kingdom, Christ reigns, and His Kingdom ceaselessly resists and makes war on the kingdom of Satan. Into this Kingdom we are transferred, not by our own power but by the grace of God, by which we are set free from the present evil age and delivered from the dominion of darkness."[71]

As a result of this conflict, two kinds of people are derived from the two sons born to Adam. The whole course of history is the intermingling of two peoples, going back as far as Abel and Cain. Cain appears to be saintly, but he is wicked and does not believe the divine promise concerning the Blessed Seed. Abel, on the other hand, does "not rely on his own worthiness, his sacrifices, or his work, but on the plain promise which had been given about the woman's Seed."[72] Just as God has a people who belong to Him, so has His opponent. "Just as the Church is the body of Christ, so there is a similar human and historical *corpus* belonging to Satan."[73]

Nations are Extinguished by God because of Their Sins

History is the account of God exalting those of low degree and putting down the mighty as He sends one nation against another nation. "The history of the nations is the history of an active God who metes out death as He wills."[74] The nations are God's delegates to destroy other, godless nations as they serve as His agents of wrath.[75]

> We see in all histories and in experiences that He puts down one kingdom and exalts another, lifts up one principality and casts down another, increases one people and destroys another; as He did with Assyria, Babylon, Persia, Greece and Rome, though they thought they should sit in their seats forever.[76]

"It is profitable to observe and note such examples . . . [since] they are intended to frighten the proud and to humble us, that we may learn that our lives and all that we have depend on God's approval, who is disposed to give grace to the humble but to destroy the proud. . . . All times, all courts, and all countries abound with such examples. . . . Blessed, therefore, are those who take note of such things and, admonished by the examples of wrath, humble themselves and live in the fear of God."[77]

Thus the historical process moves along these interpretive lines. God allows the ungodly to become[78] great and the mighty to exalt themselves. Then He withdraws His power from them and lets them puff themselves up in their own power alone.[79] "When their bubble is fullblown, and everyone supposes them to have won and overcome, and they themselves feel safe and secure and have achieved, then God pricks the bubble and all is over." They "do not know that even while they are puffing themselves up and growing strong they are forsaken of God, and God's arm is not with them."[80] Therefore, God tolerates even the wicked and sinners to declare His great goodness and tolerance, but only up to the time that has been set for punishment. When their iniquities have been filled up, He withdraws His hand. Therefore, men must either live under the shadow of God's wings and trust in His mercy, or they must perish.

Hence, history is the stage upon which God executes His judgments and the stage in which He works His salvation. Nations do not perish of themselves, but God wipes them out because of their sins. When the ungodly world has scorned both tables of the Law, God, who is a consuming fire and jealous, comes to inflict judgment. "The Flood came, not because the Cainite race had become corrupt, but because the race of the righteous who had believed God, obeyed His Word, and observed true worship had fallen into idolatry, disobedience of parents, sensual pleasures, and the practice of oppression."[81]

As God works in history, He is disguised[82] and concealed, as a man may hide behind a mask. All events in history, all persons of history, and all forces of history are masks of God. There is no war that He does not wage, no peace that He does not conclude, no man whom He does not lead; thus every action derived from God gives unity and meaning to history. Because man is the instrument of God, every person is denied the luxury of being a spectator.

A significant force in history is the interpretive principle that history is made and changed by great men[83] or heroes. These men are used by God to bring about the necessary changes of the existing political and social conditions. "God, who guides their hearts and gives them courage, also gives success to the works of their hands."[84]

Leah's Story: God Remembers Those of Low Degree

One of the familiar stories of the Old Testament is the story of how Laban deceived the deceiver, Jacob. Jacob's first choice in marriage is Rachel. But Laban did a spousal switch on Jacob's wedding night and Jacob ends up marrying Leah before he is permitted to marry Rachel. But in this story, as the married lives of Jacob, Leah, and Rachel play themselves out, the historical principle of God exalting those of low degree and putting down the mighty is demonstrated.

> For no one cares about [Leah]; no one has any regard for her, not even Jacob himself. But the LORD alone must look into the matter, must break and crucify Jacob's disposition, and must also break Rachel's spirit. The Lord has regard for her, and in such a way that He crucifies Jacob's love and disposition, and breaks Rachel's pride by *exalting Leah*, who is odious and despised. In this way one must learn that *God sees and governs all things* but has regard solely and in a special manner for what is despised and cast off.[85]

For it is certain, notices Luther, that He does not want the great ones to boast or to be proud, but He also does not want those who are downcast to despair, for they have One who has regard for them and receives them. Thus God has regard for and blesses the downcast, weeping, odious, and saddened woman; but He humbles the one who is proud. The Lord closes Rachel's womb and lets her be barren, which was no smaller cross. Indeed, it was death itself for Rachel, but He honors the one who is cast off by opening her womb and making her a mother. "For this is the title and the most proper definition of God: *He who regards the despised and the humble.*"[86]

Temporal and Spiritual Authority

In his treatise *Temporal Authority: To What Extent It Should Be Obeyed,* Luther dealt with the divine origin and nature of spiritual and temporal authority. These two authorities constitute "the two means by which God rules the world. For man they represent the two different ways in which he encounters the divine reality."[87]

Therefore, as long as the world endures, both authorities are to remain. The spiritual one is to produce an evangelical righteousness and the temporal is to bring about external peace and prevent evil deeds. Luther's sober admonition is for each sphere of authority to operate within its own boundaries: spiritual authority is to give its life in the proclamation of the Gospel and the salvation of souls, and temporal authority is to give its life in the protection of good and the punishment of evil.

Heilsgeschichte

Throughout the nineteenth century in Germany it was generally assumed by theologians that the Christian faith could be defended only by interpreting it as an expression or symbol of the religious experience of Christians (and not upon the Christ revealed in Gospel history). In response, the Heilsgeschichte theology understands the apostolic witness as the testimony of "actual witnesses to the acts of God in history for the sake of us and for our salvation."[88]

The Heilsgeschichte theology takes the biblical proclamation of God's action in history, not as mythology, not as pre-scientific way of announcing existential truth, but as ultimate and factual truth. This truth, of course, is not verifiable by the techniques of scientific historical investigation because the action of God, precisely because it is God's action, is not accessible to man's scientific enquiry. God cannot be made an object of scientific investigation as if He were one factor amongst many within the universe; He cannot be detected by telescopes and microscopes, or yet by critical historiography.[89]

2

MAJOR WORLDVIEWS
on External Reality

Buddhism

Introduction

Buddhists believe that all phenomena in the universe belong to the realm of anicca, which is impermanent and perpetually changing. These phenomena are the result of ever-changing, interrelating skandhas that lend present but transitory form to existing phenomena and, in the case of some creatures, consciousness. Nothing, neither man nor beast, neither mountain nor star, has its own separate and distinct existence.

Nothing remains the same. The whole of the cosmos that presents itself to sense perception is in a state of continual flux. All things, without exception, are impermanent and pass away in the course of time. All human experiences are only processes of change and decay, of becoming and passing away, of appearing and disappearing.

Thus, for Buddha, nothing in the universe is exempt from the gnawing tooth of time and change. Wherever he looked, Buddha found change and decay, and he concluded that universal flux is the law of the universe; people only mistakenly consider things to be permanent.

The Universe

Buddhism teaches that the universe evolved out of the dispersed matter of a previous universe, and when our current universe is dissolved, its dispersed matter will, in time, give rise to another universe in the same way.

Karma–samsara

The universe is one of lawful order in which events are governed by laws of cause and effect, and whose consequences extend from one incarnation to the next, and so on endlessly. The Hindu believes that man must strive obediently through many successive incarnations to achieve emancipation; Buddha, however, believed that by the Four Noble Truths and the Eightfold Path there is a power strong enough to break the chains and liberate the believer immediately in a single moment of insight.

The Chain of Causation

Human suffering comes out of a twelve-linked chain[1] of causes and effects; the first two links belong to the previous life, the middle eight to the present, and the last two belong to the future existence.

The first and most fundamental cause of suffering in every individual is ignorance, which is carried over from one's previous life and manifests itself from the start. From birth, a person's individuality expresses itself through the mind and senses and makes contact with other selves and other things. These, in turn, give rise to sensation. These sensations cause desire or craving, and from these cravings one clings to existence. The clinging to existence entails the process of becoming, which brings on a new state of being different than the one preceding it. Finally, this new state of being experiences old age, death, grief, suffering, and despair.

As one is successful in eliminating attachments to this illusory existence, then the effects of karma will have nothing to attach themselves to, which releases the individual from the realm of illusion and ignorance. At that moment of enlightenment, the person achieves the state of nirvana. Nirvana means "blown out," suggesting that the fires of desire have been extinguished. Nirvana is also believed to end karma and rebirth after the present life. To reach nirvana, Buddhism recommends following the Eightfold Path.

Confucianism

The World was Created by Shang Ti

According to rituals connected with the ancient Border Sacrifice,[2] Shang Ti is the god who created the universe. Shang Ti decreed and called into existence heaven, earth, and man. The first human being on earth, according to ancient Chinese writings, was a fully-grown adult man who was made from the soil of the earth and became a noble man. As a noble man, he resembled his creator by living out his existence in filial love toward others.

Again, according to the ancient Chinese writings, Shang Ti gave a garden to the first couple and made them his tenant landlords of this garden. The garden became their imperial domain. Two important trees were located on a mountain in the center of the garden and the first couple went there to be with Shang Ti and receive his blessings.

A Chaotic and Turbulent World

Confucius lived during a time when the social order that had glued China together was dissolving. During the period of the Warring States, from 500 BC–221 BC, the authority of the central government collapsed and the country descended into anarchy. The chief question of his day was, "How can society be saved?"

Confucius believed that heaven had given him a job to do and that the meaning of his life was to carry out this divinely given assignment, that is, to reestablish good order. Confucius sifted through the records of remote antiquity and drew out those principles that he felt worthy of promotion. He believed that excellent individuals would keep society harmonious and a harmonious society would nurture excellent individuals. His primary models of virtue were Yao and Shun, emperors of the early legendary period.

An Orderly World

Confucius believed that the world really exists and operates according to fixed natural laws. This predictable order can be messed up if things are not spoken of and understood according to their proper names. Consequently, Confucius taught the necessity of describing external reality in accordance with the truth of how things really are (the Rectification of

Names). If the way we "name" things is not correct, then the relationships among human beings in society will not be administered properly, order and harmony will not flourish, and justice will be arbitrary.

Good Government Rests upon Te

Under the Shang dynasty, Te (or power) was the force that permitted a ruler to overcome his enemies, win the support of the people, and achieve influence. With the Chou dynasty, Te became the power that the king used to bring justice and harmony to the land; it was believed that if the king had Te, it would flow out to the people.

Thus "the chief power of government in Confucius's view is not so much its power to enforce its will by law, but its moral power, that is, its power to influence the inner character, the heart and soul of the people by its own moral example."[3] For example, if the ruler is a man of Jen, one who embodies compassion for others, the people will become a people of Jen, also showing compassion for others.

The Family Foundation

If a society is to be healthy, the family life of its citizens must be healthy. Of all the relationships in society, the chief relationship is between father and son. The father must love his son and care for him, and the son must respect and obey his father. A father who neglects his son may achieve many personal goals and accomplishments in this life, but because he failed in his relationship to his son he cannot claim to be truly human. Similarly, a son who does not respect his father may become quite famous and successful in the eyes of some, but he, too, is not truly human.

Yin and Yang

The doctrine of Yin and Yang was formulated during the fourth century BC. This is the view that everything in nature is composed of two different but complementary cosmic forces. All objects in the universe are made up of both. Evil and disharmony result from an imbalance between them.

Hinduism

The Configuration of the Universe

Hindus consider Brahman to be an impersonal force of existence, therefore the universe is viewed by most Hindus as being continuous with and extended from the being of Brahman. In other words, the universe is a manifestation of the one Brahman. The Rig Veda[4] records that the origin of the universe emerged from a division and cosmic sacrifice of Purusha.[5]

Maya

One of the significant teachings in the Upanishads is that the material world is less than real. Although the external world is a manifestation of the one Brahman, this knowledge of the external world as it is experienced through the senses is an illusion, for we fail to see the "Really Real" behind it all. Thus all phenomena, which are accessible to the human senses, are illusory (maya) and only the hidden Brahman is utterly real and imperishable.

The Law of Karma

The word *forgiveness* is rarely found in Hindu writings. Everything is neatly tied up in the doctrine of karma. The ordinary Hindu regards forgiveness as impossible because the iron law of karma cannot be broken. Everyone gets exactly what he or she deserves, and creates the future into which he or she will move. In essence, a person reaps what that person sows.

As a teaching, karma is the moral law of cause and effect. The universe is strictly just and impartial. The present condition of a person's life is an exact product of what one has wanted and receives from the past; and equally, present thoughts and actions determine one's future. Consequently, each individual is wholly responsible for his or her present condition and, in the future, will have exactly what he or she is now creating.

Samsara[6]

Every human being must eat the fruit of ancient deeds until they are wholly consumed, that is, each person must atone for his or her wrongful deeds. If there has not been time in one's life for a debt to be fully paid, then the one who has incurred the debt must be born again upon the earth, and so on endlessly until the uttermost part has been paid.

Moreover, the only way for the atman[7] to get back where it belongs is through samsara, the ever-revolving wheel of life, death, and rebirth. We are reaping in this lifetime the consequences of the deeds we committed in previous lifetimes. A person's karma determines what kind of body, whether human, animal, or insect, into which he or she will be reincarnated in the next lifetime. A person's atman may begin as a worm, then through death and rebirth it goes higher and higher in the order of things until it becomes a human being. Once the atman becomes a human being, he seeks to attain higher social classes by following his dharma, that is, his duty to do certain things according to the class that he is in.

The goal of one's life is liberation (moksha) from the wheel of life, death, and rebirth. One way to release the soul is through yoga, a discipline that causes one to hold his or her passions in check so that the atman can escape the cycle of death and rebirth and be joined with Brahman. Within Hinduism, there are three other ways to achieve liberation from samsara: the way of works by following one's dharma; the way of knowledge as taught by the Upanishads; and the way of devotion to a god such as Brahma, Vishnu, or Shiva.

Caste System

The Aryans were an active, warrior-dominated, patriarchal society who entered India between 2500 and 1500 BC. When the Aryans conquered a people, they generally placed the conquered people, whom they called servants, below their own classes of priests, warriors, and commoners. In addition to this rigid caste system, the foundation of many Hindu beliefs and practices were introduced into Indian culture through the poetry and oral traditions of the Aryan priests.

Every individual who has any claim to the Hindu name is a member of one of the many castes into which society is divided and is pledged to its rules by his membership. Each caste has its own traditions and its own way of living, that is, what its members wear and what they eat, the words they use, the gods they worship, and the manner in which they order their social relationships. The Bhagavad-Gita teaches that it is better to carry out the duties of one's class badly rather than those of another class well.

There are four basic castes or social classes within Hinduism. At the top of the social pyramid are the Brahmins, the priestly caste. Second in rank are the Kshatriyas, the warriors and rulers. Third in rank are the Vaishyas, the peasants, merchants, and craftsmen. Fourth, and last in rank, are the Shudras, the laboring class. Outside of the caste system are the untouchables, groups who are judged to be altogether exterior to the scope of Hindu society. Burke further details that the "chief duty of the Brahmin is to study and teach, to sacrifice, and to give and receive gifts. The duty of the Kshatriya is to protect the people. The duty of the Vaishya is to breed cattle and till the earth, to pursue trade and to lend money. The duty of the Shudra was to serve the other three."[8]

These four castes are subdivided into several thousand smaller divisions. Each caste or subcaste lays down detailed rules for its own members regarding food, marriage, and occupation. This caste system is considered sacred and forms a part of the cosmic order. Within this cosmic order, the person who lives the good life will be reborn into a higher caste while the one who has lived an evil life will return to a lower caste.

Islam

Allah as Creator

The world was created by the will of Allah and everything is subject to him. This world is real and there is nothing that happens in life except by the decree, will, and power of Allah.

The Ka'ba

At the time of Muhammad, Mecca was already a center of religious pilgrimage. Located in Mecca was a black meteorite that had fallen to earth during the time of Adam and was venerated because it was believed to have been sent from heaven. A squarish shrine, the Ka'ba, was constructed to contain it. "By Muhammad's day, as many as three hundred and sixty religious images of tribal gods and goddesses had been placed within the Ka'ba, and tradition tells that twenty-four statues, perhaps associated with the Zodiac, stood around the central square of Mecca."[9]

The Ka'ba is the center of the world for Muslims. It is "the navel of the earth," the first creation of Allah and the beginning of all creation. Muslim cosmology locates it on the same axis with seven Ka'bas directly above it in the seven heavens. These Ka'bas, earthly and celestial, are directly below the throne of Allah, which is encircled by angels even as the Meccan Ka'ba is encircled by pilgrims.

Angels

Muslims believe one function of angels is to serve as mediators between god and man due to god's transcendence. For example, Allah sends Gabriel, as his go-between, to bring the words of the Qur'an to Muhammad.

A second function of angels is that they are needed on the day of judgment in order to present a record of one's life. Islam teaches that every person has two recording angels constantly with them: the one on the right side records good deeds and the one on the left side records evil deeds. There is a third angel who is present in the mosque to record all who attend worship.

Jinn

Jinn are spiritual beings who were created from fire 2,000 years before Adam. They are invisible, but can become visible at will. They also are capable of assuming animal or human forms as well as sexual relations. There are good and bad jinn. They do die and they are in need of salvation just like human beings. Because Islam rejects original sin in humankind, it is the jinn (and a devil called Iblis) who are held accountable as the instigators of evil thoughts and intentions.

The Muslims do believe that Iblis's function it to obstruct the plans of Allah and to lead humankind astray from him. Iblis is called "the whisperer" in Surah 114 of the Qur'an because of his work of encouraging and tempting humankind from obeying Allah. It is Muslim belief that Iblis was cast out of heaven and put under a curse because he refused to prostrate himself before Adam after Allah had created him.

Heaven and Hell

Hell, for the Muslim, is the place of eternal punishment and torment to which all infidels will be condemned. According to the Qur'an, it is a place of graphic torment and presents a strong warning to reject evil and to obey the message of Muhammad.

Heaven is the eternal abode of bliss in the presence of Allah. Islamic paradise is characterized by physical pleasure. It is a place of extreme luxury, filled with wonderful fruits and rivers of wine, honey, and milk. It is also a place of rampant sexual activity and wine that never intoxicates.

Dar al-Islam and Dar al-Harb

For the Muslim, the world is divided into two realms. One realm is called Dar al-Islam and refers to the community subject to Islam and obedient to Muhammad's message. All others are the disobedient, the infidels, and become the Dar al-Harb, which means "the house of war." It is the work of the Muslim to propagate and establish Allah's virtues in the world and to wipe evil off the surface of the earth.

Government is to be guided by the Qur'an and is to establish and enforce Islamic law. There is no need to distinguish between "religious law" and "civil law," between the sacred and the secular. The whole world is to be a mosque and unified under its submission to the will of Allah.

Tribalism

God Is the Creator

It is generally believed in Tribalism that the universe was created by the Supreme God. In many tribal languages, the name for the Supreme God even means "creator". There is no agreement, however, on how the creation of the universe took place.

The Nature of the Universe

In many tribal societies it is believed that the universe is two-tiered, with the heavens and the earth.[10] Some tribal peoples, though, believe that the universe consists of a three-tiered creation with the heavens, the earth, and the underworld.

This universe is considered to be unending in terms of both space and time appearing to have no edge or end to its space. In terms of time, the symbol of the circle is used to express the eternity and continuity of the universe.

The Universe Is Orderly

Tribal societies view the universe as orderly and, as long as this order is not upset, there is harmony. The order in the universe operates at several levels: (1) there is order in the laws of nature; (2) there is moral order at work among people, given by the Supreme God, so that they might live good lives, know what is good and evil, and live in harmony with one another; (3) there is a religious order in which God and other invisible beings are actively engaged in the world of humans; and (4) there is a mystical order that governs the universe as shown in the practice of traditional medicine, magic, witchcraft, and sorcery.

The Universe Exists for Man

Because tribal man thinks of himself as being at the center of the universe, he focuses on what the world can do for man and how man can use the world for his own good. Within this created order certain things have physical uses; some have religious uses, such as ceremonies, rituals, and symbols; and other things are used for medicinal and magical purposes.

The Universe Is Inhabited by Many Kinds of Spirits

According to the tribal view of external reality, the universe is composed of visible and invisible things. It is commonly believed that, besides the Supreme God and human beings, gods and spirits also populate the universe.

Following the Supreme God is a host of lesser gods. These gods possess specific powers and inhabit places such as rivers, mountains, forests, oceans, and so on. Some gods exercise power over human affairs such as business, marriage, and death, whereas other gods oversee nature through storms, rain, and so on. These gods expect homage from human beings and often serve as mediators between man and the Supreme Being.

Whereas nature spirits[11] have no direct physical kinship with people, human spirits once were ordinary men, women, and children. Human life does not end at the death of an individual, though, so spirits live beyond death. Most of these human spirits are not remembered in their human form, so people often fear and dislike them because they do not know their capability. However, the human spirits of those who were once leaders, heroes, warriors, clan founders, and other outstanding men and women continue to be respected by the clan and community and are actively remembered through story, ritual, and song.

Those who are recently deceased are remembered by their families and friends for up to four or five generations. These living dead are the spirits that matter most on the family and individual level and they are considered to still be part of their families. "They are believed to live close to their homes where they lived when they were human beings. They show interest in their surviving families and, in return, their families remember them by pouring out portions of their drinks and leaving bits of food for them from time to time. The living dead may also visit their surviving relatives in dreams and visions."[12] When people face sickness and misfortune, the cause may be attributed to the living dead unless magic or witchcraft is involved.

The Universe as an Integrated Organism

The world in which humankind finds itself is seen to be an integral organism, throbbing with life and animated by spiritual beings and forces that pervade everything. This spirit world, though usually invisible, is just as real as the physical world. Because these spirits have a greater knowledge of things typically hidden to man or beyond his realm of experience, they become important sources of information and insight. These spirits can possess, or be induced to possess, people for the purpose of divining causes of sickness or for prophesying about unknown things. They, especially the lesser spirits, are subject to manipulation or control by men using the appropriate formulae.

In addition to spirit beings, there exists in the external world a power that is called "mana." Mana can be possessed and it can also be made to adhere in objects such as charms or medicines. To use it, people must first acquire this power and, when they do, they can perform supranatural deeds, such as causing someone to become ill, lightning to strike, crops to fail, or putting up a barrier of protection from other magic, and so on. The mechanism for manipulating this impersonal force is magic or witchcraft. It is usually employed by specialists who have been given, or who have acquired, the secrets that enable them to harness this mana power for either good or evil through the making of charms, fetishes, or medicine.

Modernity

Nature Is the Sum of All Things

One of the core assumptions of humanism is naturalism, which is the view that nothing exists except nature, and nature comprises the whole show. According to naturalism, only matter exists. This present universe did not get here because a supernatural god created it, but because its present form just happened as a result of chance events way back in time. Naturalism assumes that the matter that makes up the universe has never been created but has always existed.

Naturalism presents nature as a dynamic evolutionary process with a very long history of emergent novelty, characterized throughout by chance and natural laws. It is the view that everything began with an impersonal beginning—the impersonality of the singularity—and then everything, including the life of man, comes forth by chance from that. Thus the total configuration of the universe is the combinations of the impersonal, time, and chance.

Big Bang

Following the publication of ideas from Albert Einstein in the 1920s, the majority of scientists have accepted the view that the universe started with an explosion of some dense particle. The idea of the big bang hypothesis is that billions of years ago all the matter of the universe was concentrated in a single mass. Then that very dense mass exploded and caused all of the other parts of the universe to expand into space continuously.

Initially, the universe was so hot that the four fundamental forces (electromagnetic, strong nuclear, weak nuclear, gravity) were unified as one force and existed as high-energy radiation. This expansion quickly yielded a temperature cool enough for gravity to separate, followed soon by the separation of the strong nuclear force. The separation of these two forces released enough energy for a sudden inflation in the size of the universe. Since that inflationary period, the universe has gone through three stages: the particle stage lasted ten seconds, the radiation stage lasted 500,000 years, and the present matter stage has lasted 15 billion years. This dispersed matter collected into galaxies from which the stars began their life cycles. Around the second or third generation, stars and planets formed. On at least one planet, our earth, life occurred.

The Universe Is a Closed System

The early scientists of the modern period, including Galileo, Copernicus, Francis Bacon, Johannes Kepler, and Isaac Newton, believed that the world was created by a reasonable God and that we could discover the order of the universe by reason. However, as the methods of science achieved greater and greater triumphs in explaining the nature of external reality, the picture derived from the Bible was replaced by a quite different one.

Scientists in the seventeenth and eighteenth centuries continued to use the word *God*, but they pushed Him more and more to the edges of their explanatory systems. It was not a shift of newly discovered facts, however, but a shift in presuppositions grounded in an emerging worldview of materialism and naturalism. In this new worldview, the only kind of reality[13] is the observable and testable kind that exists as occurrences in space and time. This reality conforms to the mathematical-mechanical world of natural laws, within a closed system of cause and effect, and can be totally explained by mathematical and experimental analysis.

God had become the "God of the gaps" where He was still used as a hypothesis. At best, God's involvement "was conceived of as an almighty clock-maker who had constructed the clockwork universe of the scientists, wound up its mechanism, and left it running."[14] He was a sort of Prime Mover standing behind the processes of nature.

Step by step, however, scientific knowledge expanded to the point where the gaps became closed. Finally, scientists in this stream of thought moved to the idea of a completely closed system[15] that functions only by cause and effect. There is no need for a transcendent Being above or outside the cosmos.

The Universe Is a Machine

Despite all the new discoveries in physics, such as quantum physics and Heisenberg's uncertainty principle, the vision of the real world in the mind of ordinary people is one derived from Newtonian physics. In the Newtonian physics, "reality was composed of billiard-balls, whether little ones (atoms) or big ones (planets), all obeying the Newtonian laws of motion."[16] Prior to Newton, people assumed that God's providential hand kept the moon, planets, and stars in place. The Newtonian laws led to a view of the universe as a great machine whose parts were subject to universal laws that behaved in perfect order and harmony.

Thus, with the rise of modern science, nature itself began to be seen as a machine. However, because the universe is such a gigantic machine, with parts so numerous and processes so complex, we have only been able to achieve a partial and fragmentary understanding of how it all works.

The Universe Is a Single Plane of Existence with No Purpose

Since the seventeenth century, science has been committed to an understanding of the universe and its workings that is non-teleological. The consensus of the Western world in the twentieth century is that the universe had an impersonal beginning. In much modern thought, everything began with the impersonality of the atom or the molecule or the energy particle, and then everything—including man—comes forth by chance from that.

The universe, observed Diogenes Allen, has been reduced to a single plane of existence where there is no sense of mystery and wonderment. Instead, the universe operates on the assumption of a simple, mechanistic, billiard-ball-type causality. All the movements of tangible bodies, whether they be celestial, terrestrial, human, or atomic, and all the changes in the visible world can be explained without reference to purpose and in terms of efficient cause. The real world disclosed by science is one governed not by purpose, but by natural laws of cause and effect; to have discerned the cause of something is to have explained it. Consequently, "there is no reason to involve purpose or design as an explanation" because everything is to be understood and explained by the laws of physics and in terms of their causes.[17] Every particular event happens because some other event has happened.

Transcendence has been Reduced to a Rumor

According to Peter Berger, we live in a world in which transcendence has been reduced to a rumor.[18] It is rumored that He might exist, but who knows? There appears to be no eternity and no eternal perspective. All reality seems to be restricted to the here and now.

In a large measure, significant findings and theories derived from natural science have made it difficult to believe that there is such a being as a transcendent God. For example, Copernicus and Galileo, by discovering the structure of our solar system, displaced the earth as the center of the universe. Newton's theory of gravity challenged the daily providence of God. Darwin's theory of evolution challenged the entire doctrine of creation, especially the special nature of humankind as created in God's image. Freud challenged man's entire religious experience and judged it to be psychological and illusionary. As science evolves, the credibility of notions of a causally intervening God has been increasingly reduced.

Consequently, modern man lives in a de-created world. But if the Creator has been removed from His creation, asks Eugene Nida, who or what can man look to for answers about his past, present, and future?[19]

The Reigning Plausibility Structure

The coherence of every society depends upon a set of what Peter

Berger calls "plausibility structures."[20] These are patterns of belief and practice accepted within a given society that determine which beliefs are plausible to its members and which are not. The reigning plausibility structure within modern, Western society is that there is no way that God could enter and act in this closed system. The premoderns understood the events in their lives to be the result of interventions by supernatural beings (God, good and evil angels) whereas modern people believe that these same events are to be understood in terms of natural laws that are unchanging and mathematically fixed in space and time.

A Biblical View of External Reality

The First Article of the Apostles' Creed

Luther begins his teaching on the First Article of the Apostles' Creed by inquiring what kind of being God is and what kind of things He can do. Because the source and nature of external reality is clear, Luther can say, "If you were to ask a young child, 'My boy, what kind of God have you? What do you know about him?' he could say, 'First, my God is the Father, who made heaven and earth. Apart from him alone I have no other God, for there is no one else who could create heaven and earth.' "[21]

Everything that is, was created by God. In the beginning, and before every creature, there is the Word and it is such a powerful Word that it makes all things out of nothing. This "omnipotent Word, which was with God from the beginning" and which was "uttered in the divine essence,"[22] was heard spoken only by God Himself.

This Word is God (John 1:1–14) and yet is a person distinct from God the Father. Therefore there is a distinction of persons[23] in the creation account. It is revealed to us that God is the speaker who creates heaven and earth out of nothing; not by making use of matter but solely by His Word.[24]

> This Word is God; it is the omnipotent Word, uttered in the divine essence. No one heard it spoken except God Himself, that is, God the Father, God the Son, and God the Holy Spirit. And when it was spoken, light was brought into existence, not out of the matter of the Word or from the nature of Him who spoke but out of darkness itself. Thus the Father spoke inwardly, and outwardly light was made and came into existence immediately.[25]

Creation Is Ongoing

This created universe, in all its grandeur and immensity, is neither self-sufficient nor self-sustaining. God has not created the world as though He were a carpenter "building a house that He could walk away from when finished and let stand the way it is. On the contrary, He remains with and preserves everything He has made. Otherwise it would neither hold up nor endure."[26]

Not only does God actively preserve His creation, His creative labors are ongoing for He did "not create everything at once, but bit by bit, without stopping."[27] In the beginning whatever God wanted to create, He created when He spoke. The fruit of His creative speaking can be seen daily as we "see the birth into this world of new human beings, young children who were nonexistent before; we behold new trees, new animals on the earth, new fish in the water, new birds in the air. And such creation and preservation will continue until the Last Day."[28]

So God, through His Word, extends His activity from the beginning of the world to its end. For when He once said, "be fruitful," that Word is effective to this day and preserves nature in a miraculous way; "For the growth of the fruits of the field and the preservation of various kinds, this is something just as great as the multiplication of the loaves in the wilderness."[29] "For whatever the world has, exists and is preserved by the Word of God."[30]

All His Works Are Words of God

"God, by speaking,[31] created all things and worked through the Word, that all His works are some words of God, created by the uncreated Word."[32] In His creatures we recognize the power of His Word and how everything came into being: the human race, the animal race, the fish and the birds.[33] So God, through His Word,[34] extends His creative activity from the beginning of the world to its end.[35] But He did cease creating new classes,[36] and species of creatures, as is reflected when God said that He "rested from all His work (Genesis 2:3)."

A Special Place for Humankind

After God had prepared the heavens and added light, He prepared a piece of ground and made it fit for the habitation and activity of humankind. Even before the human being was created, God provided an attractive dwelling place where man found a ready and equipped home.[37] The heaven is as a roof; the earth is the flooring; the animals are the possession wealth; seeds, roots, and herbs are food. Man himself has been created and is the lord of these. Nothing is lacking. All this generosity is intended to make humankind recognize the goodness of God and live in the fear of Him.

The Tree of Life

The "tree of life" was created by God in order that man, by eating of it, might be preserved in full bodily vigor, free from disease and free from weariness. The tree of life was given to humankind to preserve perpetual youth. By eating of this tree, man would never have experienced weaknesses associated with old age. This tree would have been a medicine to keep man's body forever healthy and strong.[38] Likewise, "the remaining trees of Paradise were all created for the purpose of helping man and maintaining his physical life sound and unimpaired."[39]

The Tree of the Knowledge of Good and Evil

The tree of the knowledge of good and evil was so named from the event that lay in the future, the fall of humankind through sin and rebellion. Adam was to demonstrate his reverence and obedience toward God by not eating anything from this tree. It was a tree of divine worship and the place for man to bear witness through his obedience that he knew, honored, and feared God.[40]

Therefore, this "tree is put before Adam in order that he may also have some outward physical way of indicating his worship of God and of demonstrating his obedience by an outward work."[41] If Adam had obeyed this command, he would never have died; for this tree was not deadly by nature, it was deadly only because it was stated to be so by the Word of God. This one tree "killed Adam for not obeying the Word of God, not indeed because of its nature but because it had been so laid down by the Word of God."[42]

The Earth Is Cursed because of Adam

Because of the sins of Adam and Eve, the earth, which is innocent and committed no sin, is nevertheless compelled to endure a curse and not bring forth the good things it would have produced if man had not fallen. Before sin, the sun was brighter, the water purer, the trees more fruitful, and the fields more fertile.[43] The human body was healthier than it is now. Proof of this lies in the length of life among people before the flood.[44] The earth also produces, since the fall, many harmful plants that it would not have produced. This can be seen in the fields where, along with the good seed that is sown, weeds quickly spring up and seek to choke the seed.[45]

Thus the earth, along with the farmer, must work hard to yield those things that are necessary for our life. The earth "would gladly produce the best products,[46] but it is prevented by the curse which was placed upon man because of sin. . . . This curse was made more severe through the Flood, by which all the good trees were all ruined and destroyed, the sands were heaped up, and harmful herbs and animals were increased."[47]

Creation Is a Sign of His Goodness and Activity

Among the many miracles of God's continuing activity and goodness is that the sun shines, fire warms, water furnishes fish, the earth yields grain, cows calve, and hens lay eggs. In these daily acts of goodness, "the face of God shines forth in all His creatures because they are works of God and testimonies of God's will and presence."[48] The upright recognize these wonders and they give to God the honor He deserves as their Creator and Preserver. The majority of people, on the other hand, are ignorant of these works of God. They are so

> permeated with them as an old house is with smoke; they use them and wallow around in them like a sow in an oats sack. Oh, they say, is it marvelous that the sun shines? That fire heats? That water contains fish? That hens lay eggs? . . . You dear dolt Hans, must it be insignificant because it happens daily? If the sun ceased to shine for ten days, then its shining would surely be regarded as a great work. If fire were to be found only in one spot in the world, I judge that it would be esteemed more precious than all gold and silver . . . If God created all other women and children of bone, as He did Eve, and but one woman were able to bear children, I maintain that the whole world, kings and lords, would worship her as a divinity. But now that every woman is fruitful, it passes for nothing . . . God showers man with such great and rich miracles but man ignores them all and thanks God for none . . . Only the eyes of the upright . . . accord God the honor [as they] recognize God's wonders.[49]

Thus, "the entire world is full of miracles. But clear eyes are needed; otherwise, the most excellent works of God become ordinary because of their frequent occurrence, and the glory of the Word and the works of God is obscured."[50]

Creation Serves as a Sign and as an Instrument of His Wrath

Creation not only functions as a sign of His activity and goodness but also serves as a divine instrument in "the execution of the judgments of God's wrath."[51] The judgments of God's wrath reside in nature so that all God needs to do is withdraw His protective hand and the judgments are in effect.

For example, "to the disobedient Jonah, who was seeking to escape God and from doing His will, the sailors and the storm were instruments of divine wrath, the means by which God struck at his conscience."[52] As his conscience was convicted by the Holy Spirit through the storm's fury, and the accusing question "What is this that you have done?" by the captain and the sailors (Jonah 1:10), Jonah understood that he was being confronted by the living God in all that was happening to him.

> Jonah no longer thought that the sailors threw him into the sea. No, "You [the Lord] threw me into the deep, into the heart of the sea" (Jonah 2:3). And he did not say, "the sea's waves and billows rolled over me," but rather, "Your waves and Your billows," because he felt in his conscience that the sea with all its waves and billows served God and His wrath, to punish sin.[53]

Another example of a living creature who functions and serves as God's instrument of wrath would be the "hangman." The hangman is a mask of God's wrath "against the wicked, and a source of comfort for the good and oppressed."[54] A second example from nature would be the rainbow, which serves as a sign that "preaches to the entire world with a loud voice about the wrath which once moved God to destroy the whole world."[55]

Or whenever Adam and Eve, along with their descendants, dressed for the day, they were reminded of the fall, their lost bliss, and of God's judgment upon sin. They were clothed, "not in foliage or in cotton but in the skins of slain animals, for a sign that they are mortal and that they are living in certain death."[56] Through this daily ritual of dressing and undressing, they were to be constantly afraid of sinning, to repent continually, and to sigh for the forgiveness of sins through the Promised Seed.

"Collectively and individually, are not all of them [thorns, thistles, water, fire, flies, fleas, and bedbugs] messengers who preach to us concerning sin and God's wrath, since they did not exist before sin or at least were not harmful and troublesome?"[57] "Therefore, whenever we see thorns and thistles, weeds and other plants of that kind in a field and in the garden, we are reminded of sin and of the wrath of God as though by special signs."[58]

Not only in churches, therefore, do we hear ourselves charged with sin. All the fields, almost the entire creation is full of such sermons, reminding us of our sin and of God's wrath, which has been aroused by our sin. Human nature, observed Luther, has need of such reminders and signs, for we readily forget the things that are gone by, both good and bad.

God's Ordered Power

God is an active God, and as the almighty One He preserves and governs His entire creation through the power and effectiveness of His Word. God could act in accordance with His absolute power, but He works primarily through His created orders[59] of church, home, and government. His working is not limited to these three orders, though, for all creatures are His masks and disguises, and are "the hands, channels, and means through He bestows all blessings."[60]

In and through these orders, God seeks to protect the human race against the devil, the flesh, and the world.[61] They are the means through which God seeks to govern His world for humankind's good and to reveal, in a daily fashion, His care and goodness toward humankind.

These three social classes have been given the command not to let sins go unpunished.

1. Parents, who maintain discipline in their home.
2. Governmental rulers and officers, who bear the sword and exercise authority that both willing and unwilling citizens obey the laws of the land.
3. The Church, who governs solely by the Word of God.

As Luther explains, "In the church one seeks the glory of God; in the state, peace; and in the household, the rearing of children."[62]

If some are remiss in their calling and do not enforce punishment in earnest, Luther warned, "they take the sin of others upon themselves. [For example,] if a father does not censure the sin of his children, it becomes the father's own sin. [Likewise,] the sins of adulterers, murderers, and usurers are the sins of the citizens who commit them; but if the government does not punish them . . . those personal sins of the individuals become the sins of the city . . . and public disasters are always wont to result from them."[63]

Marriage

Marriage is "the inseparable union of one man and one woman, not only according to the law of nature but also according to God's will and pleasure."[64] Marriage is the divinely instituted and lawful union of a man and a woman in the hope of offspring, or at least for the sake of avoiding fornication and sin, to the glory of God; but if no children result, you should nevertheless live content with your spouse and avoid promiscuity. The ultimate purposes of marriage are to obey God and to be a remedy for sin,[65] "to desire, love, and bring up children to the glory of God; to live with one's wife in the fear of the Lord; and to bear one's cross."[66]

Marriage is, according to God's will and design, "the source of human society and of the human race"[67] as men and women are lawfully united and bring up their children to serve God and their neighbor.[68] The world views marriage as insignificant and nothing else than sexual intercourse,[69] kisses and embraces,[70] observed Luther, despite the impending harm to those who dishonor marriage through promiscuous relationships: "Property is squandered, bodies are damaged by serious diseases, God is provoked to inflict horrible punishments, and, worst of all, states and households are destroyed."[71] But it is a lawful union not only of bodies, but also of hearts, and was created by God for lifelong, inseparable union and companionship.

The Church

In the command not to eat from the tree of the knowledge of good and evil, "we have the establishment of the church before there was any government of the home and of the state; for Eve was not yet created." Moreover, the Church is established without walls in a very spacious and delightful place. In this order, God desired humankind to know that He was created for a relationship with God, and for immortality and eternal life with God.[72]

God's Church is wherever God's Word[73] is proclaimed and heard, for it is God's Word that establishes the Church. The Church is made up of those who have the promise and believe it, and the Church exists only where the Word is and where there are people who believe the Word. "Therefore, those who want to be the people of God or the church must have the Word of Christ, that is, the promises of God;" and they must believe and keep them.[74] The Church is "not a people that should be judged on the basis of a large number, of size, of wisdom, of power, of wealth, of prestige;" no, it is a people of promise who believe the promise.[75]

Therefore, "[d]irect your step to the place where the Word resounds and the Sacraments are administered, and there write the title THE GATE OF GOD."[76] As we gather at these external places to hear a sermon delivered through a human voice and gather at temples built of stones and wood to receive the Sacraments, we must always remember that here is the house of God and the Gate of heaven; for God Himself is speaking.

Luther identified two primary ministries for the Church in this world. First, this Church would be a hospital for healing in which the people who feel sin, death, and the terrors of an afflicted and wounded conscience are healed.[77] Second, "the Church is the house of God which leads from earth into heaven."[78]

Therefore God, in order to accomplish these purposes of bringing comfort to wounded consciences and of leading people into the kingdom of heaven, has always preserved for Himself a people who would cling to the Word, would be the guardian of religion and of sound doctrine in the world, and bring His love and comfort to people terrified and troubled by their sins. But, if His people are to possess a true knowledge of Him and to be able to share a Gospel message grounded in God's revelation, they must be pupils of Christ and of the Scriptures that testify of Him. They must be a people, writes Luther, who sit at the feet of Jesus and listen to His Word.

The Church is also a wall against the wrath of God as the Church sustains the world through its teachings and prayers. Until the Day of Judgment, the Church "grieves, it agonizes, it prays, it pleads, it teaches, it preaches, it admonishes" much like the preacher Noah before the days of the great flood.[79] It is a hidden reality to the non-Christian that the nations of the world are preserved through the daily prayers of God's people, for God is patient, hoping that all might come to salvation; also, the world is preserved so that His people might have a place of lodging in this life.

Within this assembly of believers, the duty of the pastor is to instruct God's people concerning the will of God, admonish them to lead a holy life, strengthen them in their faith, fortify their hope of future blessing, and pray with them. His ministry is done so "that they might learn that God is merciful and benevolent toward the human race, since He promises a Seed by whom His wrath is to be removed and the eternal blessing that was lost in Paradise through sin is to be restored."[80]

The Home

After the Church was established, God brought the ordered power of the home into existence when Eve was created and given to Adam as his companion.[81] In this ordered power, God, through the instrumentality of husband and wife, bestows the blessing of physical life as children are born to them, even though He is able to make a human being out of clay as He did with Adam.

"God has placed in woman His creation of all human beings."[82] All kingdoms, empires, prophets, and fathers have had their origin from this source. Yet how great is the wickedness of the human nature, grieved Luther, that so many girls were in his day, as in ours, preventing conception by killing and expelling their "tender fetuses."[83]

In the management of the household, father and mother are the instruments through which the house and household affairs are governed. Parents should not only feed and look after the material needs of their children but, above all, bring them up to praise and honor God and to communicate the hope of the Promised Savior.[84] In the home, children are to honor and love their parents because their parents have been given to them by God and stand in for God.

In summary, the family is the nursery not only for the state but also for the Church and the kingdom of Christ. It is God's design that, through the father and mother, He Himself governs in the home. It is God's deepest concern that we bring up people who will be of service to the world by helping it know God, live in harmony with Him, and produce all kinds of fine qualities in the struggle against evil and the devil.

Government

Before the fall, "There was no need of civil government, since [man's] nature was unimpaired and without sin."[85] If man "had not become evil through sin, there would have been no need of civil government."[86] With the sinful condition of humankind, God foresaw that there would be a great abundance of evil in the world and that an outward remedy would be required to hold sin in check by the bonds of laws and penalties.

These laws are not inventions of man. They describe accurately how things are and are indicated in the moral codes of all nations and peoples. They order the relationship of parents and children and they order the relationships of life. There are laws about sexual relationships and laws that protect truth and property. Laws of humankind attempt to codify the law of God that confronts men in the very structure of the world.[87]

This is the foremost function of government, to hold sin in check, and it is the role and scope of government to punish all the sins of the Second Table. With this hedge, these walls, God has given protection for our life and our possessions.[88] Hence, the most important duties of government are to uphold the law, to maintain peace, and to preserve justice.

Before the flood, God reserved all judgment for Himself and did not permit one human being to kill another human being as the examples of Cain and Lamech show (Genesis 4:14–15; 23–24). "It was for this reason He Himself finally exacted punishment from the wicked world by means of the Flood when He saw that the world was daily becoming more and more corrupt."[89]

After the flood, God shares His power over life and death with man, provided that the person is guilty[90] of shedding blood. Whoever does not have the right to kill human beings, that is, anyone who is not a magistrate or hangman, God makes liable not only to His own judgment but also to the human sword. Therefore, if such a guilty person is killed, he is said to have been killed by God[91] through the instrument of the "hangman."

Good terms for persons of the government are *saviors* or *healers* as they "cure the abscesses and ailments of the body, put thieves and robbers to death, and defend their people against acts of violence"[92] through holy justice.[93] For God wants evildoers to be condemned and the godly defended.[94] Without these masks, peace and discipline could not be preserved.

Here we also have the source from which stem all civil law and the law of the nations. If God grants to humankind power over life and death, surely He also grants power over what is less, such as property, the home, wife, children, servants and fields. All these God wants to be subject to the power of certain human beings in order that life might be preserved and the works of the devil be restrained and abolished.

However, if government does not punish the sins of the citizens who commit them, warned Luther, "those personal sins of the individuals become the sins of the city or public sins, and public disasters are always want to result from them."[95] Therefore, government is God's rod, as it were, and the servant of God to execute His wrath on the wrongdoer;[96] and, without the law of civil government, we would accomplish little in our sermons.[97]

A Fatherly Face Perceived

In these three orders, it is God's will that we perceive a Fatherly face as others patiently rule over us.[98] Through His ordered power, God desires to be graciously seen and known as He works all things through His creatures, accomplishes His purposes and will in the world,[99] and meanwhile remains present yet hidden.[100] Therefore, God's winsome face "must be recognized in His promises, in the sacraments, and likewise in external blessings and gifts, in a gracious prince, a neighbor, a father, and a mother. When I see that the face of my parents is gracious, I see at the same time the winsome face of God smiling at me."[101]

The Twofold Office of Angels

As God works all things through His creatures, everything, "including empires, states, and households . . . are all governed by the ministry of holy angels."[102]

The "lower office" of the angels is to govern God's creation as they fight for the safety and welfare of the world and control the world's empires. Luther saw behind and in all the works of God that He was bringing everything to pass through angels who are perpetually engaged in conflict with Satan and his evil angels.[103] If we were without their protection, and the Lord did not restrain the fury of Satan[104] through their protective labors,[105] the godly would not remain alive for a single moment.[106]

Their "higher office" consists in singing praises to God for His great mercy and grace toward a fallen humankind.

Therefore let us learn that our *best and most steadfast friends are invisible*, namely, *the angels*, who in their faithfulness, goodwill, and friendly services far surpass our visible friends, just as the invisible wicked angels and devils are enemies more dangerous than those who are visible.[107]

"Because we have the God of heaven and earth, the angels are our protectors, guardians . . . wherever we are. . . . It is certain that they are not only waiting for our arrival in our future fatherland, but that they are actually abiding with us in this life, concerning themselves with and directing our affairs."[108]

3

MAJOR WORLDVIEWS
on the Nature and Orientation of Man

Buddhism

Five Skandhas

Buddhism believes that a person is a temporary collection of aggregates: the physical body, emotions, perception, volition, and consciousness. In other words, man is not a separate self but a combination of skandhas, a transient bundle of forces or energies of attachment that come together at birth, giving the appearance of substantive reality, which separates at death. These five changing skandhas set up the complex interplay that constitutes the personal life of an individual.

The first skandha is rupa, which is all that presents itself to us as the visible properties of our physical bodies. The other four skandhas are grouped together as nama, the immaterial properties of sensation (emotions), perception, mental formations (volition), and consciousness. At the end of life, our desires and attachments are a karmic spark that ignites a new round of desires and attachments and, with them, a new ego-illusion.

Man Has No Soul and Lives a Karmic Existence

Buddha denied the soul as a spiritual substance; instead, he replaced the atman (soul) of Hinduism with the teaching of anatta (no-self), illustrated by the image of a flame being passed from candle to candle. Each life is in the condition it is in because of the way the lives that have led into it were lived. In other words, man is what he is in this existence because of what he has been in past existences. And what man is now will, in part, determine his future existences. There is no escape from this law of cause and effect (karma) short of nirvana. Yet in the midst of this journey, man's will remains free and he is always at liberty to do something to affect his destiny. He can undertake to traverse the path of ultimate enlightenment in accordance with the teaching of the Buddha or he can choose to remain in ignorance.

Life Is Suffering

The orientation of man is that his life, from birth to the grave, is filled with dukkha (suffering). Dukkha is like an axle that is off-center from its wheel, or like a bone that has slipped out of socket. There are six occasions when life's dislocation becomes most evident: the trauma of birth, the pathology of sickness, the challenges of getting old, the fear of death, the frustration of being tied to things that we abhor, and the pain of being separated from what we love.

The cause of life's suffering is desire (tanha). It is the thirst for the impermanent and the unsatisfying. The problem is that we desire that which is temporary, which causes us to continue in the illusion of the existence of the individual self. From this thirst man must be set entirely free, but how is this to be accomplished?

Life's cure is found in overcoming selfish craving. It is understanding the diagnosis that life is out of joint and that the course of treatment is through the disciplined training of the Eightfold Path. The solution is to cease all desire in order to realize the nonexistence of the self, thereby finding permanence.

Man Lives in Ignorance and Needs Liberating Knowledge

Man, from his birth, possesses a false view of the reality of the world and of his self, that is, he believes that the world and his self are permanent and real. He clings to these objects of desire because they seem real.

From this ignorance, he needs the liberating knowledge of the Buddha to set him free. His salvation consists in passing from ignorance to knowledge, or as it happened to the Buddha, of waking up from the dream of appearances to the truth and reality of nirvana.

For the foolish man, the wheel of life continues in its endless revolutions. But to the wise man, the human condition is the opportunity to rid himself of the burden of past misdeeds and to place himself on the Middle Path where sorrow and misery give way to joy and reality. It means to be emancipated from this worldly life and become absorbed into what is true and timeless, for that is man's chief end.

Man Needs to Be Cool

For the Buddhist, the human life is a life consumed by passion and desire. The solution is for a person to achieve a state of coolness, a life free from passionate cravings. It is a life that is tranquil and undisturbed. Such a person, being a master of himself, cannot be provoked and is free from all the lower and baser desires.

Where is such a man to be found? The only one who has attained this level of coolness is Buddha himself, but he has left behind an ideal after which all people should strive. The means to the solution is the Middle Path and the outcome is Nibbana, that is, nirvana.

Nibbana, the Final Deliverance

Man's problem is his compulsive attachments to things that seem real but are not. Salvation consists of passing from the dream of appearances to the truth and reality of Nibbana. It is to pass existentially from the karma-samsara world to the Nibbana world, a state of being beyond all mortal craving.

Nibbana simply means extinction, such as when the flame of a candle has been blown out. The implication is that a person, at the end of his or her days, experiences absolute nothingness. Many Buddhists, however, are unwilling to accept the thought that one's ultimate destiny is nothingness. For them, what has been blown out is man's desire, and it is this extinction that sets him free from the bonds of desire.

Confucianism

Man Is Innately Good

Man has an innate capacity for good. For 2,000 years the first sentence a Chinese child learned to read was, "Man is by nature good." He is born with potential and it is possible for man to get better through learning and through the practice of virtue. Thus all men are born essentially alike but, over time, they grow apart depending on how they work with their human nature; some men develop into gentlemen or cultured men while others move toward their base natures. The gentleman grows upward whereas the common man grows downward.

So while people start out equal they do not end up that way. Yet through the system of proper education anyone can succeed and become the ideal man whose life is based upon virtue (Jen), righteousness (Yi), and propriety (Li).

Jen

Jen is the greatest of virtues and means "largeness of heart." It involves a simultaneous feeling of humanity toward others and respect for oneself; thus it respects life wherever it appears. Its most fundamental act is one of compassion toward those in distress. Within the family, a person of Jen is, for example, a true father, son, and brother; in public life, he always does what is right toward the welfare of others. Jen begins at home, and once it is learned and practiced there it naturally extends itself to every area of life.

Yi

Yi means righteousness and is the virtue that consists in doing what is right in our dealings with others. It means, above all, not causing harm.

Li

Just as the inner life of the noble man is governed by Jen, his outer life is directed by Li. Li is the ideal order with everything in its place. It is based on heaven and patterned on earth. Li orders and regulates the five principal human relationships in our common life together: ruler and subject, father and son, husband and wife, the oldest son and his younger brothers, and elders and juniors. If these five relationships are lived out in their proper way, then the highest propriety (Li) will be realized and harmony will reign between all individuals.

This Li orientation to life's relationships covers all conduct that is fitting or appropriate for the situation that one is in. It includes such things as dress, demeanor, and manners toward others. At all times one should ask oneself what kind of behavior is appropriate for this social setting. By the practice of Li, complete harmony may reign in every home, village, and throughout society. Ultimately, the goal is to obtain cosmic harmony between humankind and earth and heaven.

The Mean

The Mean is the way of life that is constantly between life's extremes, and advises a person to do nothing in excess. For example, pride should not be allowed to grow into arrogance, desires should not be indulged but held in moderation, will should not be gratified to the full, and pleasure should be enjoyed but not carried out to excess.

Chuen-tzu

Chuen-tzu is the Confucian understanding and definition of the ideal man. The ultimate goal and wish that all thoughtful human beings dream of and strive for is Chuen-tzu; personhood at its best. One may hope for it, but it is very difficult to achieve.

Chuen-tzu is a person who always maintains integrity and trustworthiness. In his thoughts and actions he knows his precise place and status. He is a cultured person of honor and a great man of virtue. He is the true gentleman who as a son is always filial, as a father just and kind, as a citizen loyal and faithful, as a husband righteous and caring, and as a friend sincere and true.

His way of life is equipped with Tao and Te, which are necessary for the cultivated person. Tao is the ability to live in harmony with nature and others and Te is the personal moral force that shapes and influences the lives of others. The ultimate purpose of learning and training is to be equipped with Jen, a large and compassionate heart, which enables him to live rightly in all relationships and in all circumstances.

The Destiny of Man

Confucianism does not speculate about life after death. The destiny of man is simply to lead a life on this earth that will embody harmony. What lies beyond the grave is hidden from us and we must leave it in the hands of heaven.

Hinduism

Man Is Atman[1] and Atman Is Brahman[2]

According to Hindu tradition every human being is like a king who, falling victim to amnesia, wanders about his kingdom in tatters not knowing who he really is. The reality is that each person is atman and atman is Brahman.

Humanity's primary problem is that we are ignorant of our divine nature. Although to all appearances you and I are separate beings, this separation is only an appearance. In our inner selves we are one, for there is only one being. Burke explains, "This reality takes on one appearance and becomes what we call you, and it takes on another appearance and becomes what we call me. In our innermost self you and I are an identical being."[3]

Man Begins His Journey as Jiva

Because of a person's attachments to his or her desires and individualistic existence, we have become subject to the law of karma. An individual soul (jiva) enters this world mysteriously and begins the process of transmigration.[4] When the jiva first enters the body, it wants to taste widely the sense delights of a physical body. Next, the jiva looks beyond these sensations to the social conquests of wealth and success. With time, the jiva will leave this path of desire and reach out for something more satisfying. Duty can meet this need for a time, but eventually the only good that can truly satisfy is one that is infinite and eternal, the complete identification of one's jiva with Brahman.

Four Goals toward Moksha (Liberation)

Thus, based upon these four common journeys of the soul, there are four basic goals that a person may legitimately pursue. The first legitimate goal is that of pleasure (kama), particularly the pleasure received and given in love and sexual desire. As long as the basic rules of morality are observed, you are free to seek all the pleasure you wish. Sooner or later, however, everyone wants more from life than momentary pleasures.

The second legitimate goal is that of wealth and success (artha). Worldly success is necessary for the keeping of a household and raising a family. Worldly success also brings a sense of dignity and self-respect.

The third legitimate goal is that of moral duty (dharma) in which one renounces personal pleasure and personal wealth in order to seek the common good. These obligations are moral obligations, guided by the Code of Manu, toward others, but they also are duties associated with one's class, caste, and station in life. Faithful performance of duty brings the praise of peers and brings personal satisfaction that one has done his or her part toward the civic good.

The fourth legitimate goal, and the final aim in life, is liberation (moksha) from the endless cycles of karma-samsara and into the fullness of nirvana. It is the goal toward which the wise man ultimately directs all his actions so that he may experience complete identification with Brahman.

Four Stages in Life

Every life passes through four stages, each calling for a certain kind of lifestyle and set of behaviors.

1. The Student Stage

Traditionally this stage begins with the rite of initiation for males[5] between ages 8 and 12 and typically lasts for twelve years. The student lives in the home of his teacher and serves him in exchange for the instruction that he receives. The primary aim of this stage is to learn many facts for one's future occupation, cultivate habits, and acquire character. Celibacy is a necessary part of this training.

2. The Householder Stage

This stage of life begins with marriage and permits a man to devote his life toward his family, his vocation, and to the community in which he belongs. This is the time for fulfilling the first three basic goals of life: pleasure through the family, especially in marriage; wealth and success through vocation; and duty through his responsibilities to family and community.

3. The Retirement Stage

Anytime after the arrival of the first grandchild, and when his hair turns white, a man may withdraw from his family and social obligations into the forest and live the life of a hermit in order to read, to think, and to ponder life's meaning without interruption.

4. The Sannyasin Stage

Ultimately man is to find his way to God in isolation. This stage of life seeks to cultivate an orientation where one neither hates nor loves anything. It is the final stage where a man has no fixed place on earth, no obligations, and no belongings except for a staff, a begging bowl, and a few pieces of clothing. "The purpose of this kind of life is to hasten mystical insight, to free oneself of all attachments, to end rebirth, and to attain moksha."[6] Such a man takes no thought of the future and is indifferent to the past but only seeks to identify with, and become one with, the Brahman.

Man Lives Out His Existence according to Certain Stations in Life

There is an ancient social order that governs the Hindu way of life. During the second millennium BC a people from the north and west entered the Indus valley and, with them, introduced a social order that divided society into four groups: seers, administrators, producers, and laborers.

The Brahmins are the seers,[7] the ones who understand and know the values that matter most in life; consequently, they are the ones who lead and guide the Hindu people both through teaching and the arts so that they may know life's meaning and purpose. The administrators are the social agents who organize and promote the affairs of men in such a way as to bring the best results out of the many diverse labors taking place within Hindu society. The producers are the craftsman, artisans, farmers, and anyone else skilled at producing the material things on which life depends. Finally, the laborers are those workers who are capable, under supervision, of hard and devoted labor but lack the will and drive to sacrifice in the present for the sake of the future.

In salary and social influence, the administrators stand first, but the Brahmins stand first in terms of honor and coercive power. Within each caste there are subcastes and many rules and punishments[8] that govern one's interaction with others. One enters into his caste at birth and remains in his caste until death, hopefully living in such a way that, in the next life, he will enter into a higher caste and ultimately reach nirvana.

Islam

All Humankind was Created by Allah and have Descended from Adam and Eve

All humankind is the special creation of Allah (Adam was fashioned by Allah out of clay) and have descended from Adam and Eve. Adam and Eve originally dwelled in paradise, but they were misled by Iblis (the devil) to transgress God's prohibition not to touch a certain tree and were sent out of paradise.

Man was Appointed by Allah to Be His Vice-regent on Earth

Man was created for and appointed by Allah to be his vice-regent on earth. This exalted position was confirmed by Allah's command that the angels, at the time of Adam's creation, were to prostrate themselves before Adam.

Man Can Choose Good or Evil

Man is, by nature, born in a state of natural purity (fitra). Islam regards all children as being born Muslims, and it is only later, through the influence of parents, that a child grows up to remain Muslim or to be either a Jew, a Christian, or an idolater.

Thus each person is born pure and perfect and it is possible in our earthly existence to remain perfect. Human beings are not in need of being born again in order to do what is right; they only need the proper guidance, which is found in believing in Allah's oneness and submitting faithfully to his laws and guidance.

Man Is to Surrender to Allah

A Muslim is one who submits himself to Allah. The word *Islam* means "to accept," "to submit oneself," "submission," or "surrender." The physical posture of prostration illustrates well the Muslim attitude of total surrender to Allah.

Everything is defined and revolves around this central tenet of faith and devotion embodied in the confession of Islam: "There is no God but God," and in the call to prayer that sounds forth over the community five times a day: "God is most great . . . I bear witness that there is no God but God." At these words Muslims interrupt all else to perform the salat prayer, bowing down in surrender to Allah.

As Muhammad is the final prophet, his life also displayed the ideal life for humankind. Besides fulfilling the obligations of the five pillars, the daily life of a Muslim is guided by the example of Muhammad. Muhammad, as one committed to the teachings and values revealed in the Qur'an, is a proper, living example of how Allah wanted his will to be lived out for every Muslim. Thus, as one studies the values recorded in the Qur'an, and reflects upon the recorded sayings and practices of Muhammad, one is given guidance for the straight path[9] regarding personal life, family life, social life, economic life, and political life. Moreover, by imitating the details of Muhammad's outward life and by imitating what he said and did, Muslims hope to be able to acquire the interior attitude of perfect surrender to Allah.

On a final note, a Muslim is to strive to promote the message of Islam through his words and actions. This life of action is reflected in jihad, namely, the exertion of one's self to the utmost in order to personally follow the teachings of Islam and to work for their establishment in society. This commitment may even require that a Muslim give his life for the sake of Allah.

Tribalism

The Creation of Man

According to most tribal traditions, humankind was created by the Supreme God. In some creation stories, the first human beings were created in the sky or heaven and then lowered to the earth. Within this same tradition, the first human pair was thrown out of the sky to the earth as a punishment for doing wrong things.

The majority of creation stories tell about the Supreme God creating men on this earth. In some societies, it is believed that he used clay to make the first man and wife. In other traditions, it is said that he made the first man and woman in water or marshes and then pulled them out to the dry ground. Still other stories relate how the Supreme God made people inside the ground and then let them out of a hole in the ground or in a rock.

Whatever the creation story may be, three ideas are commonplace: (1) man was created by the Supreme God, (2) the human pair was male and female, and (3) the creation of man took place at the end of the creation of other things.

The Relationship of God and Man

In the very beginning, the relationship between the Supreme God and man was very close. He was a parent and our first ancestors were his children. He supplied them with all the things they needed and with the knowledge of how to live; what was permissible and what was not. This close relationship was lost due to an action of man that either caused them to be sent away or for the Supreme God to withdraw from them.

A tragic consequence is that humans lost many of the original benefits that they once received from the Supreme God. Man's direct link with him was severed, the closeness between the heavens and the earth was replaced by a vast gap without a bridge, and death, disease and disharmony came and have reigned ever since. Yet through religion people are still able to approach him.

The Relationship of Man with Others

Man, within a tribal society, does not live alone but exists only as part of a group. In contrast with the individualism of modern Western culture, a person with a Tribalist worldview summarizes his or her existence in this phrase: "I am, because we are, and since we are, therefore I am."[10] A person owes his existence to other people, including those of past generations and of his contemporaries.

The primary social group to which man relates, and which defines his place in society, is the nuclear and extended family. This social network means that each person has numerous "mothers" and "fathers," which encompass aunts, uncles, and senior cousins, a multitude of "brothers" and "sisters," and "children," which includes cousins, nieces, nephews and even aunts and uncles. All major decisions, such as choice of spouse, work, education, and religion, are family decisions rather than the decision of a sole individual.

A person's family even extends to those who have died and yet live as ancestors. These ancestors are still respected for their life within the family and are depended upon for their parental oversight and protection. Consequently, it is proper for a person to continue filial duties toward their ancestors by offering them the first portions of meals, consulting them before acquiring or distributing land, making offerings of appeasement if they are found to be offended, and invoking their names in household and family rituals.

Rites of Passage

1. Birth

There is great joy when a wife finds out that she is expecting a baby. "Immediately steps begin to be taken to ensure the safety of the baby and mother during and after pregnancy."[11] The pregnant woman has to observe certain regulations and taboos in order that all may go well with her and the baby. It is very common for the expectant mother to wear charms that are believed to protect her and her baby from harm. Should the expectant mother begin to have problems, the traditional doctor or diviner is immediately consulted to find out the cause and take the necessary measures to cure the trouble.

After the baby has been born, certain rituals are performed to give protection to the baby as it begins its long journey in life. It is believed that "the child needs protection against magic, sorcery, witchcraft, the evil eye, disease, malicious spirits, and any other source of harm. This ritual of protection is usually performed by the local traditional doctor or diviner,"[12] and in most cases something is tied around the neck, waist, wrist, or ankle as a physical sign of protection.

A second occasion is when the mother and baby leave the seclusion of the house and are introduced to their family, relatives, and friends. They now come out into the open to be received by society. Now it is up to the community to integrate the baby into its life.

A third occasion is when the baby is given a name. In tribalistic societies a name is considered to be very much a part of the personality of the person. Therefore, it is taken seriously and chosen with great care and consideration.

2. Initiation

The second major point in the life of the individual comes when the young person goes through the initiation period; this is a time of public recognition that the individual is now passing from childhood to adulthood. Initiation also gives an opportunity to the young people to prepare for marriage as they are taught many things concerning the life of their people, its history, traditions, beliefs, and above all how to raise a family. Upon completion of their initiation, the young people return to their homes, and often this is a great occasion of rejoicing and feasting in the community. In some tribal societies, they are given new names following their initiation to show the radical change they have undergone.

3. Marriage

In most tribal societies, marriage is a sacred duty that every normal person must perform. Failure to do so means, in effect, stopping the flow of life through the individual because marriage is the meeting-point for three layers of human life: the departed, the living, and those to be born.

Through marriage and childbearing, human life is preserved, propagated, and perpetuated.

4. Death

Death is recognized as the point when the spirit separates from the body, though it is thought to linger around the body or homestead. For that reason, the correct funeral rites must be performed in order to send it away and let it join other spirits. In some tribal societies, the departed remain in the neighborhood of their human homestead, but other societies believe that the departed live in the woods or hills in the country, or even underground or far away from the homestead.

While surviving relatives remember the departed, the spirit more or less leads a personal continuation of life. After four or five generations, the dead are forgotten personally by the living and they become a member of the spirit beings.

In terms of explaining the cause of a person's death, there are always physical causes surrounding every death such as sickness, disease, old age, accident, or animal attack, but it is a central tribalistic belief that even though a physical cause was involved, the death was brought about by means of a curse, witchcraft, magic, etc. If the death was not caused in one of these ways, spirits may be blamed or God may have called the person to leave this life, but God rarely causes the death of a person.

Three Primary Needs: Belonging, Security, Harmony

First, a man without a family and a community to which he belongs is lost and is as good as dead. Second, in the very unpredictable world filled with magic, sorcery, ill-minded spirits, and ill-minded men, a man is ever aware that his well-being and his very life are always at risk. Whether security is measured in terms of provision and food, fertility of farm or family, health, peace, or wealth, these things are of unending concern.

Third, harmony must be maintained between God and man, the spirits and man, and the departed and the living. Consequently, human beings must understand the existence and ways of the spirit world around us so that they can avoid harm and incur blessings. When this balance is upset, people experience misfortunes and sufferings and the proper rituals must be performed to restore harmony.

Modernity

Man As Cosmic Accident

The major questions of the nineteenth century dealt with God, His nature, and His activity in the world. The major questions of our day deal with man. "The abolition of man as man, so deeply felt by the person who sees himself as a Social Security number" in a computer, "is the problem of our time."[13]

Except for being the highest form in the evolutionary sequence of existence, man is no longer viewed as unique by science: a science that treats and understands man as less than man made in the image of God. In the evolutionary scheme of things, man is just a chance parade from the impersonal energy particle to man. Man is merely a different arrangement of molecules made complex by blind chance.

According to the evolutionary teachings of science, man is a cosmic accident. He emerges from the slime by chance. He is a grown-up germ. All that man is comes from the properties and forces of matter organized by the processes of natural evolution. Man is basically a highly evolved animal.[14]

As he looks at the world around him, he has difficulty distinguishing himself from the world around him. Thus man is no longer seen as being qualitatively different from non-man, but just a different arrangement of molecules. Or, man is only part of the larger cosmic machine, a bit more complicated than most machines, but a machine nonetheless.

Therefore, the dilemma of modern man is simple: man, in the grand scheme of things, is a zero. "First Copernicus removed him from the center of the cosmic stage to some minor planet circling a minor star." Then Darwin took man and robbed him of his specialness within the created order; he no longer is a little lower than the angels but just a bit higher than the monkeys. "Then Freud proceeded to show that the former 'master of his soul and captain of his fate' is actually determined by a vast subconscious over which he has no control."[15] Man comes from nothing and man goes to nothing. His origin is meaningless and his destiny is meaningless. At death, human existence ends totally, except perhaps figuratively in the memory of others and in the genes passed down to offspring.

Man Is Autonomous, a Law unto Himself

The Renaissance was not so much "the rebirth of man; it was the rebirth of an idea about man."[16] It was a change that placed man in the center of all things. In the modern worldview, man becomes a law unto himself. Nothing is to be judged in relation to an absolute or a revelation or a transcendent being, for there is no absolute or revelation that is capable of guiding man.

Men, living in the absence of God, must find the courage to be gods in a world without God. Man must carve out his own destiny as he learns to be a law unto himself and acquires the moral courage to do his own thing. Without the truth claims provided by a transcendent deity, there are no absolutes by which to define and explain the particulars of life. Therefore I alone am the source of whatever meaning, truth, or value my world has. In such a world, man is condemned to be free because there is nobody who stands on a solid foundation upon which to advise man. As an autonomous conscious being, I alone am responsible for the meaning of the situation in which I live and I alone give meaning to my world.

In theory, nothing is sacred and nothing is beyond the reach of questioning and remaking, such as homosexual and bisexual relationships. Modern individualism encourages each person to define his own social reality, apart from consideration about how creation is ordered by the Creator. Any law, any institution, any figure of authority that tries to tell me what to do is an unjust oppressor of my liberty. Thus man is the autonomous ruler of himself, able to define right and wrong and frame statutes according to whatever he defines as just.

One of the most influential thinkers in the modern period is Jean Jacques Rousseau who believed that "man was born free, but everywhere he is in chains." The freedom that he advocated was not just freedom from God or from the Bible but freedom from any kind of restraint. "Rousseau's concept of autonomous freedom led to the Bohemian ideal in which the hero is the man who fights against all of society's standards, values, and restraints."[17] It is the insistence that experience is to have no boundaries to its cravings.

It is a master morality that refuses to follow the herd but sails his ship into unchartered waters and is defiant toward conventions. Ernest Hemingway is the perfect example of an author who understood the modern orientation of humankind; he is the old man who challenges the sea, he is the soldier who ignores the tolling bell, he is the man not intimidated by the slopes of Kilimanjaro.

Man Is a Useless Passion

Jean-Paul Sartre understood man to be a "useless passion." That is, a person's life is filled with passions but they are ultimately proved to be useless and meaningless. Man is viewed not so much in terms of his mind, soul, or body, but of his will and feelings. Man is a creature of passion who feels strongly and who cares deeply about life. "He cries, he sings, he yearns, he curses. Human life cannot be reduced to the elementary structures of biology,"[18] nor can it be simply understood by his intellectual activity and capacity; man is best explained by his passions.

Hemingway is the quintessential twentieth century man. In his books, Hemingway's characters drink everything, see everything, feel everything, and do everything. Yet these passions are futile and without enduring significance since all of our deepest concerns and aspirations are ultimately meaningless in light of our extinction, which will come about either through an endless cold or intolerable heat when our sun depletes its energy sources.

Man Is Determined by Forces Within or Outside of Himself

For others, man is only part of the larger cosmic machine. Man is more complicated than the machines that people make, but he is still a machine nevertheless. In such a world there is no place for man because people, and all that they do, become only a part of the machinery. Because man is only a part of the greater cosmic machine that encompasses everything, everything people are and do can be explained by some form of determinism, some type of behaviorism, some kind of reductionism.

Most twentieth century scientific thinking sees man as determined by chemical, psychological, and sociological forces.[19] In chemical determinism, man is a pawn of chemical forces.[20] In psychological determinism, every decision that man makes is already determined on the basis of what has occurred to him psychologically in the past. In environmental determinism, we are only a product of our environment.[21]

Man Possesses a Temporal Orientation and Lives in a Sensate Culture

Richard Tarnas, in *The Passion of the Western Mind*, notes that the direction and quality of the modern character is reflected in "a gradual but finally radical shift of psychological allegiance: from God to man, from dependence to independence, from otherworldliness to this world, from the transcendent to the empirical, from myth and belief to reason and fact, from universals to particulars, from a supernaturally determined static cosmos to a naturally determined evolving cosmos, and from a fallen humanity to an advancing humanity."[22]

As a result of this radical shift, a singular dimension is forming that is sensate and in which modern culture has become worldly, pragmatic, utilitarian, epicurean, and hedonistic. At its worst, this kind of orientation makes an idol of one's sensuality, body, and immediate pleasures, expressing itself in a narcissistic hedonism that has an excessive interest in one's own comfort and importance.

Man Lives As a Mystic

Even people who believe that they are machines cannot live like machines. All men have a deep longing for significance and to believe that he is more than just one more cog in a vast cosmic machine. He longs to be more than merely "a stream of consciousness or a chance configuration of atoms observing itself by chance."[23] Therefore he must, observed Francis Schaeffer, "leap upstairs" against his reason and try to find something that gives meaning to his life. In other words, modern man cannot tolerate to be stuck in the machinery and so he becomes a mystic.

Man Lives in a Lonely, Absurd Universe in which There Is No Exit

For many who gaze upon a cold, impersonal universe, their judgment is that there is nobody home in the universe but man; man is the only conscious observer. There is no god and no other conscious life in the universe. There is nobody to love man and nobody to comfort man. Consequently, he seeks desperately to find comfort in the finite, horizontal relationships of this life.

Man is simply here, thrown into this time and place. There is nothing that structures his world. He exists, but his existence is nothingness. There is no exit from the confines of this present world. He must make his decisions, live his life, and make his plans all within this closed arena of this time—the here and now. Death is the final nothingness and is only another witness to the absurdity of human existence.

Consequently, he experiences nausea, the pointless quest for meaning in a universe devoid of purpose. Man's absurd existence is like an actor walking out on stage and not recognizing the scenery or knowing the lines of the play he is supposed to speak; it is a sense of permanent displacement and not belonging. He has great need for unity and meaning in his life but the world is silent. Thus because modern man does not have any foundation upon which to build, human existence is purposeless, meaningless, and contingent. There is no source of absolute truth to which man can turn to in order to provide meaning for his life. Man is alone and is the source of whatever meaning, truth, or value exists in his world.

Man Lives in Anguish and Is Forever Condemned to Be Free

Because man believes that he is the only conscious observer, he alone is condemned to make decisions and there is nobody who stands on a solid foundation who is able to advise man. Man alone is responsible for the meaning of the situation in which he lives—he alone gives meaning to his world.

Being totally free, man can only make decisions in anguish, alone, and without any help from any moral principles or moral authority. Anguish is the realization that man's freedom is also his responsibility to choose the meaning of his world. He defines his very existence by his own day-to-day actions, in his doing good to others and in his being an example to everyone of the goodness that is possible for man to accomplish.

Man Lives in a Culture of Diversion

Popular culture exerts a powerful influence upon the modern man. Ken Myers, in his assessment of pop culture,[24] calls this culture a culture of diversion, one that prevents people from asking questions about their origin and about the meaning of life. Instead, man's quest is for novelty and a desire for instant gratification. The meaning of human existence is the self and attendance to its needs.

The quest for novelty is not simply a search for new distractions, but it involves the notion that a new thing will be definitely better than the old thing as it seeks out new sensibilities. Not only is the modern man preoccupied with the new, he also wants the new immediately.

Man Dwells in a Secular City

According to Harvey Cox, two motifs characterize the style[25] of many modern cities and the people who dwell there: pragmatism and profanity. Pragmatism is symbolized in man's question, "Will it work?" Modern man does not occupy himself much with mysteries but instead judges ideas by the results they will achieve in practice. He experiments by trial and error and the truth is determined by what works for the individual and/or society. Profanity refers to man's wholly terrestrial horizon; profane man is only concerned with his world. Technopolitan man does not ask religious questions because he fully believes he can handle this world without them.

Man Lives Outside of Himself

Traditionally, the values and religious commitments of both family and community provided the context for a person to experience his own individuality. Cut off from family and community by mobility, privatization, and individualism, there is a new urgent necessity to "find" oneself. And yet, contemporary individualism is reluctant to draw values from the past and searches to be like others in the larger culture. The certainties that had been once acquired through socialization within the family are now replaced by the impersonal images that flicker across one's television screen for an average of a little over three seconds each.

Consequently, man frequently looks outside of himself to both radio and television[26] for answers on how to think about human issues and how to live. These media are the other-directed individual's stream of consciousness. He scans "others for the social signals they emit, regarding what is in and what is out, what is desirable and what is not."[27] He finds comfort in listening to the reality-definers of our day who guide him in knowing what constitutes the approved lifestyle, tastes, fashions, and thoughts. Thus modern man does not live by bread alone but by every catchword and revelation that comes from the lips and private lives of his heroes.[28]

Man Lives for Personal Peace and Personal Affluence

As the more Christian-dominated consensus weakened in the modern world, the majority of people adopted two impoverished values: personal peace and personal affluence. That is, they want to make enough money to practice their chosen lifestyle undisturbed by the demands of others.

Personal peace simply means wanting to have my personal life pattern undisturbed in my lifetime. Man wants to be left alone and not be troubled by the troubles of other people, whether across the world or across the street. He wants to "live with minimal possibilities of being personally disturbed."[29]

Personal affluence means a bountiful and ever-increasing level of prosperity. It is a life made up of things and more things. Success in life is "judged upon an ever-higher level of material abundance."[30]

A Biblical View of the Nature and Orientation of Humankind

Man Is Created and Cared for by God

Man is, based upon the witness of Genesis 2 and 3, a creature of the divine Creator and is preserved by God's daily activity. This means that God has given and constantly sustains

> my body, soul, and life, my members great and small, all the faculties of my mind, my reason and understanding, and so forth; my food and drink, clothing, means of support, wife and child, servants, house and home, etc. Besides, he makes all creation help provide the comforts and necessities of life—sun, moon, and stars in the heavens, day and night, air, fire, water, the earth and all that it brings forth, birds and fish, beasts, grain and all kinds of produce. Moreover, he gives all physical and temporal blessings—good government, peace, security.[31]

Man was Made in God's Image

Man was created "a living soul" from the dust of the ground (Genesis 2:7). He is earthy. He is called Adam because he is from the ground and of the earth. This is the "animal life" of man, but this is not all there is to man. Man was created in God's image, that is, "we were made according to the image of those Makers who say 'Let us make.' These Makers are three separate Persons in one divine essence. Of these three Persons we are the image."[32]

According to Luther, God's statement in Genesis 1:26, "Let us make,"[33] shows an obvious deliberation and plan, and indicates that there is "an outstanding difference between man and all the other creatures."[34] Adam not only knew God and believed that He was good, but he also lived a life that was wholly good—without the fear of death or any other danger[35]—and was content with God's favor.[36]

Before the fall, Adam's original nature, both the inner and outer sensations, were all of the purist kind. The image of God was that Adam knew God and believed that God was good. "For just as it is the nature of the eye to see, so it was the nature of reason and will in Adam to know God, to trust God, and to fear God."[37] "Therefore the image of God was something most excellent, in which were included eternal life, everlasting freedom from fear, and everything that is good."[38]

"In Adam there was an enlightened reason, a true knowledge of God, and a most sincere desire to love God and his neighbor." Added to this, Adam possessed "a perfect knowledge of the nature of the animals, the herbs, the fruits, the trees, and the remaining creatures."[39] Before the fall Adam was able to view all the animals and arrive "at such a knowledge of their nature that he [could] give each one a suitable name that harmonizes with its nature."[40] Adam and Eve, living in His image and knowing God, became the rulers of the earth, the sea, and the air. Therefore the naked human being—without weapons or walls—was given the rule over all birds, wild beasts, and fish.[41] Moreover, the one who was to cultivate the earth came from the earth.[42] In this garden man was to till and apply himself to reap his livelihood.[43] Thus God assigns to Adam a twofold duty: "to work or cultivate this garden and . . . to watch and guard it."[44]

Therefore, man's original virtue meant that "man was righteous, truthful, and upright not only in body but especially in soul, that he knew God, that he obeyed God with the utmost joy, and that he understood the works of God even without prompting."[45] If Adam had remained in the state of innocence, he would have given his descendants instructions about the will and worship of God and, on the other days, he would have tilled his fields and tended his cattle.[46] "Adam would have lived for a definite time in Paradise, according to God's pleasure, then he would have been carried off to that rest of God."[47]

But in his sin Adam lost this image and died. Through the fall, "we have lost a most beautifully enlightened reason and a will in agreement with the Word and will of God."[48] As a consequence, man's nature is subject to varieties of death, sinful lusts and passions, and emotions such as apprehension and terror.[49] Man's intellect has become darkened so that we no longer know God and His will.[50] Man's will is depraved so that we do not trust the mercy of God but, as the conscience is troubled and despairs, unregenerate man adopts illicit defenses and remedies.[51] The end result is that sinful man in the presence of a holy God does not love Him but instead flees from Him, hates Him,[52] and desires to be and live without Him.[53]

There is good news, however, for the Gospel has brought about the restoration of that image through the new birth of the Holy Spirit. We are reborn not only for eternal life but also for righteousness in this life and "are zealous to obey God as we are taught by the Word and aided by the Holy Spirit. But this righteousness has merely its beginning in this life, and it cannot attain perfection in this flesh. Nevertheless, it pleases God, not as though it were a perfect righteousness . . . but because it comes from the heart and depends on its trust in the mercy of God through Christ."[54]

Man's Nature Consists of Three Parts

It was Luther's understanding that man's nature consisted of three parts: spirit, soul, and body. "The first part, the spirit, is the highest, deepest and noblest part of man. By it he is enabled to lay hold on things incomprehensible, invisible, and eternal. [The spirit] is the dwelling place of faith and the Word of God."[55]

"The second part, or the soul, is this same spirit, so far as its nature is concerned, but viewed as performing a different function, namely, giving life to the body and working through the body" even while a person sleeps. The soul is the seat of life, for "the soul may live without the body, but the body has no life apart from the soul." Whereas the spirit deals with incomprehensible, invisible, and eternal things, the soul embraces the things of reason by which man can see and administer the things of the world. "unless the spirit, which is lighted by the brighter light of faith, controls this light of reason, it cannot but be in error" concerning invisible and unseen things.[56]

"The third part is the body with its members. Its work is but to carry out and apply that which the soul knows and the spirit believes." Thus everything depends on the faith of the spirit; for if the spirit is holy, then everything becomes holy. In the life of the Christian, his spirit is to be the place where God dwells in faith; his soul is the place where he possesses reason, "knowledge and understanding of visible and bodily things;" and his body is the place where all "men may see his works and manner of life."[57]

Man Is, after the Fall into Sin, a Lost and Condemned Creature

When God created man in His image, He graciously endowed him with a free will. Satan attacked man, and man, in the exercise of his freedom, chose to disobey God and gave heed to the temptation of Satan. It was Satan who caused the fall, but it was man who sinned. His sin was simple transgression of God's command, but at the bottom lie unbelief and the exaltation of self in which man seeks himself to be God, and would have God be nothing.

The sin of Adam became the sin of the whole human race. Man is flesh and this flesh is all that is contrary to the Spirit of God unless he is born anew of the Holy Spirit. This flesh includes all that belongs to a person: soul, body, mind, reason, and judgment. Every imagination of the thought of the heart is only evil every day, for if one could look into the heart of a person, one would see that he did it for his own glory. Also, the more numerous the gifts with which one is endowed, the greater one's pride is. "This is a common fault of our nature. Unless it is restrained by the Holy Spirit, it cannot keep from becoming puffed up by the gifts God has bestowed upon it."[58]

Man is the Battlefield between God and the Devil

Man, unless he is born of the Spirit, is a member of Satan's kingdom and in all his actions is under Satan's sway. His will, power, and exercise of choice is enslaved to sin and Satan. Man's will is like a beast standing between two riders. "If God rides it, it wills and goes where God wills . . . if Satan rides it, it wills and goes where Satan wills; nor can it choose to run to either of the two riders or to seek Him out, but the riders themselves contend for the possession and control of it."[59]

Man, without the Spirit of God, Does Evil Spontaneously and Voluntarily

Without the Spirit of God man does evil spontaneously and voluntarily, and he cannot, of his own strength, do otherwise.[60] The essential problem for man is that his unregenerate reason is evil and ungodly and this can be seen in his effort "to live without God, to live independently, and in revolt against God."[61] His enslaved will "wants and does none of the things God wants and commands."[62]

Moreover, man "does not have to learn revolt; he is born in a state of revolt against God."[63] As noted earlier, man, unless he is born of the Holy Spirit, is a member of Satan's kingdom and in all his actions is under Satan's control. Consequently, "if God is in us, Satan is absent, and only a good will is present; if God is absent, Satan is present, and only an evil will is in us."[64]

Yet "the omnipotence of God makes it impossible for the ungodly to evade the motion and action of God, for he is necessarily subject to it and obeys it." Consequently, "God cannot lay aside His omnipotence on account of man's aversion, and ungodly man cannot alter his aversion."[65] Luther explains this state of affairs in this way: "For although God does not make sin, yet He does not cease to fashion and multiply the nature that has been vitiated by sin . . . Thus as is human nature, so are men made, God creating and fashioning them out of such a nature."[66] Thus when God works in and by evil men, evil deeds result; yet

> God cannot act evilly although he does evil through evil men, because one who is himself good cannot act evilly; yet he uses evil instruments that cannot escape the sway and motion of his omnipotence. It is the fault, therefore, of the instruments, which God does not allow to be idle, that evil things are done, with God setting them in motion. It is just as if a carpenter were cutting badly with a chipped and jagged ax. . . . Hence it comes about that the ungodly man cannot but continually err and sin, because he is caught up in the movement of divine power and not allowed to be idle, but wills, desires, and acts according to the kind of person he himself is.[67]

Therefore unregenerate man, like his prince and father Satan, cannot will good but is ever turned in the direction of self and its desires. "[H]e does not seek after God or care about the things that are God's, but he seeks his own wealth, his own glories, works, wisdom, power, and in short his own kingdom, and these he wishes to enjoy in peace."[68] Amidst their abundance, they lay up provision against future hunger and need so that they no longer have any need of God and His providential care.

Man Possesses Freedom in Earthly Things

"By divine commission we have been appointed lords of the fish of the sea, of the birds of the heavens, and of the beasts of the field."[69] In the realm below him, God has granted humankind "the free use of the things according to his own choice, and has not restricted him by any laws or injunctions."[70] For example, "with regard to his faculties and possessions he has the right to use, to do, or to leave undone, according to his own free choice."[71]

At table one is at liberty to take either pears or apples, to drink either beer or wine, to dress either in white or in black, and to go either to the one friend or to the other. In such matters man has a choice, and it is certain that even these optional works become a worship of God and please God if you walk in the faith and abide by the commands of God or have a good conscience.[72]

Even those who are not Christians can be praised because of all sorts of good qualities: moderation, generosity, justice, and many other positive virtues that human discipline can bring. What Scripture does complain about is that they do evil before the Lord, for they disregard His promises and worship idols.[73]

Consequently, "in those matters that pertain to God and are above us no human being has a free will;" that is, man is not free but is led by the will and council of another, whether God or Satan. He is "like clay in the hand of the potter, in a state of merely passive potentiality, not active potentiality. For in those things that are above us, regarding God and His Word, "we do not choose, we do not do anything; but we are chosen" by His grace, we are born again by His Spirit, and we are equipped for works of service.[74]

Man Delights in Idolatry

Adam and Eve sinned when they forgot they were God's creatures. When they were tempted to be as gods, they sought to judge God and do those things that were proper for God alone.[75]

As a result of the fall, man has lost his proper knowledge of God, of grace, and of righteousness. Unless he is enlightened by the Spirit of God through the Word of God, he remains in his state of unbelief and blindness. Because he is incapable of loving a God he does not know, man loves an idol[76] and the dream of his own heart.[77] Thus "When the light of the Word and these signs of grace . . . have been lost, men run, of necessity, after the desires of their hearts."[78] Moreover, it is man's pride and unbelief that keeps him from jumping into the outstretched arms of God.[79]

Unregenerate Man or Godly Man

An ungodly man is a perverted lover of God who loves his salvation but not his Savior. In every religious action, he seeks his own advantage in God and has an eye to himself, and only considers the good things that he receives from God. The perversion of his love becomes evident when God hides His face and withdraws the rays of goodness, then his love cools immediately and he is unable to love the bare, unfelt goodness hidden in God.[80] Thus God has many lovers "in times of peace," when all things are going well,[81] but "the situation is however different 'in times of war,' that is, when God strikes and destroys men and when my neighbor injures me and is everything else but loveable."[82]

Contrary to this ungodly spirit, Christians love God Himself and not only the good things that He freely gives to His children.[83] God's children do what is good because they want to, and not for selfish reasons. They seek no reward except to be praised by God and to do His will. Christians understand that God's favor is not grasped "from things that will perish, such as wealth, power, and victories but from eternal benefits."[84] Christians know how transitory the goods and riches of this world are "since no human being can be sure of his life for a single moment!"[85]

For the elect all things work together for good, even the rods and the cross. The believer, living a life placed under the cross, experiences God's goodness as his "flesh is mortified, faith is strengthened, and the gift of the Holy Spirit is increased." On the other hand, "when the ungodly are burdened with a cross, they become worse" and "drive God to the extreme punishment of utterly destroying them."[86]

The Ungodly Experience Only a "Repentance of the Gallows"

"[T]he repentance of the wicked is such that they grieve more about the prohibition of their evil desires and sins than about the mortification of their corrupt desires and sins."[87] Luther liked to call this kind of repentance the "repentance of the gallows." For if he were free of the fear of the cross and punishment, the thief would much prefer to steal than to abstain from stealing another's property. Consequently, it is a superficial repentance because he repents in such a way that he is not ashamed of offending God, but he is ashamed because he has done harm to himself.

A truly repentant heart is so affected by sin and having offended his God that it dreads nothing else but the wrath and indignation of God. Thus "to repent is to feel seriously God's wrath because of sin, so that the sinner is troubled in his heart and plagued by a desire for salvation and for the mercy of God." It earnestly desires that He be appeased, and it is willing for God to make whatever example He must of the self, provided that He forgives and pardons the sins.[88]

It Is Hard for Man's Nature to be and Remain Humble

The ungodly "assume that they are the cause of the blessing, and they attribute everything to their own wisdom and righteousness."[89] Through sin Satan has put this evil into all men so "that the richer, the more learned, and the more beautiful one is, the more arrogant one becomes."[90] When God bestows outstanding gifts, the old Adam exalts himself and becomes proud because he sees that others do not have similar gifts.[91] Because of our sinful nature "we cannot avoid being haughty because of the gifts of God, just as, conversely, we despair when His gifts are taken from us."[92]

For example, riches are fraught with danger. In the Gospel they are called thorns and the unrighteous mammon; and if the Holy Spirit is not there, a rich man goes along "in his affluence and most certainly lapses into arrogance and into contempt for God and men, makes flesh his arm, and worships mammon instead of God. Thus wealth becomes an idol."[93] The entire fault lies, not with God's gifts and blessings, but with one's lust and depraved will.[94] Unless our nature "is restrained by the Holy Spirit, it cannot keep from becoming puffed up by the gifts that God has bestowed upon it."[95]

The Godly, When this Life Is Ended, Find and Experience Rest

The loved one who departed in the faith is not in sorrow or distress; he or she is at rest. There he or she is sleeping[96] and is waiting for a better life just like those who are still living. Thus "it is our comfort that wife, son, and parents are sleeping and are not affected by hardships and afflictions but are *resting* gently in peace."[97]

> For in Christ death is not bitter, as it is for the ungodly, but it is a change of this wretched and unhappy life into a life that is quiet and blessed.[98]

4

MAJOR WORLDVIEWS CONCERNING
Truth and Ethics

Buddhism

Introduction

Buddhism was founded upon the experiences and teachings of Sid-dhartha Gautama, the Buddha, the "Awakened One." Buddha actively sought an answer to his life's question: how to overcome the four passing sights (an old man, a sick man, a dead man, an ascetic) so that one might achieve enlightenment.

In his quest, Buddha explored and rejected several widely-held teach-ings before undertaking and achieving his own original philosophy. First, he rejected the aristocratic world into which he was born, a world filled with compulsive desires and cravings. Second, he rejected Brahmin meta-physics as a meaningless and useless word game. Third, he rejected Jain asceticism as an error equal and opposite to worldly indulgence. Finally, he rejected bhatki yoga and its dependency upon an outside savior; Bud-dha believed that man must save himself.

Buddha called his path to enlightenment the Middle Way because it avoided the extremes of both affluence and asceticism. Buddha had sought an answer for six years and would spend the next forty-five years after his enlightenment teaching others by precept and practice what he had found as the truth to enlightenment and emancipation.

The Four Noble Truths

Shortly after his enlightenment, Buddha traveled to Benares, and in the Deer Park there he preached his first sermon—the contents of which have come to be known as the "four noble truths." The four noble truths are a linked chain of truths about life:
(1) suffering exists, (2) suffering has causes, (3) suffering has an end, and (4) there is a way to attain release from suffering.[1] The four noble truths are cast in the language of ancient Indian medicine. The first two noble truths constitute the diagnosis and the last two noble truths constitute the therapy. Thus man is a disease and his cure involves a complete transcending of the human condition.

The first noble truth is that all mortal existence is characterized by dukkha. The term covers a whole range of meanings such as "ill," "evil," "imperfection," and "disease." It basically conveys the thought that things are neither what they should be nor as one would wish them to be. To live means to experience anxiety, loss, pain, decay, disease, and death; in other words, living means suffering and sorrow.

The second noble truth is that of samodaya, which is an uneasiness that arises out of personal desire and cravings. Suffering comes "from wanting what we cannot have and from never being satisfied with what we do have."[2] We suffer because we desire those things that are impermanent. It is the perpetual thirst of the human spirit to consume, whether things or experiences or ideas. Yet no matter how much we acquire, we cannot be permanently satisfied because desire is insatiable.

The third noble truth is that of nirodha, or cessation, that is, the cessation of desire. The way to liberate oneself from suffering is to eliminate all desire and to stop craving that which is impermanent. The cessation of personal desire results in the cessation of the experience of suffering. To be in this ideal state is to experience nibbuta, a state of "coolness" in the sense of being cool after a fever. It is the state of being healthy and well and no longer subject to or consumed by the heat of passions, hatred, greed, and illusion.

The ultimate goal of Buddhism is nirvana: the end of suffering, the state of inner peace, and liberation from the limitations of the world. The fourth noble truth is that there is a way to the cessation of desire and to personal wellness; the path pioneered by the Buddha, the Eightfold Path.

The Eightfold Path

The Eightfold Path may be compared to an eight-rung ladder. The rungs or steps of the ladder are right understanding, right aspiration, right speech, right action, right mode of livelihood, right endeavor, right mindfulness, and right concentration. This way of living, if followed consciously, will eventually lead to the goal of nirvana.

1. *Right understanding* is the comprehension of the four noble truths. If one is to take up the path, one must be convinced that suffering abounds, that it is occasioned by desire, that it can be cured, and that the means of the cure is the Eightfold Path.

2. Whereas right understanding calls us to make up our minds as to what life's problem basically is, *right aspiration* advises us to make up our hearts as to what we really want. Right aspiration aims for the renunciation of all desire. It includes ahimsa,[3] the resolve to not harm any living thing and to foster thoughts of non-violence and love. It involves thoughts and motives that are pure and not tainted by selfish desires.

3. *Right speech* is to abstain from lying, slander, unkind words, and foolish talk. It is to engage in the kind of speech that causes no harm; it is to speak pleasantly and benevolently or to not speak at all.

4. *Right action* is to abstain from wrongdoing in the world of the senses. It is the kind of behavior that helps others. One avoids causing harm by not taking life, not stealing, and not defrauding.

5. The *right mode* of livelihood forbids the earning of one's living by any trade that causes bloodshed or harm to other beings, such as dealing in firearms or selling liquor. Because one's occupation engages most of our waking attention, Buddha considered spiritual progress to be impossible if one's occupation pulls in the opposite direction.

6. *Right endeavor* aims to eliminate evil mental states of mind and to bring into existence good mental states of mind.

7. *Right mindfulness* means that everything needs to be seen as it really is, and one needs to remain fully aware of what one is about and what is happening, in order to be free of ignorance and proceed always toward nirvana. In other words, to be clearly aware of the body as a body, to be aware of feelings as feelings, of the mind as mind, and of mental states as mental states.

8. *Right concentration* aims to root out all turbulent emotions, thereby attaining peace of mind. It is the step that involves a transmutation into a different kind of creature, just as something happened to Buddha under the bo tree, so something will happen to the adherent who has overcome the hindrances of the sense-desires and entered absorption into nirvana.

Buddha, in teaching and modeling the Middle Way and the Eightfold Path, proposes a rigorous system of habit formation in order to release the individual from the repressions imposed by impulse, self-ignorance, and suffering.

Thus right understanding and right thought serve as the foundation from which the other points flow. For example, when one has right understanding, he or she sees the universe as impermanent and illusory and is aware that the "I" does not, in reality, exist. Right thought follows right understanding by meaning to renounce all attachment to the desires and thoughts of our illusory selves.

As a person attains such a selfless perspective, he or she finds the power to speak well of others (right speech), to obey Buddhism's moral commands or abstentions (right action), and to avoid making his or her living through an occupation that breaks the moral precepts of Buddhism (right livelihood).

The final three points of the Eightfold Path refer to mental discipline and addresses one's attitudes and state of awareness in which all sense of personal identity ceases. Through right endeavor one prevents evil thoughts from entering the mind; through right mindfulness one is especially conscious of the events in one's life; and through right concentration one can attain the bliss of enlightenment.

The Ten Precepts

There are five basic moral observances for monks and lay people alike. Followers must abstain from causing injury to living things, from stealing, from sexual immorality, from falsehood, and from the use of alcohol and drugs. In addition to these five moral injunctions, there are three moral observances: followers must abstain from taking food after midday, from dancing and singing and amusements, and from the use of cosmetics and personal adornments. Two additional moral precepts are also assumed: refraining from accepting gold and silver and from the use of a luxurious bed. These ten precepts are observed by all members of the Sangha order.

Confucianism

The Scriptures of Confucianism

During the period of the Warring States, a number of books were compiled that are still considered the classics of Chinese civilization. There are five classics that provide important background to understanding the Confucian worldview: (1) the Classic of Changes, *I Ching*, a book of divination; (2) the Classic of History, *Shu Ching*, which contains the Chou theology; (3) the Classic of Poetry, *Shih Ching*, a collection of three hundred poems; (4) the Classic of Ritual, *Li Chi*; and (5) the Spring and Autumn Annuals, *Ch'un Ch'iu*.

The teachings ascribed to Confucius can be found in the "four books." *The Analects* contains a collection of Confucius's thoughts and were compiled after his death. *The Doctrine of the Mean* develops the religious aspects of Confucius's views, dealing particularly with the relation of human nature to the underlying moral order of the universe. *The Great Learning* is a short treatise on moral education. *The Mencius* is a collection of the teachings of Confucius's outstanding disciple, Meng Tzu. These four books, together with the Five Classics, are the basic scriptures of Confucianism.

Truth Is the Moral Law

For Confucius, truth is the moral law. When lives are lived out according to this truth, a person is rewarded with a good life. A wise and great man simply follows the natural law of things. However, when things are not going well, there are various ways to discover, through divination, what needs to be done in order to bring oneself back into conformity with the natural order of things. One of these methods of divination is the use of a Shang oracle bone in which a question was inscribed and heat was applied so that the bone cracked. The shape of the crack was believed to give the answer to the inscribed question.

Five Key Ethical Relationships

Confucius believed that everyone should treat everyone else fairly and respectfully in accordance with his or her station in life. Social harmony is established when people live out their social roles properly. This sense of social responsibility was codified in five great relationships:

1. The father is kind and the son is respectful; the father must love and care for the son and the son must respect and obey the father.

2. The older brother is good and the younger brother is respectful; the elder brother must care for the younger and the younger must respect the elder.

3. The husband is righteous and the wife is listening; the husband must treat his wife fairly and the wife must respect and obey her husband. The husband is an authoritative protector and the wife is a protected homemaker and mother.

4. The elder is gracious and the junior compliant; those who are older must show due consideration toward those younger than them, and those who are younger must respect those who are older than them. All older people have responsibility for younger people because younger people need care, support, and character formation. Younger people must show respect to those older than themselves and be open to their advice.

5. The king or ruler is benevolent and the subjects are loyal; the ruler must be concerned with his subjects' well-being and the subjects must obey and be loyal to the ruler.

The key to the five relationships, and the attitude upon which all good society is built, is the son's filial attitude toward his father. This piety can be fulfilled in two ways:

- Do your best to please your father by bettering your character and doing what he wishes you to do.

- Do not disgrace your father by disgracing yourself and do not do what he would not wish you to do.

Filial piety requires that a person be respectful and affectionate toward his parents while they are alive and to keep them in respectful memory when they have died. Our parents have given us life and we would not be where we are today without their care and concern. Therefore, in thanksgiving for their efforts, we should respond by living morally and righteously.

The Art of Living

The central theme of Confucianism is the art of living: how to live and what to live for as one lives with oneself and others. The Confucian method of reasoning is that a good son at home will become a good citizen in the state because the sense of order and discipline, and sense of duty and loyalty, are already established in his childhood. The goal of good government is to provide the proper societal order so that the family ties can function smoothly and cultivate these virtues within the home.

Just as social harmony comes from living out of the five great relationships, so personal excellence comes from the manifestation of four virtues. *Jen* means to think of others and to be considerate of others through one's actions and words. *Li* means knowing and using the proper words and actions for social life. For every situation, there are appropriate words to say, proper ways to dress, and correct things to do. *Shu* is reciprocity and seeks to answer the question, "How will my action affect the other person?" It is putting jen into practice and living out the silver rule: do not do unto others what you would not wish done to yourself. Finally, *hsiao* is filial piety and is the devotion that all family members have toward their family's welfare. It involves doing what would please one's parents and bring them respect. Ideally, "it means valuing the entire extended family—of past, present, and future."[4]

The Rectification of Names

If the five relationships are to be lived out in the proper way, they must correspond to their intended reality in the eyes of heaven. This means, for example, that a father should act in the way that is fitting and appropriate for fathers to act, and that a son should act in the way that is fitting and appropriate for a son to act. Every station and relationship in life should live up to its name and live out its name.

Hinduism

The Various Sources of the Hindu Truth Claims

Hinduism has its roots in the interrelationship of two basic religious systems: that of (1) the ancient civilization residing in the Indus river valley from the third millennium BC and (2) the religious beliefs brought to

India by the Aryan people who began migrating into the Indus valley sometime after 2000 BC. With the passage of time, two types of sacred and authoritative sources developed within Hinduism: the shruti ("that which is heard") are primary and the smriti ("that which is remembered") are secondary. These writings form the basis for Hindu beliefs and reveal a gradual development of religious ideas.

The Vedas[5] are shruti scriptures and consist of four collections of writings composed between 1500 and 500 BC: the Rig Veda, the Sama Veda,[6] the Yajur Veda,[7] and the Atharva Veda.[8] Attached to these collections are treatises called Brahmanas that are devoted to explaining the hymns, rituals, myths, and sacrifices of the Vedas. Vedic literature is completed by the inclusion of the Aranyakas and Upanishads.[9]

Besides these primary scriptures, there are the smriti scriptures, such as the Ramayana and Mahabharata epics (for example, the Bhagavad-Gita is a story within the Mahabharata epic), codes of law, genealogies and legends of the gods, rules of ritual and social conduct, and writings on how to obtain occult power.

Man Lives in Ignorance

Hinduism teaches that we live in a state of ignorance, an ignorance created by selfish desire. The universe as we experience it is fundamentally deceptive, for it conceals its true nature from us. In truth the world is Brahman and yet the world presents itself to us as being multiple and limited. Salvation consists in piercing through the veil of maya[10] and reaching the truth and reality of Brahman concealed within it. Thus if we could get rid of our self-centered desire, then illusion would fall away, our apparent self would be shed, and Brahman alone would reign.

The Four Paths to Salvation

The Gita teaches that there are four paths to salvation: works, knowledge, devotion, and experiment. These various paths, or yogas, are methods that can be used to help people live spiritually and to perfect their union with the divine.

Karma Yoga:

The first path is the way of works. This is a very popular way of salvation and is based upon the belief that liberation can be obtained by fulfilling one's family and social duties. The Code of Manu prescribes a long list of sacramental rites for each significant episode of life: birth, name-giving, the first time one sees the sun, the first hair-cutting, the initiation into manhood, marriage, and so on.

The head of the household must also see to it that the household deities are properly worshiped each day and that they are presented with portions of prepared food. Among the most important of these rites pertains to the dead and is directed to the ancestral spirits. These rites involve offerings of memorial prayers and food substances. For women, the way of works is to meekly serve the men in her life and occupy herself with household duties. In childhood a female must be subject to her father, in youth to her husband, and when her husband is dead, to her sons. A woman must never be independent.

Jnana Yoga:

The second path of salvation is the way of knowledge. This way of salvation is based upon the belief that the cause of our bondage to karma-samsara is ignorance, especially the ignorance that "atman is Brahman." The evil of man's situation is that he persists in thinking of himself as a real and separate self and does not understand that he is, in reality, Brahman-atman. For man, then, salvation comes from right understanding and the saving knowledge that one has reached a state of consciousness where karma ceases to exert its effects and rebirth reaches its end; to reach this state of consciousness requires long preparation and self-discipline and is outlined in the Code of Manu.

Bhakti Yoga:

The third path of salvation is the way of devotion. This is the most popular way among the common people of India and involves the ardent and hopeful devotion to a particular deity in grateful recognition of aid received or promised. It also involves the surrender of self to the divine being and acts of devotion in temple and private worship.

For countless Hindus the personal lord is Krishna, but any choice in a deity, sincerely and wholeheartedly followed, will obtain salvation both here and hereafter. Such devotion is expressed through acts of worship at the temple, in the home, through participation in the many festivals in honor of one's god, and through pilgrimages to one of the many holy sites. In this path of devotion, the focus is on obtaining the mercy and help of one's god in order to find release from the cycle of karma-samsara.

Raja Yoga:

Raja yoga is designed for persons who possess a scientific bent, for it is the way to salvation through psychological experiment. These experiments are conducted upon one's own self, body, and spirit, and involve special postures, methods of breathing, and rhythmical repetition of the proper thought-formulas. There are eight steps to the process:

1. To practice the five abstentions: from injury, lying, stealing, sensuality, and greed
2. To practice the five observances: cleanliness, contentment, self-control, study, and prayer
3. To sit in the proper posture, with the right foot on the left thigh, the left foot upon the right thigh, and with the hands crossed and the eyes focused on the tip of the nose
4. To develop complete mastery of the breathing mechanism, while inwardly repeating the sacred word *OM*
5. To withdraw from all sense-objects and to shut oneself off from the outside world
6. To contemplate on a single idea or object until the mind is emptied of all else
7. To deepen one's concentration into meditation
8. To completely absorb one's mind in god and to be one with the "One"

Islam

Muhammad's Call

Muhammad grew up with a religious worldview that worshiped the tribal deities and believed in omens, jinn, and Satan. As he grew older, he became greatly troubled by the many idols in Mecca and the immorality of the Arab people displayed in their drinking, gambling, and dancing.

According to Muslim tradition, Muhammad would often visit a cave near Mount Hira for days at a time in order to meditate and reflect. Suddenly one night Muhammad saw a vision of the angel Gabriel who cried out to Muhammad: "Recite!" After a period of self-doubt[11] and self-examination, but with the active encouragement of his wife that these words were the very words of Allah, Muhammad began to appear in the streets of Mecca and recite the verses of revelation that he had received from Gabriel, the messenger of God.

During this time a special event occurred for Muhammad that confirmed his vocation as the prophet of Allah. One day he experienced himself being carried away to Jerusalem and ascended from there into paradise. In this journey, called the Night of Ascent, the angel Gabriel guided him upward. "As Muhammad ascended toward the highest heaven, he encountered angels and the great prophets of the past" such as Adam, Noah, Abraham, Moses, and Jesus; "at last, he entered into the presence of God."[12]

However, many of the Meccans believed Muhammad to be mad or they harbored the suspicion that, as a prophet, Muhammad wished to assert greater authority among them and over them. In the first four years of his prophetic ministry, there were only about forty converts. Throughout this period, though, the revelations continued.

The Qur'an Is the Word of Allah

The Qur'an is accepted by all Muslims to be absolute truth and the very word of Allah himself. The Qur'an is four-fifths the length of the New Testament and has 114 chapters called surahs. Its words were dictated by Allah directly to Muhammad, through the instrumentality of Gabriel, over a period of twenty-three years. The Qur'an is the last and final revelation from heaven and it completes and goes beyond all previous revelations that other religions before it have declared. The Qur'an is the very word of Allah, absolute and correct in content and language.[13] All Muslims must accept the religion that is presented in the Qur'an and follow its commands.

In Islam, Allah is the only source of truth. One of the ninety-nine beautiful names of Allah is "the truth." Allah has chosen to reveal his truth in three ways. First, there are those prophets[14] throughout history through whom God provided as prophetic witnesses to humankind, calling them out of their idolatry to worship and obey the one true god, Allah. The greatest of these prophets were Adam, Noah, Moses, Solomon, David, and Jesus. Muhammad understood himself to be another prophet, particularly a prophet to the Arab peoples. However, Muhammad's prophetic ministry was different in that he was "the seal of the prophets." Consequently, all previous prophetic revelations are subject to the authoritative message of Muhammad. This is especially so because Muslims believe that both Judaism and Christianity have corrupted God's word with false teachings.

It was Muhammad who freed the divine message from human error and offered it, purified, to all people once again.

Second, Allah has revealed through the Qur'an, recited by the angel Gabriel and recorded by Muhammad, his undistorted and final word to humankind. It is believed that the Qur'an is identical with an eternal word of Allah in heaven. The Qur'an has the final truth about all realities, all matters of life from birth to death, and all rules and regulations about religion. The primary purpose of the Qur'an is to let man know the truth about God's will, to warn him and to show him "the straight path" because human reason is not sufficient to guide man to the truth.

Third, Allah has revealed himself through the message of his special messengers to humankind; the angels.

The Articles of Faith

The most fundamental article of faith in Islamic theology is that "There is no god but Allah." Allah stands alone and supreme because he existed before any other being or thing; he alone is self-subsisting, omniscient, and omnipotent; he alone will judge on the last day. Therefore, there is no sin so grievous and unforgivable than to associate another being or thing with Allah in terms of equality.

The second article of faith is belief in the hierarchy of angels and jinn that exists between Allah and humankind. The angels are messengers or servants of Allah who, similar to the work of Gabriel, served as the mediator of the Qur'an. Angels also serve Allah by recording the good and bad deeds of every person for the day of final judgment. The jinn are usually invisible, but they do have genders and they can engage in sexual relations with humans. The jinn are typically seen as bearers of sickness or trouble to humans. While the jinn can be good, they are almost always viewed as evil and assist the evil one in instigating bad thoughts and intentions among humankind. The jinn die and also are in need of salvation; consequently, the message of Muhammad was not limited to humankind but was a message of salvation to the jinn as well.

The third article of faith is belief in Allah's holy books. Chief among these books are the Law given to Moses, the Psalms given to David, the Gospel given to Jesus, and the Qur'an given to Muhammad. Each of these books was written to communicate the same basic message of Allah's will to humankind. Of these four books, only the Qur'an has been preserved in an uncorrupted state. The Jewish and Christian scriptures were once genuine revelations of God but have since been changed and corrupted by men. Thus the Qur'an remains the only uncorrupted word of Allah for humankind.

The fourth article of faith is belief in God's prophets through whom Allah revealed his will. Each prophet was given for a particular age, but Muhammad is the only prophet who is "the seal of the prophets."

The fifth article of faith is belief that all things are the direct result of Allah's will. Things do not happen by chance or by mechanistic determinism, but everything happens according to the will and power of Allah. This includes good and evil, obedience and disobedience. Moreover, because Allah is the absolute sovereign, he has the right to do whatever he wills.

The sixth article of faith is belief that Allah has decreed that there will be a day when all will stand before him in judgment. On that day, each person's deeds will be weighed in the balance. Those whose good deeds outweigh their bad deeds will be rewarded with paradise, and those whose bad deeds outweigh their good deeds will be judged to hell.

Islamic Law[15]

As the purpose of God's truth is to guide man so that he might follow "the straight path" and achieve paradise in the end, it is not surprising that Islamic law occupies a central position in the ethical life of every Muslim and shows him what he should do and how he must act.

Muhammad is the final prophet, so he is also the final model for humankind that is pleasing to Allah. This model way of life is explained in the Shari'a and is derived from four sources: the Qur'an,[16] sunna,[17] ijma',[18] and qiyas.[19]

Major and Minor Sins

Muslims distinguish between major[20] and minor sins. There are three major sins that every Muslim seeks to avoid committing and are unpardonable in the sight of Allah. The greatest sin is shirk, which is associating any other person or thing with Allah. The second major sin is kufr, which is being ungrateful to Allah; gratitude is the only proper response to Allah for revealing to us his will and granting us temporal and eternal blessings. The third major sin is hypocrisy, that is, to claim to be a Muslim but not being sincere and fully committed to Islam. If a Muslim can avoid these three major sins, all the other sins can be forgiven because Allah is merciful and compassionate.

Finally, within Islam, there are certain things that are permitted (halal) and certain things that are prohibited (haran). For example, the drinking of alcohol and the eating of pork are forbidden. A Muslim must always distinguish between things that are haran or halal or else suffer the wrath of Allah.

Tribalism

Truth Is in the Past

For the tribalist, truth is to be sought in the past. It is in the past that we have recorded all that has happened, including the counsels of the elders and tribal heroes. Truth is not discovered, it is remembered.

Truth Is Pragmatic

Tribalists believe that nothing happens by chance or without a cause. This world is so permeated by spiritual beings and impersonal forces that there is a spiritual cause for every action. Therefore, the tribalist is always seeking the spiritual reason for earthly events, whether good or bad, but especially those events that are viewed as bad.

Frequently, divination is used in order to discover the source of the problem and then to determine the appropriate response based upon the knowledge gained. The practical use of divination as a way to achieve pragmatic truth can be illustrated in the following examples:

- to determine the best time for the wedding of a child or an application for a job
- to determine the cause of an illness and how to become well again
- to understand the wishes of the living dead so that harmony and co-existence may be maintained
- to redirect an act of witchcraft or sorcery so that those who invoked evil magic might be harmed

Socially Defined Sins

Within most tribal societies, sin can be divided along two lines: social sins and theological sins. Socially defined sins are violations of culturally defined morals and laws that destroy social harmony. These sins are offenses committed against individuals or groups within the culture rather than wrongs committed against gods and spirits.

For example, a Japanese person might feel little or no moral guilt as a result of a certain action before their god, but he or she would greatly fear losing face when caught in some antisocial act that creates social disharmony. The strong moral force is not the fear of god but the respect for public opinion.

For many tribalists, sin is an attitude of heart and mind that destroys or spoils the life-force of another and especially that of the family group. The greatest social sin in tribalist society is sorcery because it means that someone in the community is covertly seeking to kill, maim, or destroy by ritual means.

Among African and Asian peoples, socially defined sins are infractions against not only those who are living but also those who have passed into the realm of the living dead.[21] Among the Chinese, it is a great sin and an unforgivable breach of filial piety to fail to periodically offer incense and food sacrifices to the deceased ancestors.

Thus socially defined sins are understood as anything that disrupts the cohesiveness of an ordered world and causes disharmony. Human beings must live in such a way that every action is in harmony with the forces that control their world. When disharmony occurs, rituals must be performed to restore order to the universe.

Each community or society has its own set form of punishment for socially defined offenses. Punishments range from paying fines for theft of money or possessions, to death for offenses like practicing sorcery and witchcraft or committing murder. The basic moral principle is that if a person is guilty, evil will befall him.

Theologically Defined Sins

While socially defined sins are defined by culture, theologically defined sins are determined by spiritual beings. The latter are offenses that disrupt human relationships with the Supreme God and are punished by him in this life because he desires that a moral way of life be upheld.

For example, the Barundi believe that god gets angry and punishes a person who commits adultery. A Congonese tribe believes that god punishes people who steal, neglect aging parents, murder others, or commit adultery. Other tribes believe that if the chief offends god, he punishes the whole people with locusts, floods, or other ecological calamities. Or, if a man has great pride before god because of his possessions or number of children, god may punish such arrogance by taking it away. Thus people believe that if a person does wrong, god will eventually punish him and possibly the entire group.

Modernity

The Basis of Truth

Immanuel Kant, in answer to the question of what the Enlightenment was, used the phrase "dare to know" and has defined the central thrust of our modern culture. It is man emerging from his self-imposed nonage[22] and requires nothing more than the freedom to make use of one's reason in all matters. It is the summons to have the courage to think for oneself, to test everything in the light of reason and to dare to question even the most hallowed traditions. No alleged divine revelation, no tradition, and no dogma, however sacred, has the right to veto its exercise. The mark of intellectual maturity and competence is to subject every alleged truth to the critical scrutiny of reason.

For centuries the dominant pattern had been one in which the ground rules and the boundary lines had been set by theology. Philosophy had to operate within those limitations and science had to follow the lead of both theology and philosophy. Now this situation has been reversed. After the philosophical writings of Immanuel Kant, it is the thinking subject and not some external authority who defines what is to be believed—it is a shift from external authority to internal authority.[23]

Consequently, we live in a society that is not controlled by accepted dogma but by the critical spirit; we live in a time when every supposed truth must be critically examined by the acids of critical doubt and only what survives is to be retained. The old morality celebrated faith and belief and regarded doubt as sin; the new morality celebrates methodological skepticism. That is the only safe path from the darkness of superstition, dogma, and tradition to the clear light of truth. The only authority that now remains is that of private reason and experience.

Public Truths and Private Values

One significant feature of the scientific worldview is the dichotomy between the public world of facts and the private world of beliefs, opinions, and values. In the world of values, each person is free to choose what values to cherish and what values to reject. Values and styles of living are not right or wrong, but they are matters of personal choice; the values he or she will live by. However, in the world of facts, statements are either true or false. Where statements of alleged fact are in contradiction to one another, we argue, experiment, and test until we finally agree on what the facts are, and we expect all responsible and educated people to accept them. In other words, religious answers do not deal with facts, only science deals with facts.

For example, the fact that the program encoded in the DNA molecule governs the development of the individual person is something every educated person is expected to know and accept. The belief that every human being is made to glorify God and to live with Him forever is an opinion held by some people, but is not part of the entire public truth.

Thus, in the world of values, pluralism rules. But in the world of facts there must be certainty based upon scientific inquiry and testing. Knowing is essential and the schools, the institutions where public facts are instilled, are to see that everyone knows the real facts. Believing is something else and it is a personal matter for each individual.

The Nature of Truth: Pluralism

George Forell offers meaningful insight and Christian concern regarding the increasing level of pluralization within modern Western society when he notes that "Pluralism, the simultaneous existence of various and contradictory approaches to life, which can neither be uprooted nor overcome, absorbed, or ignored, is ideologically the most threatening aspect of the modern world."[24] It especially undermines the nature of one truth. The distinctive feature of modern Western culture is that there is no generally-acknowledged plausibility structure.[25] What this means is that there is diversity in this world, but we have no access to ultimate unity and therefore no way to bring the diverse things of our experience into a coherent whole.

As a result, with respect to ultimate beliefs, pluralism is key and each person has to make a personal decision about ultimate questions. "The man on the street is confronted with a wide variety of religious and other reality-defining agencies that compete for his allegiance."[26] Each of us, bombarded by these many possibilities, is tempted to create his own syn-cretistic worldview, picking and choosing the combination that meets his needs.

Thesis-Antithesis and Synthesis

Before Georg Hegel, truth was conceived on the basis of thesis and antithesis. The basic presupposition was that there were absolutes and that people could reason together on the basis of thesis-antithesis. They took it for granted that if anything was true, the opposite was false. Like-wise in morality, if one thing was right, its opposite was wrong.

According to Francis Schaeffer, the crucial years of change from truth based upon thesis-antithesis to truth based upon synthesis were from 1913–1940.[27] This new thinking was based upon the philosophy of Georg Hegel who understood truth in this way: there is a thesis that is any idea or a historical movement; there is antithesis that is a conflicting idea or movement; synthesis overcomes the conflict by reconciling a higher level of truth contained in both. Moreover, this process is ongoing and cyclical. Every synthesis becomes a new thesis that generates another antithesis, giving rise to a new synthesis. Since Hegel, and his view that the universe is steadily unfolding and that no single proposition about reality can truly reflect what is the case, truth is understood to be found in the flow of his-tory; a synthesis of thesis and antithesis.

The Spread of the Fragmentation

Francis Schaeffer, in his tracing of the movement and growing influ-ence of non-Christian ideas since the time of the Enlightenment, sug-gests that "Modern pessimism and modern fragmentation have spread in three different ways to people of our own culture and to people across the world. Geographically, it spread from the European main-land to England, after a time it jumped the Atlantic to the United States. Culturally, it spread in the various disciplines from philosophy[28] to art,[29] to music,[30] to general culture, and to theology. Socially, it spread from the intellectuals to the educated and then through the mass media to everyone."[31] Consequently, there is an almost monolithic consensus, an almost unified voice shouting at us a fragmented concept of the universe and of life.

Ethics

The Lowest End of the Food Chain

Cut off from the supernatural sanctions given by God in His Word, man has actually begun looking down to the subhuman level of existence to find authentication and validation for life. Instead of basing human values on a kind of God-given humanism, man is looking to nature.[32] One's ethical standards are to be found operative in nature. "Since it is the purpose of nature that the fit survive, everything that contributes to the survival of the fittest is good, and everything that hampers this survival and helps the unfit to survive is bad."[33]

Thus this subhuman world supplies modern man with an orientation and pattern for life. For example, Friedrich Nietzsche advocated a master-morality against the prevalent slave-morality of Christianity. Nazi Germany engaged in "the destruction of the mentally ill and the sterilization of those who were considered biologically unfit to propagate the species."[34] Likewise, Fascism has developed its understanding of and justification for modern "supermen" and "super-races" based upon evolutionary biology, that is, some individuals and races are biologically superior and are destined to rule and to dominate others.[35]

Or, since man is only one of the animals that inhabit the planet earth, it makes no sense to grant him a privileged position over other animals. To say that man is qualitatively superior to animals is to be guilty of speciesism.

Different Strokes for Different Folks

Many people make their ethical decisions not because they have thought through their decision in an intelligent way, but because their actions conform to the prevailing custom, that is, "Is this what everybody else does?" They live according to the accumulated good sense and experiences of their social group.

For others, pleasure is the gauge of what is ethical and what is not. For those who hold to this understanding of what is good, he or she believes that the goodness of an action depends entirely upon the amount of pleasure he is going to secure. "The good is identified with that which gives pleasure and evil is identified with that which gives pain."[36] Whatever this pleasure[37] might be, it is their supreme value in life.

For others, their slogan is "the greatest good for the greatest number." If my pleasure conflicts with the pleasures of the group, I must be willing to sacrifice my personal pleasure for the greater pleasure of the majority.

For still others, there is a sense of duty that is the basis for all ethical action. "We all have in us a 'sense of ought.' We all know there is a difference between what we like to do and what we 'ought' to do." It is the moral imperative to act in such a way that the rules governing your action could become the universal law.[38]

Thus, notes Forell in his study on ethics, these competing and divergent understandings of how people live out what it means to be good can be seen, for example, in the hall of one's apartment complex as "people on the other side may live in an utterly different world; a world in which there is no God, no divine law, and where only self-interest, animal instincts, and the survival of the fittest rule."[39]

A Pragmatic Style of Morality

The hallmark of secular humanism, though, is pragmatism, which is the practice of doing what seems to work without regard for fixed principles of right and wrong. Human actions and behavior, then, are not right and wrong in themselves but only because of the results they produce, and the good feelings they engender or express. In the absence of any absolute criteria of right and wrong, the self and its feelings become our only moral guide. Everything depends on how you look at it. As a result, we have situational ethics in which every situation is judged subjectively with no absolute to which to appeal.

A Personal Moral Universe

Expressive individualism is the freedom to express oneself against all constraints and conventions. "For Walt Whitman, the ultimate use of America's independence was to cultivate and express the self and explore its vast social and cosmic identities."[40] In the spirit of Whitman, modern individualism in the United States of America encourages each person to define his own social reality and to constitute his own moral universe. Therefore, in our privatized worlds, each individual is entitled to his own bit of space and is utterly free within its boundaries.

For many North Americans the self is defined by arbitrary preference. Clearly, the meaning of one's life for many Americans is to become one's own person. Much of this self-discovery process is negative, though, since it involves breaking free from family, community, and inherited ideas.

For those who hold to an existentialist bent, morality is the personal attempt of every human being, living in an apparent hopeless situation, to make the most out of life that we can. Although there is no purpose to life or love or suffering because death is the end of everything, individuals can attempt to give their own meaning to life while it lasts.

The Therapeutic Attitude

In this quest toward discovery of self, "therapy can help individuals become autonomous by affirming over and over again that they are worthy of acceptance as they are" and "by teaching the therapeutic client to be independent of anyone else's standards."[41] One must become the source of his standards and to rely on his own judgment without deferring to others.

This therapeutic attitude liberates individuals by helping them get in touch with their own wants and interests. This attitude is based upon several selfish and egocentric assumptions: that one's personal and emotional well-being is the greatest good in life, that most of the time the self is entitled to get whatever it wants, that restraints on those desires are almost always unjust and unhealthy, and that feeling good is the highest test of whether something is legitimate.

Sociological Law

We need moral universals[42] if we are to determine which actions are right and which are wrong. Not having universals, the modern concept is ultimately sociological because the majority determines moral questions. This means that the elite emerges to tell us what behavior is acceptable. Sociologically, law has no fixed base because a group of people arbitrarily decides what is good for society at that moment, and what they decide eventually becomes law.[43]

The abortion law is perfect example of an elite deciding what is sociologically good for society at that moment in history. In 1973 the Supreme Court abortion ruling invalidated abortion laws in all fifty states, even though it seemed clear that the majority of Americans were against abortion. By ruling that abortion was legal, the Supreme Court overthrew state law overnight and pressured Americans into thinking that abortion was not only legal, but ethical.

Man has No Second Boundary Condition

Eve was physically able to eat the forbidden fruit. But on the basis of the second boundary condition of the moral command of God, it was wrong for both her and Adam to eat the fruit.[44] Likewise, because modern man sees himself as autonomous, he has no universal to supply an adequate boundary condition for what he should do. He is left only with what he can do. Man has no reference point beyond human egoism.[45] It is impossible, many would say, to find a meaningful standard for determining whether any particular decision is right or wrong.[46] One opinion is as good as the next and everybody has to establish his own ethical standards that will be true for him and nobody else. People believe that what is right is what they think is right for themselves as individuals, and what is wrong is what they think is wrong for themselves. There are as many "ethics" as there are people.

As the Christian ethic dies in our culture, there are not many alternatives. There is (1) hedonism in which every person does his own thing, (2) the 51 percent vote whereby law and morals becomes a matter of averages, and (3) the elite, consisting of academic and scientific intellectuals and government bureaucrats, who determine and give authoritative absolutes.[47]

Media

There is a new, all-encompassing culture that has entered the modern world, namely, the audiovisual medium. As a result of electricity and everything that flows from it, the human being is taken into a vast network that changes habits, lifestyle, and moral behavior and is the main cause of moral change. For example, it is impossible to watch television without being bombarded with the philosophy of moral relativism, subjective experience, and the denial of objective truth.

A Biblical View of the Basis and Nature of Truth

Epistemological Certainty is Found in God's Word

God has always been known through His works of creation. All peoples have been given a general knowledge of God's metaphysical attributes, such as His omnipotence and omniscience, but most are also familiar with His ethical attributes. They have been told that God is the giver of all good; that God is orderly, kind, and gracious; that God is willing to help a man who calls upon Him in time of need; and that God is legally oriented.

Hence, unregenerate reason knows that God exists and this knowledge is written in all hearts. But who God is and what He is like is taught only by the Holy Spirit in the Word of God who alone can reveal what God thinks of us and what His intentions are toward us.

God Satisfied Our Desire to Know Him

In order that God might be known and comprehended, the Spirit of Christ meets us in simple, earthly, and concrete ways. Since the fall of man there can be no unmediated relationship between God and man (See Exodus 33:20). God must wear a "mask" or "veil" in all of His dealings with men. Moreover, this nature of ours has become so misshapen through sin that it cannot recognize God or comprehend His nature without a covering. Therefore God, in His grace and mercy, envelops Himself in His works and seeks to reveal Himself to humankind in certain forms. In the New Testament we have the visible form of the Son of God and the other visible forms of Baptism, the Eucharist, and the spoken Word.

It is the first stage of error when men disregard God as He enveloped Himself and seek to scrutinize the unveiled God. It is insane, observed Luther, "to argue about God and the divine nature without the Word or any covering."[48]

> But you must adhere to and follow this sure and infallible rule: God in His divine wisdom arranges to manifest Himself to human beings by some definite and visible form which can be seen with the eyes and touched with the hands, in short, is within the scope of the five senses. So near to us does the Divine Majesty place Itself.[49]

The person who makes use of these forms and coverings in faith does not believe in vain and does not stray from God but surely hears and finds God.[50] Luther offers four reasons why God comes to us through His concrete Spirit in the Word:

1. Since the beginning of the world, divine wisdom has so ordained and arranged things that there is always some public sign[51] toward which all people might look in order that they might find, worship, and pray to the true God and be saved.[52]

2. These outward and visible signs have been placed "alongside the

Word, so that men, reminded by the outward sign . . . would believe with greater assurance[53] that God is kind and merciful."[54] By means of these visible signs of grace God shows us that He is with us, takes care of us, and is favorably inclined toward us.

3. He presents Himself to us in these visible forms in order that we might be kept from degenerating into and following the erratic and vagabond spirits[55] who boast of visions and revelations. Since we cannot ascend to Him, He has chosen to come to us and reveal Himself "within the range of our comprehension."[56] The true God is not a wandering God but has limited Himself to a place and certain external forms.

4. As God comes to us in these concrete forms, He deals with us in a twofold manner: first outwardly, then inwardly. He draws us outwardly through Christ's Word and the Gospel and inwardly through the Holy Spirit.[57] However, there is no inwardly coming to God apart from these outwardly means.

These concrete forms of the Holy Spirit are God's way to us and a rejection of every way from man to God. These are the common epiphanies or appearances for all people. When God comes, He does not hide Himself in the corner but He appears publicly before us all. When we get to heaven we shall see Him differently, but here we see Him enveloped in an image, namely, in His Word and Sacraments.

God's Word Grants Epistemological Certainty

In Luther's debate with Johann Eck at Leibzig on the topic of penance, Eck persisted in challenging Luther with a line of questioning: "Are you the only one that knows anything? Except for you is all the Church in error?" Yet at Leibzig, Luther could boldly claim with certainty that a simple layman armed with Scripture is to be believed above pope or council without it.

Luther's certainty was based upon the truthful and reliable words of Scripture that are revealed through the Holy Spirit.[58] "Human beings can err, but the Word of God is the very wisdom of God and the absolutely infallible truth."[59] True wisdom is in the Word of God that

gives information not only about the matter of the entire creation, not only about its form, but also about the efficient and final cause, about the beginning and about the end of all things, about who did the creating and for what purpose He created. Without this knowledge of these two causes [the efficient and final cause] our wisdom does not differ much from that of the beasts, which also make use of their eyes and ears but are utterly without knowledge about their beginning and their end.[60]

For "[w]hat advantage is there in knowing how beautiful a creature man is if you are unaware of his purpose, namely, that he was created to worship God and to live eternally with God?"[61] Consequently, Luther preferred "to drink from the source, [the Word of God,] rather than from the rivulets," the interpretations and traditions of men. Luther wanted to "have the Scripture in the purity of its powers, undefiled by any man . . . and not spiced with anything earthly."[62] For "[t]he Holy Spirit is no Skeptic, and it is not doubts or mere opinions that he has written on our hearts, but assertions more sure and certain than life itself and all experience."[63] Moreover, the Holy Spirit "teaches us about most important events, which involve God, sinful man, and Satan, the originator of sin."[64]

But if the Scriptures were to be understood correctly, the interpreter must be subject to the Word of God and its authority in every respect. A person does not have the freedom to lord over the Scriptures, to build upon uncertain and unreliable interpretations of men, or to change the meaning of God's Word in order to force it to agree with personal opinions, philosophies, and presuppositions. The interpreter must allow God to be God and let Him speak in the clear, simple words recorded in Scripture.

Furthermore, Luther believed that in every age the Church has the same Spirit as the prophets and apostles. As God came to earth to save us and became flesh for us, so He comes to us in the language of men revealing Himself in His written Word. Therefore, the same meaning applies to the words of the Scriptures. This being so, advised Luther, let us learn that true wisdom is in the Word of God.

Reason

Reason contributes the essential difference between man and other living beings. Through reason, man exercises his lordship over the earth that was given to him in Genesis 1:28. Reason provides the light by which man can see and administer the affairs of this world and is the source and bearer of all culture. The majesty of human reason is that it serves this earthly life as it judges and decides the proper regulation and administration of earthly matters, such as economics and politics, and as the discoverer of all arts and sciences, of all medicine and law.[65]

The limitation of unregenerate reason is that it discusses "the works of God without the Word."[66] The result of this procedure is that the glory of Holy Scripture and the majesty of the Creator are lost since "it denies providence and concludes that . . . everything happens by accident and by chance." Just as "natural reason has no [proper] knowledge of God, it also has no [proper] knowledge of God's creation."[67]

Faith Alone Comprehends the Hidden God and the Revealed God

In *The Bondage of the Will* Luther makes the distinction between the Hidden God and the Revealed God. God in His majesty is hidden and inaccessible to man. We cannot find or see Him as He is. Yet in His grace and out of His great love He has chosen to take the form of the Word become flesh, born in Bethlehem.

In Christ's incarnation, the Hidden God becomes the Revealed God. Yet His presence can be seen and apprehended only by faith. It is only by faith, acquired through the Word, that a person can cut through the coverings of flesh and blood and see Him in Christ's incarnation and in God's daily activity and presence in the world.

The Word Is the Measure

"[I]n our whole life the Word is the measure, the standard, and the most precious thing that guides our life."[68] "If we do not have Holy Scripture lighting and governing our actions, this whole life, [with all its wisdom, is] . . . darkness and confusion."[69] Simply stated, "life without the Word is uncertain and obscure."[70]

The task of every Christian believer is to examine what the Scriptures say and see whether what is taught in the Church and in the world is true according to the Word of God. In matters of faith and life, the Christian must be captive to the Word and become drunk by the Holy Spirit.[71] Most of all, the sinners' troubled conscience must have a certain and reliable Word from God if he or she is to find peace and rest.

A Biblical View of Ethics

A Treatise on Good Works

Luther, in a treatise on good works in 1520, sought to instruct God's people in the biblical teachings concerning what kind of life is pleasing in His sight. It is only those works that have been commanded by God that are good works. "[W]e must distinguish between the glory of the Word of God . . . and fair-seeming works."[72] A clear example of this distinction can be seen in King Saul's failure to keep the command of the Lord.

> Saul *seems* to be doing the right thing (1 Sam. 15) when he does not kill all the cattle of the Amalekites but keeps the choicer animals for worship. But because God had clearly given the command that all had to be killed, this deed provokes Him to extreme anger. Therefore the fair-seeming work is nothing but an abomination, because it was undertaken against the Word of God.[73]

The primary concern of the Christian believer must be for the First Table of the Ten Commandments: "God must be loved above all things, and loved so perfectly that you love nothing in the entire world in the same way, neither your wife nor your children nor your own life."[74] "People must first be instructed about the true worship of God, [to fear, love, and trust in Him above all things, for] this produces a good tree, from which later on good fruits result."[75] But if a tree is to become good, you must become a person of promise; that is, you must accept grace and rely on mercy alone, something that cannot happen unless you apprehend the Word of the promise by faith. Wherever this is done, there will follow spontaneously the works of the Second Table.

> He who believes God and fears God, who calls upon God in troubles, who praises and thanks Him for His blessings, who gladly hears His Word, who constantly meditates on the works of God, and who teaches others to do the same, cannot harm his neighbor, can he? Or disobey his parents? Or kill? Or commit adultery?[76]

Also, it is the natural tendency of humankind to view works by considering their appearance, size, or the number of works themselves, but "God does not have regard for either the size or the quantity or even the value of the work, but simply the faith of the individual . . . for God is interested in faith alone, that is, the reliance on His mercy through Christ.[77] God has regard for faith and judges only those to be good who believe. "Through [faith] people begin to please God, and after that their works also please Him."[78]

Thus the Scriptures teach that "a person rather than his work is accepted by God and that a person does not become righteous as a result of a righteous work, but that a work becomes righteous and good as a result of a righteous and good person."[79]

[I]f the heart is full of faith, [one must conclude] that everything he does in faith, even though in outward appearances it is most unimportant—such as the natural activities of sleeping, being awake, eating, and drinking . . . is a holy work that pleases God.[80]

For example, "Because God has regard for Abel, He has regard also for his offering; and because He has no regard for Cain, He has no regard for his offering either."[81] God "had regard for Abel, not because He was moved by any work, but simply because He was moved by his faith, in which he also brought his offering."[82] God "rejects Cain, not because his sacrifice was inferior . . . but because his person was evil, without faith, and full of pride and conceit."[83]

Faith Active in Love

"Faith alone lays hold of the promise, believes God when He gives the promise, stretches out its hand when God offers something, and accepts what He offers."[84] Christianity, to Luther, represented a very simple relationship: on the one hand, God's promise; on the other hand, a believer's faith. "For faith is the firm and sure thought or trust that through Christ God is propitious and that through Christ His thoughts concerning us are thoughts of peace, not of affliction or wrath."[85] Therefore, the only faith that justifies is the faith that deals with God in His promises and accepts them.

Just as faith constitutes the proper relation of the Christian person to God, so good works and love exercised in vocation define a man's relation to his neighbor because "a true Christian lives and labors on earth not for himself, but for his neighbor."[86]

All Christian life can be summed up in two terms, "faith" and "love,"[87] whereby man is placed midway between God and his neighbor, receiving from above and giving out below, and becoming as it were a vessel or a tube through which the stream of divine goodness flows unceasingly into others. Gustaf Wingren offers a beautiful summary of Luther's understanding of vocation, for it is God's will that

Each one ought to live, speak, act, hear, suffer, and die in love and service for another, even for one's enemies, a husband for his wife and children, a wife for her husband, children for their parents, servants for their masters, masters for their servants, rulers for their subjects and subjects for their rulers, so that one's hand, mouth, eye, foot, heart, and desire is for others; these are Christian works, good in nature.[88]

126

The believer responds to the love of God and plunges himself into the world as the proper place for the activity of faith. "All Christians have been placed into the world for the purpose of serving their neighbors, not only so far as the Second Table is concerned but rather so far as the First Table is concerned, in order that they all may learn to fear God and to trust in His mercy."[89]

Finally, the Christian life demands that we love both our friends and our enemies. We are to "love all human beings equally and that we should do good to all, not only to the good and to those whom we consider worthy because of their conduct but also to the evil. For this is God's way; He pours out His benefits without distinction."[90]

Outward Obedience Follows Inward Obedience

The righteous shall live by faith. For Abraham, God spoke and he believed what God said. As evidenced in the faith of Abraham, outward obedience follows upon inward obedience. Abraham heard and believed the Word, then he became a righteous doer of works by following Christ. For Abraham

> had already been justified when he believed the promise of God that was revealed through the holy patriarchs. If he had not been righteous, he would never have . . . obeyed God when He called. Therefore he heard the Word and believed the Word; and later on, after he had been justified thereby, he also became a righteous doer of works by wandering about and following Christ, who had called him.[91]

Abraham exhibited a perfect act of obedience "as he put his faith into practice in circumcision. If he had wanted to act in accordance with reason and to argue, he would have said: 'What is the use of being circumcised in this part of the body? Why did God not choose another part, one that is more honorable?' " This way of thinking "deceived Adam. Not satisfied with God's command, he sought also to learn the reason *why* God ordered him to keep away from only one tree. When people get into this way of thinking, either the work that was commanded is left undone, or it is objected to and becomes the opposite."[92]

Thus "when you hear God's Word, see to it that you obey directly, without discussion. . . . God does not want any delay when He gives a command. . . . Abraham had weighty reasons for putting off the sacrificing of his son, but he places God's command ahead of his own thoughts."[93] Abraham could have reasoned that Isaac must be spared since the promise of the Blessed Seed resides in Isaac and his offspring. But Abraham relies on the promise and believes that, somehow, God will restore his dead son to life.

Abraham "obeys God's command without arguing."[94] He simply cuts the throat of this baneful "Why?" and tears it out of his heart by the roots. He takes reason captive and finds satisfaction in the one fact that He who gives the command is just, good, and wise; therefore, He cannot command anything but what is just, good, and wise, even if reason does not make sense of it.

"Therefore let no one add this detestable and fatal little word 'why' to God's commands. But when the command is certain, let us obey at once without any argument, and let us conclude that God is wiser than we are. He who argues about *why* God gives a particular command actually doubts that God is wise, just, and good." Therefore, "let it be enough for us that we hear the Word and understand what it commands, even though we do not understand the reason for the command."[95]

Righteous and Sinner at the Same Time

Christians are righteous because they believe in Christ whose righteousness covers them and is imputed to them, but they are sinners because they do not fulfill the law and are not without sinful desires. Hence, the Christian life is nothing else than a daily baptism, once begun and constantly followed. All that is necessary is that a man be baptized by water and the Holy Spirit and attain faith through Him. This works the new birth.

> Then I serve God by observing the three Commandments of the First Table of the Law of Moses; and then, in obedience to the Second Table, I attend to the duties of my vocation to the best of my ability, loving my neighbor and leading a decent and quiet life with my wife. And if a cross[96] should come upon me, I shall also endure it gladly, go to church, and listen to the words of Christ, my Bishop.[97]

Faith Submits to Temporal Authority for the Sake of One's Neighbor

Because the sword of government "is a very great benefit and necessary to the whole world, to preserve peace, to punish sin and to prevent evil, [the Christian believer] submits most willingly to the rule of the sword, pays tax, honors those in authority, serves, helps, and does all he can to further the government, that it may be sustained and held in honor and fear."

5

MAJOR WORLDVIEWS CONCERNING
the Social Location of Religion

Buddhism

Man Needs Salvation from Earthly, Impermanent Existence

Buddha, in response to three passing sights of sickness, old age, and death, sought to discover a way for humankind to overcome these three tragic realities. His quest led him to the Middle Way and the Eightfold Path. Out of his compassion for humankind, Buddha spent forty-five years preaching and teaching the way of deliverance.

It was the observation and teaching of Buddha that all mortal things decay. A wise man is one who places himself on the Middle Path so that he can be emancipated from this earthly, impermanent existence and be absorbed into what is true and timeless—nirvana.

The Three Jewels

Not long after the Buddha's death his followers began to recite a three-fold utterance called "the three jewels." These three statements are repeated every day by most, if not all, Buddhists, both monks and laity:

I take refuge in the Buddha.[1]

I take refuge in the dharma.[2]

I take refuge in the sangha.

The picture that lies behind this confession is the image of a crossing, the simple everyday experience of crossing a river in a ferryboat in a land with unbridged rivers and canals. Buddhism is seen as a voyage across the river of life, a transport from the shore of non-enlightenment, spiritual ignorance, desire, and death, to the bank of wisdom that brings liberation and freedom.

As one pushes off the shore and moves across the water to reach the other side, refuge is found in three ways: (1) there is refuge in Buddha for he was an explorer who made this trip and who has showed us the way, (2) there is refuge in dharma, the teaching of Buddha and the teaching to which we have committed our lives in the conviction that it is a sure guide to nirvana, and (3) there is refuge in the sangha, the order, for we have a good crew navigating the ship and we will safely reach the other side.

The Sangha

The invitation to the community of Buddha was an invitation to lose one's individual existence in the common life of the sangha. The monks depend on the sharing of food put aside by lay well-wishers and supporters of the community for their daily sustenance. In addition to food, the lay people provide the monks with robes and maintain the monastery. In exchange, the monks operate a school where the village boys and girls come to learn how to read and write. The monks also conduct ceremonies at festivals and funerals, give regular instructions in the Buddhist way of life, and act as spiritual advisors and moral counselors.

The life of the Buddhist monk is one that denounces all personal possessions and preferences and lives a common life of poverty and chastity. From very early on, a rule of life was developed and codified in what came to be known as the Vinaya—the Discipline. This Discipline consists of a list of 250 items of offenses to be avoided, beginning with the most serious, from which the penalty is expulsion from the order, and followed by those offenses from which the penalty is suspension for a time, and then by offenses of diminishing seriousness, down to matters of etiquette and decorum.

The essential rules of the order are simple: the wearing of the yellow robe; the adoption of the shaven head; the carrying of the begging bowl; the habit of daily meditation; and subscription to "the three jewels" and "the ten precepts." If any monk breaks one or more of these precepts, he makes public confession of his sin before the assembly of his chapter on the bi-monthly fast days.

Social Duties of Lay People

In addition to the moral precepts for lay people (whether five or eight precepts), there are certain social obligations that are outlined in the *Sigalovada Sutta*, a famous social discourse of the Buddha that sets out the duties of children to parents and parents to children; of pupils to teachers and of teachers to pupils; of husbands to wives and wives to husbands; of servants to employers and employers to servants; and finally of lay people to monks and of monks to lay people.

Theravada and Mahayana Buddhism

The Theravada school of Buddhism takes its name from its goal of passing on the Buddha's teachings unchanged. Its name means "the way of the elders." As a school, it has always stressed "the ideal of reaching nirvana through detachment and desirelessness achieved through meditation."[3] Although Theravada does accept that lay people can attain nirvana, the life of the monk offers a surer path.

Mahayana Buddhism emphasizes that nirvana is not only attainable by monks but is a possibility for everyone. Instead of the Theravada ideal of detached wisdom and unworldly living, the Mahayana ideal is the person of deep compassion.[4]

Confucianism

Heaven, Earth, Man, and the Central Kingdom

The values and themes of the Confucian classics[5] find expression in four recurring images: heaven, earth, man, and the central kingdom.

Heaven is the vault of the sky and is the source of the authoritative norms and values that give meaning to human life. The Mandate of Heaven (T'ien Ming) is a corollary concept that imparts a sense of vocation and mission to individuals and society; that is, the aim of life for the individual and society is to discover and to perform the Mandate of Heaven.

Through agriculture, earth is the source of material goods essential to human survival. Sacrifices to the earth therefore marked the seasons of the agricultural year. From the earliest of times, the Chinese emperor, as the son of heaven, performed elaborate and prescribed sacrifices to heaven at the summer and winter solstices, and to earth at the spring and autumn equinoxes.

In the center of the flat disk of earth lay the Central Kingdom of China. The Chinese people never called themselves Chinese but Chung Kuo, the Central Kingdom, for China has always been viewed by its people as the center of the world.

Under heaven, on earth, and in the midst of the Central Kingdom stands man. Man is to live a good life as reflected in the virtues of Jen and Li and thereby fulfill the Mandate of Heaven.

Confucian Curriculum

Confucian literature, divided into the Five Classics and the Four Books, became the core curriculum for almost 600 years in China, from 1313 to 1912. The common practice in families who could afford it was to select at least one boy in the family to receive a Confucian education and to prepare him for the civil service examination and possible governmental service.

Reverence of the Ancestors

Veneration of the ancestors was an early innovation, possibly derived from the practice of the emperor acting as high priest in the worship of Shang Ti. He was the first intercessor between God and man in China. With the death of the earthly royal intercessor, his spirit was believed to continue in mediatorial service. Originally, emperors, then later national heroes, and finally family patriarchs were revered—"not as deities but as spirit intercessors who could grant favors and take an interest in the current welfare and future benefit of the suppliant."[6]

The ancestors, even after they have died and become good spirits, remain active within the family, bringing success to the family's labors and protecting the family from harm. To this day, traditional Chinese homes have an ancestral shrine containing the Spirit Tables of the ancestors. These shrines are pieces of wood that are inscribed with the ancestors' names.

Religion Is to be Honored and Respected

Religion is accepted by Confucius as a natural part of an ordered society and it is to be honored and respected but not overdone. The real focus of humankind is in learning how to live with one's fellow man, especially within one's family. True wisdom is to devote oneself earnestly to one's duty to humanity, and to remain distant, yet respectful, of the spirits.

When Confucius was asked about his duty to the spirits, he replied, "When one is still unable to do your duty to men, how can you do your duty to the spirits?" When asked about death, Confucius advised, "While you do not know life, how can you know about death?"

Even with these statements, Confucius did encourage his followers to do their religious duties[7] according to the prevailing customs of Chinese society: to faithfully live a life of Jen and Li and to respect and honor the ancestors.

Hinduism

The Quest and the Four Paths to Nirvana

The quest that has inspired the spirit of man in India is to discover how one comes to Brahman and remains in touch with it. There are four traditional spiritual paths to nirvana because, according to Hindu analysis, there are four kinds of persons, and the way to reach nirvana is based upon the kind of person you are: some are reflective (jnana yoga), some are emotional (bhakti yoga), some are active (karma yoga), and some are experimental (raja yoga). For each kind of person, there is a distinctive yoga that is recommended and designed to match your personality in your quest for nirvana.

All four paths begin with the same moral habits and practices such as non-injury,[8] truthfulness, non-stealing, self-control, cleanliness, contentment, self-discipline, and a compelling desire to reach the goal. The aim of each path is to render the surface self-transparent to the divinity beneath. It is to cleanse the dross of one's being to the point where its infinite center, the atman, will be fully manifest. In other words, every deed I do for the sake of my own private welfare adds another coating to the ego and, in thus thickening it, insulates it further from god within and without. Correlatively, every act done without thought of self diminishes self-centeredness, and eventually no barrier remains to cloud one from the divine.

There are Many Paths to the Same Summit

It is Hinduism's conviction that the various major religions are alternate and relatively equal paths to the same oneness with Brahman. It is the contention of the Vedas that the various religions are but the different languages through which God has spoken to the human heart. Accordingly, it is possible to climb life's mountain from any side since all of the pathways merge at the top. As one can ascend to the top of a house by means of a ladder or a staircase or a rope, so there are many ways and means to approach God, and every religion in the world shows one of those ways. Thus every person should follow his or her religion; for the Hindus the ancient path, the path of the Aryan sages, is the best. It is only an ignorant man who says, "My religion is the only one, my religion is best."

Islam

Religion and Politics

In order to understand how Islam views the relationship of religion and society, it is most important to consider "the Hijra" (the migration) and the theocracy established at Medina. In AD 620, Muhammad's first wife, Khadija, and his uncle Abu Talib died. Not only did Muhammad grieve because he lost two very special people in his life but also because he lost two of his greatest tribal protectors: Khadija because of her wealth and social standing and Abu Talib because of his social influence and age. In that same year, six men from Yathrib discussed their need for a strong leader to govern their chaotic and divided city with Muhammed. In AD 622, Muhammad quickly left (some would say that he fled) the persecution in Mecca and made the Hijra to Yathrib.

The Hijra is a central event in Islam and marks the point of which "Muhammad's message was favorably received and the start of the Islamic community (umma). For these reasons, the Muslim calendar dates the year of Hijra as year one."[9] During his eight years of establishing himself as leader and governing there, the city became known as Medina, the city of the prophet.

It is at Medina that the first mosque was erected as a house of worship. The construction of a worship cultus was also developed with weekly services on Friday; prostration during prayer facing at first toward Jerusalem, then toward Mecca when the Jews in Medina did not convert to Islam; a call to prayer from the mosque's roof; and the taking up of alms for the poor and for the support of religious causes.

In January AD 630, Muhammad marched into Mecca with 10,000 men and accepted the surrender of Mecca. One of his first acts was to go reverently to the Ka'ba honoring the black stone, to ride around the shrine seven times, and to order the destruction of the idols within it. Opponents were invited to offer allegiance to Allah and to the governance of Muhammad; before his sudden death, Muhammad was well on his way to unifying the Arab tribes under a theocracy governed by the will of the one and only god, Allah.

Thus as one learns from the example of Medina between AD 622–630 and Mecca in AD 630, the will of Allah must be effected throughout all of society. Religion and politics must be unified and is properly expressed in the Islamic state. Thus Islam is not only concerned with converting the heart, but all of public life as well. It is not only concerned with teaching general principles but also with stipulating in detail how life must be lived, individually, and politically.

Five Pillars

The Muslim way of life can be outlined under three headings: articles of faith (iman), right conduct (ihsan), and religious duty ('ibadat). The articles of faith and right conduct have been set forth in the Qur'an. One's religious duty is modeled largely after the religious practices of Muhammad, the model Islamic man.

By following these five pillars, the Muslim lives in a complete dedication to the will of Allah.

Shahada: the Confession of Faith

It is the religious duty of every Muslim to recite the creed: "There is no god but Allah and Muhammad is the prophet of Allah." This confession of faith cannot be changed or altered in any way. This sincere confession is usually regarded as the basic and sufficient mark of a Muslim. A Muslim must say this confession at least once in his or her lifetime. Most Muslims say it many times a day.

This single sentence is the first sentence "whispered into the ears of a newborn infant; it is recited daily in prayer; and it is written in Arabic everywhere inside the domes of mosques and over their doors."[10]

Salat: the Five Daily Prayers[11]

It is the religious duty of every Muslim to reserve time each day for prayer: at dawn, at midday, at mid-afternoon, at sunset, and at the fall of darkness upon the land. People are called to prayer several times a day by a muezzin, a chanter who announces that Allah is great, greater than anything else. He continues his invitation by witnessing that there is no god but Allah, that Muhammad is Allah's messenger, and that they should hasten to prayer.

As part of one's prayer, a prayer rug is rolled out, one bows down facing Mecca,[12] and praise to Allah is offered in gratitude for his many blessings along with prayers of supplication. Before prayer, the individual is normally expected to perform a ritual purification with water, washing the hands, arms, face, neck, and feet. These ritual prayers mark Muslims as a people whose surrender to God is daily and constant. The postures of their bodies daily educate Muslims that they are to lay aside their pride and remember that before Allah they are nothing. In their prayers, passages from the Qur'an and other prayer formulas are recited from memory.

Friday is the special day of public prayer for all adult males. The men assemble at the call of the minaret, leaving their shoes at the entrance to the mosque. They ritually perform ablutions by going to a pool of water and washing their hands, mouth, nostrils, face, forearms, neck, and feet. The service usually consists of hearing a reader recite from the Qur'an; the imam leads the assembly in rituals of prostrated prayer and after the prayers preaches a message that expounds Muslim teaching.

Zakat: Compulsory Almsgiving

Zakat is the giving of alms as freewill gifts to the poor and the needy. In the early days of Islam, Zakat was gathered by religious officials into a common treasury and distributed to the poor and the imams so that the mosques might be maintained. Today the Zakat is 2.5 percent of one's income and is a way for the Islamic community to show compassion to the needy among them, and is an attempt to fairly distribute the community's accumulative wealth.

Sawm: Fasting During the Sacred Month of Ramadan

Except for the sick, every Muslim is expected to fast during the entire lunar month of Ramadan.[13] Once the month has begun, and as soon as it has been determined that the day has begun (there is sufficient light for one to distinguish between a white and black thread), no food or drink are to be taken until sundown (there is no longer sufficient light to distinguish between the two threads). After sundown, they are allowed to partake of all those things until sunrise.

During daylight hours in the month of Ramadan, the Muslim physically abstains from eating, drinking, smoking, and sexual relations. Spiritually, he or she abstains from all evil thoughts, actions, and sayings. The month of fasting is also a time to remember those who are poor and whose daily life is not one of eating and drinking whenever they chose.

Hajj: the Pilgrimage to Mecca

Once in a lifetime every Muslim, man or woman, is expected to make a pilgrimage to Mecca and join thousands of other Muslims in order to circle the Ka'ba,[14] participate in the Lesser[15] and Greater Pilgrimage,[16] and celebrate the Great Feast.[17] The pilgrimage concludes with everyone gathering to circle the Ka'ba once more before returning home.

During the pilgrimage, Muslims also reenact important events in the life of Abraham. Islam believes that Hagar and Ishmael lived in the region of Mecca and that Abraham visited them there. Muslims also believe that "Abraham was asked by God to sacrifice his son Ishmael, not Isaac," and that "this near-sacrifice took place in Mecca."[18]

Since Muhammad's day, all pilgrims have been required, whether rich or poor, to enter the sacred precincts of Mecca wearing the same kind of seamless white garments (ihram) and to observe the same moral imperatives: no food or drink, no harm to any living thing whether animal or plant, and no distinction of race and class.

The central purpose of the Hajj is for every Muslim to reflect on his or her position as a naked soul in the presence of Allah alone. The pilgrimage also symbolizes the unity of the Muslim community and its universal brotherhood. Every Muslim is to know that every other Muslim is his brother or sister and that they are one brotherhood. The unity and brotherhood of Islam is symbolized by the robe of Abraham,[19] worn by all who participate in the pilgrimage. Ideally, for those males who made the pilgrimage, his burial clothing is the white robe of Abraham. The face of the deceased is turned toward Mecca at the burial, and the plain stone marker that serves as the headstone signifies equality of all people in death.[20]

The Mosque

When Muhammad arrived at Medina, one of his actions was to build a simple mosque (which means "a place of prostration"). It was a rough building with three trunks supporting the roof, a stone to mark the qiblah (the direction of prayer), and a tree trunk where Muhammad would stand to preach. There was also a courtyard where the Islamic community gathered to discuss social, political, and religious concerns. No activity was excluded from the mosque. Thus while the mosque serves as a place of prayer and the reading of the Qur'an, it also is the place of education, a hospitable abode for travelers, the base of social assistance to the needy, and the center for political gatherings.

Tribalism

Religion Permeates All of Life

Every single person in a tribal society is religious. To be human is to belong to the whole community and to do so involves participating in the beliefs, ceremonies, and festivals of that community. One's whole life is permeated by its religious beliefs and practices. From conception to death, from morning until night, from springtime until harvest, and from the start of any enterprise until its end, supernatural forces are present and must be properly dealt with, or failure is inevitable.

Every religious activity and practice are significant as they place individuals, families, and groups in right relationships with gods, ancestors, other human beings, and nature. In the maintenance of these right relationships, the shaman serves as an intermediary between the visible, ordinary world and the spirit world. The shaman can contact this realm, receive visions of it, and transmit messages from it; sometimes the spirits even speak through the shaman. Shamans also experience "a shared identity with animals and the rest of nature. Thus the shaman can interpret the language of animals, charm them, and draw on their powers."[21] Shamans can also command and manipulate spiritual forces to do good and bad things through incantations, potions, and figurines used for sympathetic magic.

All Life Is Connected

The first assumption of most tribalists is that reality is all of one piece.

Animals may be ancestors of men, people may change into animals, trees and stones may possess souls, and the mana of a stick may be transferred to a man. In fact, almost every object in the universe is viewed as possessing some amount of life force—the spiritual substance without which nothing could exist.

In addition to mana, the souls of the living dead still exist and participate in a man's life, protecting him from danger and keeping him faithful to the traditions. Each man must pass on this vital force to his descendants. Therefore, he must have children who can, in turn, honor him in the spirit world and for whom he can be a protecting spirit.

Thus tribalists believe that the seen world is related to the unseen world. There is no sharp distinction between these two realities: what happens in the one world affects the other. Within this spiritual-physical world, humankind seeks to be an integrated member, living in harmonious symbioses with the rest of the external world. Yet at the same time, humankind sees the external world as full of many hidden dangers and threats that cause them to live with many fears. In order to live successfully, the tribalist seeks out various means of being protected and blessed, such as rituals and charms prepared by religious spiritualists, to counter the dangers and to promote personal prosperity within his physical-spiritual environment.

Religion without Ethics

For the tribalist, religion is essentially non-ethical. If the spirits are offended because of adultery or theft, then one must avoid such "sinful behavior" because harmony must be maintained with the spirits. Religion is primarily a technique for procuring the best advantage in the power struggle in the spirit world. Thus if one knows the right formulae, the spirit world can be made to do one's bidding, whether for good or for evil. The tribalist is not concerned about seeking the will of his god or spirit, but in compelling, entreating, or coercing his god to do his will.

Modernity

Religion in Society

Religion is an illusion, according to Sigmund Freud, a hope inspired by certain wishes within the human psyche. In order to make life more bearable, frustrated individuals invent the illusion that there is a loving, providential God who cares for humankind and who grants immortality to those who believe in and serve Him. Thus "most people seek to neutralize the harshness of life by seeking consolation through the narcotic known as religion."[22]

For Ludwig Feuerbach, since gods are a product of man's creation, all religious ideas are projections of human needs and desires into an imaginary other world.[23] Man clings to God and his religion because he desires that consolation that will enable him to get through life and to have a hope. Religions owe their success to the promise of happiness and bliss in the world to come. Feuerbach's goal was to destroy this religious illusion and help people see that whenever they speak of God, they are in reality saying something about man.

For Karl Marx, "religion is the opium of the people."[24] The reason human beings invent gods is because they have not mastered their world and so they look for alliances with, and consolations from, imaginary beings called gods. Religion is the balm that enables us to put up with an unbearable life. At its deepest level, though, religion is harmful because it turns man away from this world and from finding his true fulfillment here.

For Friedrich Nietzsche,[25] religion is the greatest sin on earth because it teaches man to live for another world and to forget the earth. Religion was invented by the sick and decaying, who despised the body and the earth, and who invented the heavenly realm so that they could escape their misery. Religious people, instead of living a full, adventurous life, are despisers of life who seek to carry immense burdens, like a camel carrying a heavy load in the desert. Instead, man should be encouraged to play, live, govern, and die as though God doesn't exist.

Three Key Pressures

The rise of the modern world has brought three key pressures to bear on the social location of religion: secularization,[26] privatization,[27] and pluralization.[28] Due to these social forces operative in the West as a result of modernization, more and more cultures have been freed from the influence of the Christian faith so that Christian institutions and Christian ideas, and religion in general, are displaced from the center of modern society and relegated to the margins of society.

As a result of secularization, religion no longer presides over much of society as it did in the past, nor is it involved in all facets of life as the Christian faith requires. Sector after sector[29] has been successfully removed from the influence of the Christian faith so that for all practical purposes the heartland of modern society (labor, education, big business, technology, science, government) is thoroughly secular. Simply stated, secularization achieves a "world without windows," that is, a world shut off from transcendence and transcendent referents.

Privatization seeks to domesticate the activity of the Triune God in the world by developing the understanding that faith is ultimately personal.[30] Privatization is the posture that religion is to be privately engaging but socially irrelevant. One direct consequence of privatization is that the individual finds sources of identity increasingly only in the private sphere. Privatization also produces greater individual autonomy and has expanded the area in which the individual is free to make his own choices about what is good and evil, about what kind of life is to be admired or despised, and about what code of ethics should govern one's private life.

Historically, religions were monolithic. They established the worldview of their society and had a monopoly over the ultimate legitimation of individual and collective beliefs and life. Religion has been described as a "sacred canopy" that arched over all of society, defining the world and determining the ways of those who lived under its shelter. The pluralistic situation relativizes the competing worldviews, depriving them of their taken-for-granted status, and undermines the notion of "one truth." As a result, "the man in the street is confronted with a wide variety of religious and other reality-defining agencies that compete for his allegiance."[31] Each of us, "bombarded by these many reality-defining possibilities, is tempted to create our own syncretistic worldview, picking and choosing the combination that meets our needs."[32]

The Impact of Modernization upon Christianity

According to Os Guinness, there are three significant ways in which modernization has impacted Christianity in a negative way.[33]

1. There has been *the loss of certainty* that Christianity is the one, true saving faith; instead, due to pluralization, Christianity seems less real and is but one choice among many belief systems. Christianity is now seen as one of the great religions and must take its place among all the other religions in humankind's pantheon.

2. There has been *the loss of comprehensiveness* that Christianity speaks to all areas of life and to all areas of knowledge; instead, due to privatization, the Christian faith possesses relevance only for the private sphere and only in dealing with private matters such as personal belief and values.

3. There has been *the loss of compelling power* since, due to secularization and the end of Christendom in the West, the biblical worldview is no longer permitted in many areas within the public square, which silences its corrective and evangelical voice.

Unless Christianity is able to break these three chains, warns Guinness, it will never be more than a harmless, though popular, folk religion. Unless there is dramatic societal change and evangelical fervor, soon all that will remain will be a little philosophy, a little morality, a little architecture, and a little experience.

The World has Come of Age

Dietrich Bonhoeffer, in his *Letters and Papers from Prison*, observed that "man had come of age" in which the "religious hypothesis" is no longer needed by man since he can get along very well without it. Bonhoeffer observed that, "as people have to use 'god' as an explanation less and less and have to call on 'god' for help less and less, this 'god' is being edged out of the world, to the periphery of people's conscious world."[34]

Bilingual Education

This displacement of the "religious hypothesis" is promoted through what Lesslie Newbigin calls the bilingual nature of public education.[35] For most of our early lives, through the accepted systems of public education, we have been trained to use a language that claims to make sense of the world without the hypothesis of God. For an hour or two on Sunday mornings, we use the other language, the language of the Bible, but for the rest of the week we use the language[36] imposed by the occupying power.[37]

A Biblical View
of the Social Location of Religion

Introduction

For Luther, the *coram* relationships[38] present a framework for understanding the place that religion plays in the organization of life. The fundamental situation of man is that he lives out his life in the presence of God (*coram Deo*), in the presence of other human beings (*coram hominibus*), and in the presence of the created world (*coram mundo*). The important element in this situation is not the way in which someone else is present before me in my sight, but the way that I am before someone else and exist in the sight of someone else. Hence, the *coram* relationship reveals that the fundamental situation of man is that of a person on trial. The basic experience of man is that a demand is always being made upon him both by God and by the relationships that he has with others in the world.

Coram Deo: Man Is Always in the Presence of God

Coram Deo is a teaching that seriously treats the depth and tragedy of the human predicament because it considers man and his world in the presence of the living God. In everything that happens to us,[39] it is God Himself who is at work dealing with us, whether in His grace or in His wrath.[40]

"Since God works all things everywhere, we are always in His hand. No matter where one goes, one can fall only into God's hands."[41] This inescapable living presence of God in all that exists is either the most blessed or the most terrible reality for a man, depending on his relationship with God.

GOD'S ALIEN AND PROPER WORK

Man, in the presence of God, is a sinner. In order that humankind might be saved and come to a saving knowledge of Christ, the triune God, in His mercy, works in two ways to bring fallen humankind to Himself.

First, God comes to man in order to perform His alien work, that is, He comes to unregenerate man with the Law[42] so that man might be brought to a true knowledge of himself as a sinner in the presence of God. "When the Law comes, then the eyes are opened, and man becomes aware of what God has commanded and what punishment He has established for the transgressors. When the Law thus gains control in the conscience, then there is the true knowledge of sin."[43] "Only after the Law has come, does it become clear what we have done."[44] Therefore, "God cannot accomplish anything among us through His grace unless He has first broken and crushed"[45] our sinful and stubborn hearts. The Law is like a taskmaster: it cures no illness but helps sick people to realize they are sick and in need of a doctor. Then follows true repentance and the looking about for the help of another, a mediator and savior.[46] The Good News is that man's situation is not hopeless. God was in Christ reconciling humankind to Himself. "For God so loved the world, that He gave His only Son, that whoever believes in Him should not perish but have eternal life" (John 3:16).

Thus when a person is bruised and afflicted and the Law has tormented sharply, then it is the time for grace and the time to hear of Christ. The Gospel, the proper work of God, proclaims the actions of a merciful Father who, seeing us to be oppressed and overwhelmed by the curse of the Law and knowing we could never be delivered from it by our own power, sent His only Son into the world and laid upon Him all the sins of humankind.[47] God is the only one who could die for the sin of all humankind. It was the "will of His good pleasure" to take upon Himself our sins and to bear the punishment and wrath of God. This Gospel proclamation is the proper work of God whereby He draws unregenerate man to Himself so that man might know and believe that he is justified freely by grace through Christ's redemption.

Therefore, by the law comes "not righteousness but knowledge of sin." The law makes the conscience guilty before God and is "such a light as reveals sickness, sin, evil, death, hell, the wrath of God, though it affords no help and brings no deliverance from these."[48] As long as sins are unknown, there is no room for cure and no hope of a cure. Thus the law is necessary to give knowledge of sin so that the sinner, "who imagines himself well may be humbled and may sigh and gasp for the grace that is offered in Christ."[49]

The Gospel points the sinner not to his works but to God's work, the works of Christ, and bids him confidently to believe that for the sake of His Son, God will forgive his sins and accept him as His child. Therefore, through faith in Christ and His work the heart of the sinner is immediately cheered and comforted. The heart will no longer flee from God but rather turn to Him. By this gracious act of God the believer experiences His mercy and is drawn to Him and commences to call upon Him and to treat and revere Him as his beloved God.

The Alien and Proper Work of God in the Lives of Adam and Eve

Wherever "the Word of God is, there Satan also makes it his business to spread falsehood and false teaching; for it grieves him that through the Word we . . . become citizens of heaven."[50] This being so, as soon as God had given His Word concerning the tree of the knowledge of good and evil, Satan visited Eve with his own word so that she was tempted to doubt God's goodness and to listen to another teacher.

In his rebellion, when Adam is bringing the fruit to his mouth, he gives no heed to the Word. If you were to look into his conscience, "you would observe that he is no more concerned about God and His Word than if God were something dead and nonexistent." It is the nature of sin to lie still and be quiet for a time, while lust and sin reign, and to live as if God were sleeping. "[R]eal terror arises when the voice of the wrathful God is heard, that is, when it is felt by the conscience."[51]

Thus after their consciences had been convicted by the Law, Adam and Eve were terrified and lost their confidence in God and hid. They found the entire world too narrow to be a safe hiding place. When God came to them and asked, "Where are you?", He spoke words of Law to their conscience. God wanted "to show Adam that though he had hidden, he was not hidden[52] from God, and that when he avoided God, he did not escape God."[53]

After the fall, when Adam heard God's voice he was afraid. But had he not heard the voice of the Lord before, Luther wondered, when God forbade him to eat from the forbidden tree? Why was he not afraid then? Why did he not hide then? But after the fall he was terrified. Adam should have said: "Lord, I have sinned." But he did not do so.

Instead, when he was convicted, he tried to defend himself with the claim that if You had "not burdened me by making me live with her, I would have remained without sin."[54] But God continued to work in Adam's life so that he might know his sin, be thoroughly frightened by it, and then be given courage through the promise of the remission of sins through faith in the Promised Seed. Therefore, advises Luther, let us learn that

> When you feel in your conscience that you are guilty . . . Do not flee from God when He is pointing His spear at you, but flee to Him with a humble confession of your guilt and a request for forgiveness. Then God will draw back His spear and spare you.[55]

Faith in the Promised, Blessed Seed

The Seed of the Woman

After Adam and Eve had sinned against God and brought upon themselves the just penalty of their sin, Luther saw the victorious irony of the situation in that

> Through the woman you, Satan, set upon and seduced the man, so that through sin you might be their head and master. But I, in turn, shall lie in wait for you through means of the same instrument. I shall snatch away the woman, and from her I shall produce a Seed, and that Seed will crush your head.[56]

Through the very flesh in which sin had entered the world, God would bring forth a Man who would crush Satan along with all of his powers. In this veiled promise, Luther saw a second irony in that

> this promise and this threat are very clear, and yet they are also very indefinite. They leave the devil in such a state that he suspects all mothers of giving birth to this Seed, although only one woman was to be the mother of this Blessed Seed. Thus because God is threatening in general when He says "her Seed," He is mocking Satan and making him afraid of all women.[57]

In this promise "there is *hope* of a procreation through which the head of Satan would be crushed, not only to break his tyranny but also to gain eternal life for our nature, which was surrendered to death because of sin."[58]

Comforted by these words, Eve gained the sure hope of salvation. Adam, "by assigning [the name Eve] to his wife he gives clear indication that the Holy Spirit had cheered his heart[59] through his trust in the forgiveness of sins by the Seed of Eve."[60]

When Eve had given birth to her firstborn son, she hoped that he would be that Crusher. Although she was deceived in this hope, she saw that eventually this Seed would be born from among her descendants. "In this hope our first parents live and die, and because of this hope they are truly holy and righteous."[61] From that time on,

> men began to call upon the name of the Lord, that is, that Adam, Seth, Enos, exhorted their descendants to wait for their redemption, to believe the promise about the woman's Seed and through that hope to overcome the treachery, the crosses, the persecutions, the hatreds, the wrongs, etc., of

the Cainites; not to despair about their salvation but rather to thank God, who one day would deliver them through the woman's Seed.[62]

In the faith of Abel, we have the first example of the believer's victory over death since, in Abel's blood being heard by God,

> God shows that the serpent does not harm Abel even though it succeeds in having Abel killed. This is indeed why the serpent lies in wait for the heel of the woman's Seed. But while it bites, its head is crushed. Because of Abel's trust in the promised Seed, God inquired after Abel's blood when he was dead and showed that He is his God.[63]

Out of this promise of the Blessed Seed has "flowed all the sermons of the prophets concerning Christ and His kingdom, about the forgiveness of sins, about the gift of the Holy Spirit."[64] Through Abraham it was linked to a certain race, thereafter through the patriarch Jacob to the specific tribe of Judah. "Now the devil was unconcerned about other nations and tribes; and with amazing cruelty and treachery he pursued this one single line of descendants. [By the time of Christ] it had been reduced to the utmost poverty, like a hopeless stump from which no one ever hopes for either leaves or fruit. For this reason Scripture also calls it the root of Jesse, a decayed and hopeless stump."[65] Yet out of this hopeless stump God brought forth a shoot.

The Seed of Abraham

Because God is good, He seeks to deliver sinful humankind from His curse and wrath. In order to effect this, He promises that this salvation will be accomplished through the seed of Abraham, not only for the descendants of Abraham, but for all the families of the earth.[66]

In order for this Seed of Abraham to be able to bless the nations, He must necessarily be a true human being[67] by nature; on the other hand, "if He blesses others, even all the families of the earth, He must necessarily be something greater than the seed of Abraham, because the seed of Abraham itself stands in need of this blessing on account of its sin."[68] Therefore

> the blessing fits the Creator alone and not any creature. Hence He who blesses must be true God, because to deliver all nations from the curse is the work of God, not of man or of angels. And so that Seed is true God and man in one Person. He is man because He is the Seed of Abraham; He is God because he bestows the blessing.[69]

And it is the Seed of Abraham who is "the principal, effective cause of that blessing."[70] And He is not only the effective cause, but He is also the formal cause which is the blessing itself. For from Him and in Him we are the blessed of Christ and are saved. This is the ground and the nature of the Christian faith: "to believe with certainty that we are blessed, not through ourselves but through Christ, who is our blessing."[71]

In this promise to Abraham, the "Holy Scriptures implies not only the divinity[72] of Christ but also the distinction of Persons. It is the Father who promises; but the Seed is the Son, who is promised; and He is distinguished from Him who promises. Accordingly, there are two distinct Persons: the eternal Father, who promises, and the eternal Son, who is promised."[73]

This Seed is divine, for the prophet David calls Abraham's Seed his Lord. He sets Him at the right hand of God: that is, he assigns Him power equal to that of God because He does work equal to the works of God. "But because He is the Seed of Abraham, He must take on human nature; for otherwise God, in His own nature and essence, cannot be called the Seed of Abraham."[74] Thus "He who is the Son of God, the Destroyer of hell, the Victor over death, the Abrogator of the Law, and the Restorer of eternal life comes from the seed of Abraham."[75]

The Seed of Jacob

The dream of Jacob, whereby he sees a ladder set upon the earth with its top reaching into heaven with angels descending and ascending, reveals the mystery of the incarnation in which the same Person is both true God and true man:

> the highest divinity is the lowest creature, made the servant of all men, yes, subject to the devil himself. On the other hand, the lowest creature, the humanity or the man, sits at the right hand of the Father and has been made the highest; and He subjects the angels to Himself, not because of His human nature, but because of the wonderful conjunction and union established out of the two contrary and unjoinable natures in one Person.[76]

> This is a wonderful ascent and descent of the angels, to see the highest and the lowest completely united in one and the same Person, the highest God lying in the manger. Therefore the angels adore Him there, rejoice, and sing: "Glory to God in the highest." On the other hand, when they consider the lowliness of the human nature, they descend and sing: "And on earth peace."[77]

This, then, is the ascent and descent of the angels of God, as seen on the day of the nativity. They adore Him as He now lies in the manger at His mother's breasts. Indeed, they adore Him on the cross, when He descends into hell, when He has been subjected to sin and hell, and when He bears all the sins of the whole world.

As they ascend, they behold the Son of God from all eternity. If they look down, they see God and the Divine Majesty subject to demons and to every creature. If the angels lift up their eyes, they see the incomprehensible majesty of God above them. Thus the ladder is the wonderful union of His divinity with our flesh. "And whether ascending or descending, the angels adore Him."[78]

Yet if He is to be the Savior of the world and not just of the Jewish people, "Gentile seed [must be] mixed with that of Abraham" so that He could be born of and for all people.[79] His father's side was Israelite but His mother's side was Gentile, Moabite, Assyrian, Egyptian, and Canaanite. By this, God wanted to demonstrate "that the Messiah would be a brother and a cousin of both the Jews and the Gentiles, if not according to their paternal genealogy, at least according to their maternal nature. Consequently, there is no distinction between Jews and Gentiles, except that Moses later separated this people from the Gentiles by a different form of worship and political regime."[80]

According to His nature, Christ has the same flesh that we have; but in His conception the Holy Spirit came and overshadowed and purified the mass[81] that He received from the Virgin so that He might be united with the divine nature. The One who comes to bless all nations must be God. Yet He must be born from a flesh outstandingly sinful and contaminated by sin. Because of this, He comes from the line of Judah, who beget twins by an incestuous relationship with his daughter-in-law, Tamar.

> [Tamar] was made pregnant by the most shameful act of incest, and the flesh from which Christ was to be born was poured from the loins of Judah and was propagated, carried about, and contaminated with sin right up to the conception of Christ. That is how our Lord God treats our Savior. God allows Him to be conceived in most disgraceful incest, in order that He may assume the truest flesh, just as our flesh is poured forth, conceived, and nourished in sins.[82]

In summary, this Promised Seed would be a human being whom people could see, touch, hear, and feel.[83] This Jesus is indeed the Right Man who was set plainly before our eyes. At the same time, He must be true God because only the Son of God is able to reveal God and to show us the way.[84] This Blessed Seed "will bring a blessing so long and wide that it will reach all the families of the earth." "If the Seed of Abraham does this, He must necessarily be a true human being by nature; on the other hand, if He blesses others, even all the families of the earth, He must necessarily be something greater than the seed of Abraham."[85]

Finally, this dream was given to Jacob that he might understand His incarnation would take place in a definite place, namely, Jerusalem.[86] This very place would also become the place of His earthly ministry as He preached, healed, and taught.[87] He would also be crucified at this very place, sleep in the sepulcher, and rise from the dead where the angels ascended and descended.[88]

Larvae Dei, the Masks of God

The angels see what is happening at Jesus' birth in Bethlehem and they know what God is doing there. But how can humankind know and see what God is doing? To the eyes that are blind, that do not see and understand, they only see the baby in the manger or a man being crucified on the cross. How, then, can a person know what God has done in order to save them? God, in His gracious activity, makes Himself known in His masks, the *Larvae Dei*.

"Man shall not see me and live" (Exodus 33:20). As a result of the fall, and man's sinful nature, man cannot see God's naked transcendence and survive. There can be no unmediated relationship between God and man. God must disguise Himself under a type of mask or veil in all of His dealings with men. So, after the fall of Adam and Eve into sin, God—in His mercy—enveloped Himself in a gentle breeze. He did this so that He could reveal Himself to Adam under a cover, and also that by coming in a very soft breeze, He could bring a fatherly reprimand.[89]

OLD TESTAMENT SIGNS

It was a great comfort for Adam that, after he had lost Paradise, the tree of life . . . [God gave him] another sign of grace, namely, the sacrifices." In this sign, Adam "could perceive that he had not been cast off by God but was still the object of God's concern and regard."[90]

Later, circumcision was enjoined upon Abraham in order that it might be a sacrament through which his descendants would be made righteous if they believed the promise that the Lord attached to it. In addition, circumcision itself was a sign[91] to the nations that the promised Savior would be born from this circumcised nation. In this way, God has always provided some public sign whereby the nations might find the true God. Therefore circumcision, like the sacrifices, was raised up as a sign "to be looked at by those who were to be saved."[92]

NEW TESTAMENT SIGNS

Since the coming of Christ, God continues to speak to us in a fatherly manner through the ministry of the Word, His sacraments, and His promises of eternal grace. It is a great gift of His mercy that He is found, not in some faraway place, "but in Baptism, in the words of the Gospel, in the use of the Keys, and indeed also with any brother who with me confesses and believes in the Son of God. These are the epiphanies or appearances that are common to all Christians."[93]

These signs, along with the Word, are our light bearers today, and wherever these are, there we find Christ, the forgiveness of sins, and eternal life. As His people worship, Christ is present in and with His gifts of grace. As His Word is preached and Sacraments are administered, Christ imparts the Word through the medium of human tongues and voices. In the pulpit He speaks through the mouth of the preacher, at the font He Himself is the Baptizer, at the altar He imparts the remission of sins through the hands of the minister. It is God alone who operates, but He operates through us.

> It is true that you hear a human being when you are baptized and when you partake of the Holy Supper. But the Word which you hear is not that of a human being; it is the Word of the living God. It is He who baptizes you; it is He who absolves you from sins; and it is He who commands you to hope in His mercy. It is great ingratitude to slight these faces of God, as Scripture calls them, and meanwhile to look for other appearances and revelations.[94]

Where these signs of grace are not present or where they are despised, there are all sorts of errors and false forms of worship. Those who want to be saved must hold "to the form, the signs, and the coverings of the Godhead, such as His Word and His works. For in His Word and in His works He shows Himself to us."[95]

When we get to heaven, concludes Luther, we shall see God differently. But here we see Him enveloped in an image, namely, in His Word and Sacraments. These are, and will remain, His "masks" until the Day of Judgment. Meanwhile, "He is certainly present in these, Himself working miracles, preaching, administering the sacraments, consoling, strengthening, and helping."[96]

Four Aspects of Our Lives as His Masks

You Are the Salt of the Earth

The Christian believer is God's salt to a corrupt and rotten world. Salt is an active ingredient and it is never neutral. It is also a characteristic of salt that it has to bite, that is, "If you want to preach the Gospel and help people, you must be sharp and rub salt into their wounds . . . and denouncing what is not right."[97] There is no greater injury or decay in Christendom than when the salt, which should season and salt everything else, has itself lost its taste.

During the time of Sodom and Gomorrah, six patriarchs were then living: Shem, Arphaxad, Salah, Eber, Serug, and Abraham. Despite the preaching ministry of these ancient leaders,[98] the people of Sodom and Gomorrah abandoned all fear[99] and knowledge of God, "live[d] in luxury, [did] violence to their guests, and [were] altogether unconcerned about their own destruction.[100] This story is recorded in Scripture so that it might serve as an example for others to be salt in the world, in order that people might learn to fear God[101] and to shun the kind of sins that were the cause of such a great evil. For within the Church we must teach not only about the future life, "but we should regulate our life according to the Law and teach men how to lead a godly and honorable life until the last day."[102]

You Are the Light of the World

The Christian is not only His salt but also His light in the world. Once sin has been denounced, the believer is to instruct other souls and guide them to eternal life. In this world, encouraged Luther, "you must be like a burning and shining lamp, in order that the others may be illuminated" and saved.[103] This "life should be devoted to the service of one's neighbor, in order that as many as possible may be brought to the knowledge of God,"[104] that is, to fear God and to trust in His mercy.

An Evangelical Priesthood

In his treatise *Concerning the Ministry*, along with *The Reform of the Christian Estate*, Luther presents some of his clearest teaching on the priesthood of all believers.

All Christians are truly of the spiritual estate for it is baptism, Gospel, and faith alone which make us 'spiritual' and a Christian people; and it is through Baptism that all of us are consecrated to the priesthood. Consequently, there is no difference between laymen and clergy "except that of office[105] and work; but not of 'estate'."[106]

In the narrow sense, the duties of a priest are twofold: (1) to turn to God and pray for himself and for his neighbor, and (2) to turn from God to men by means of doctrine and the Word. As God's priests, it "behooves every Christian to espouse the cause of the faith, to understand and defend it, and to rebuke all errors"[107] and to spread God's Word. It is also the duty of every priest to strengthen the faith of others, to teach them the Word of God so that they can know the true and only God and to give Him thanks for His saving grace and many other gifts.[108]

And yet, "just because we are all in like manner priests, no one must put himself forward and undertake" to be the pastor of the community without the consent and election of God's people. "For what is common to all no one dare take upon himself without the will and command of the community."[109]

Thus it would not be possible for every member of the community to publicly administer the Word and Sacraments. Therefore, the pastoral office is necessary for the sake of order so that everything in the community should be done in an orderly way. For this reason, and according to Christ's institution of the pastoral office, "the community of believers must call an individual to this special office of the public ministry of Word and Sacraments."[110]

Vocation: the Link between Heaven and Earth

Every Christian occupies a number of offices[111] and positions at the same time. For example, a person might be a father, husband, and employee. As one works within one's office, he participates in God's own care for human beings. God pours out His gifts to us, and "our only care ought to be what we should do with all the good that God has made so that it may benefit our neighbor."[112]

Every person is created and born for the sake of others. This means that everyone is born to love and serve his neighbor . . . If I do not use everything that I have to serve my neighbor, I rob him of what I owe him according to God's will.[113]

The purpose of our callings in life is that one's neighbor is served as God reaches down, through His servant, for the well-being of humankind.[114] The Christian "is a conduit or channel that receives from above, from God, through faith and then gives forth below, to others, through love."[115] Thus God clothes Himself in the form of an ordinary person who performs His work on earth. Through vocation the person serves as a "mask of God" behind which He can conceal Himself as He scatters His gifts to humankind. "God works both through the Christian and through an Alexander the Great; they both are His instruments and in this is their unity."[116]

Based upon Ecclesiastes 3:1–17, "all human labors and efforts have their fixed time to be started, to be effected, and to be concluded."[117] The God who moves and commands us to work in our vocation is also "the same God who holds the outward course of events in His hands and thus prepares the opportune occasion in which the things commanded are to fit;"[118] thus, God has His purpose for every hour.

Since the course of our life is shaped by factors beyond our own plans and ideas, we are to address ourselves to the present hour, to whatever is at hand, to whatever is presently waiting for us [119] and belongs to our vocation. To use the moment and the time God gives is to enter into one's vocation. "[T]here is no other way of serving God than to walk in simple faith and then to stick diligently to one's calling and to keep a good conscience."[120]

6

THE ORDERS AND ROOT METAPHORS
of the Modern and Postmodern Condition

Introduction

Using the anthropological concepts of social order, cultural order, and root metaphors,[1] Paul Hiebert[2] developed a way of organizing and making sense of the modern and postmodern condition.

	Modernity	Postmodernity
Social Order	Factory	Pluralism
Cultural Order/ Root Metaphors	Dualism	Deconstructionism
	Mechanistic Understanding of Reality	Fragmentation
	Individualism	Mind Over Matter/ Deification of Self
	Materialism/ Consumerism	Therapeutic Self
	Welfare State	Relativism

Within a given society, there are various social systems of relationships in which people live. These systems define our identity in society and shape our lives. They are essential for human life but can be used for either good or evil, and they also have economic, political, and legal dimensions.

Within the economic dimension, theorists have understood the financial market as a self-operating mechanism modeled on the Newtonian universe that, from time to time, needs fine-tuning by the Federal Reserve and the World Bank. It is also the freeing of society from traditional Christian morality through the pursuit of covetousness so that individuals might better their material condition.

Within the political dimension, social activism is often pursued through the courts instead of through the legislative process. Power and pull is most important as various social political groups align themselves with legislative and legal entities so that they might have their values enacted within society.

Within the legal dimension, with the loss of a Reformational foundation based upon natural law, we have the hedonistic, subjective whims of the 51 percent majority, or the assertions of a political-scientific-intellectual elite who decide the moral laws.

The Social Order of Modernity: the Factory

According to sociologist Peter Berger,[3] a central feature of the modern social order is the factory. Since the rise of the industrial period, work has moved from the home to the factory, where we reduce humans to machines and use them to do our work. Thus factory workers are related to each other anonymously as units in a mechanical process, and within this process they are viewed as replaceable parts.[4] In this mechanical mode of production the focus is on tasks, production, efficiency, control, profit, and success. People are expected to conform to the impersonal roles as anonymous components in the production process.

The Social Order of Postmodernity

The social order of postmodernity is the growing pluralism of Western societies. It is the acknowledgement that truth is larger, richer, and more complex than can be contained in any one religious or cultural tradition. No longer can one group remain dominant and control the social order, with a myriad of other voices[5] being heard. But postmodern society is more than the fact of pluralism, it is the acceptance of pluralism as the ideal way to organize society in the long run, that is, a society not controlled by accepted dogma.

This pluralism can best be illustrated in the field of architecture. During the modern period,[6] architects designed and constructed buildings that expressed one unified, essential meaning such as the International Style that became dominant throughout the world by the 1950s. These buildings gave expression, in the forms and materials used, to the brave new world of science and technology that typified the industrial age.

In contrast, postmodern architects purposely designed buildings that incorporated the concepts of diversity and pluralism. Postmodern architecture returned to the past to combine and incorporate different styles that emphasized decoration and symbolism and reflected both regional styles and local cultures and traditions.

The Cultural Order of Modernity

Our worldview gives us both a synchronic and diachronic understanding of reality: Synchronically, our worldview gives us the categories with which we think, provides us with the logic we use to explain reality, and defines the fundamental values and allegiances that demand our commitment. Diachronically, our worldview provides us with the big story. It includes root myths that help us interpret our lives. It also includes the cosmic story that provides meaning to all our corporate and personal stories.

According to Hiebert, the root metaphors of modernity are dualism, a mechanistic understanding of reality, individualism, materialism/consumerism, and the welfare state/civil religion. The root metaphors of postmodernity are deconstructionism,[7] the deification of self, the therapeutic society, and relativism.

The Synchronic, Cultural Order of Modernity

Dualism

Dualism is the split in Western culture between spirit and matter. One consequence of this split is the division of life into the public and private sectors. A second consequence is the division of the world into natural and supernatural realms.

The Division of Knowledge into Public Facts and Private Values

Western society, in the past, largely rested upon the metaphysical and philosophical foundation that God exists and that the Bible is true. The secular humanistic worldview, on the other hand, holds that the biblical truth-claims are unscientific, cannot be proved, and belong to the realm of faith. As a result, religious answers do not deal with facts, only science deals with facts.

Consequently, one of the key modern divisions in life is described by Lesslie Newbigin through the societal division of knowledge into public facts and private values. It is our cultural way to make our choices while realizing that there is a public world of what our culture calls "facts" that is distinct from the private world of "beliefs, opinions and values."[8]

Within such a division of knowledge, the public world is a world of facts that are the same for everyone, whatever a person's values may be, and with which every intelligent person is expected to agree. The private world, however, is a world where all are free to choose their own values,[9] provided that personal values do not prevent others from having the same freedom to choose.[10]

What are the sources of public knowledge and private values? It is the truth claims derived from science that are permitted legitimizing authority in the realm of public truth; the truth claims of religion are relegated to the private sphere, for "science is what we know; religion is what some people believe." Therefore, knowing is one thing, and everyone is to know the real facts based upon science, whereas beliefs and values are predicated upon a decision based upon religion and personal preferences.[11]

For example, one view of the origin, nature, and destiny of human beings may be taught in public schools—the big bang and evolutionary theories; but another may not be taught—creation by a supernatural being. "If it is science it may be taught—true or false; if it is religion, it may not be taught—true or false."[12] The idea that the development of the individual person is governed by the program encoded in the DNA molecule is a fact every educated person is expected to know and accept. The belief that every human being is made to glorify God and live with Him forever is an opinion held by some people, but it is not part of public truth. Yet if the universe and man is the special creation of God, and if man is created to glorify God and to live forever with Him, it is at least as important as anything else in the preparation of young children at school and the living of a people within its culture.

As you can see from just these two examples, the Christian faith has become, for many people in our society, a private and domestic matter strictly separated from the public worlds of facts. In modern Western culture, the Church and its preaching have become marginalized to the world of "values."

The Division of the World into the Natural and Supernatural Realms

The people of premodern Western culture understood their lives to be the result of supernatural interventions by God and the devil, whereas modern Western culture interprets that the same events are to be understood in terms of natural laws. How did this shift in the perception of external reality come about?

Scientists in the seventeenth and eighteenth centuries continued to use the word God, but they pushed God more and more to the edges of their explanatory systems. Step by step, however, scientific knowledge expanded to the point where the gaps of knowledge became closed and there was no place left for God. One need only to remember the famous reply Marquis de Laplace made after Napolean complained that Laplace had omitted God from his explanations of nature: "I find no need of that hypothesis."[13]

Mechanistic Understanding of Reality

The mechanistic understanding of reality divides the world between mind and matter, thereby allowing scientists to treat matter as dead and completely separate from themselves, and to see the material world as a multitude of different objects assembled into a huge machine.

Despite all the changes in physics in the present century (Planck's quantum world, Einstein's theories of relativity, and Heisenberg's uncertainty principle), the vision of the real world in the mind of the ordinary man on the street is the one derived from Newtonian science. The model of reality that emerges from a mechanistic worldview is a vast machine where fundamental characteristics can be understood by an analysis of its parts and the laws that govern their working. The popular way to explain things is to analyze them into their smallest parts and show how everything that happens is ultimately governed by the laws of physics. "Things are not explained in terms of purpose, because purpose is a function of the beliefs and values of the person whose purpose it is. Things are to be explained in terms of their causes, of what makes them happen."[14]

Even the sciences that deal with human behavior in society have likewise been enormously influenced by the mechanical model. Most of twentieth century thinking sees man as determined by chemical, psychological, and environmental determinism. For others, man is no more than a part of a cosmic machine. Either way, "human life is ultimately to be understood as the product of an endless series of random happenings in the physical world."[15]

A mechanistic understanding of reality creates a society in which there is less and less room for the transcendent, the magical, and the supernatural. In other words, the modern world has been undergoing a process of disenchantment.

Individualism/Self

The third root metaphor of North American culture is individualism, the concept of the individual as an autonomous person. Our culture no longer refers to a person as a soul but instead uses the language of self. The implication is that a soul is dependent upon God, whereas the self is autonomous and free. The term "self" gave rise to the concept of the "self-made man," then to self-achievement and self-fulfillment.

It was during the Age of Reason that this autonomy began to be developed as individuals became increasingly bold in testing all external claims to authority. Immanuel Kant, in the phrase "dare to know," has defined this anti-authority attitude in which no alleged revelation, no tradition and no dogma, however hallowed, has the right to veto its exercise. Man has emerged from his dependency upon other authorities and is now free to make use of his reason in all matters.

What is the chief end of this freedom? For most people it is being happy. Each individual has the right not only to pursue happiness but to define it as he wishes. For those who grew up in the 1960s, freedom was its primal cry. Each person had the right to be free from tradition, custom, authority, and all that inhibited the spontaneous expression of the autonomous individual in that moment.[16]

Materialism/Consumerism

The fourth root metaphor of our culture is materialism. Between 1890 and 1910, writes Paul Hiebert, a new morality entered the culture that subordinated the old goal of transcendency to new ideals of self-fulfillment and immediate gratification. Personal meaning became tied to acquiring things with borrowing, which is replacing saving as the way to fund our lifestyle.[17]

Premodern people believed that final happiness lay on the other side of death. In place of the joys of heaven, modern man looked forward to happiness here on earth. This would come within the reach of all through the cumulative work of science, liberating societies from bondage to dogma and superstition, unlocking secrets of nature, and transferring the holy city from another world to this one. "No longer would it be a gift of God from heaven; it would be the final triumph of science and the skill of the enlightened people of the earth."[18]

And yet Kierkegaard saw the modern age as a greed-ridden and narcissistic era that fetishizes money[19] as "an ultimate source of value in an abstract and unreal world."[20] Significant meaning in life would be found in acquiring things and be measured by the abundance and quality of these things. As Francis Schaeffer observed, man pursues personal peace and personal affluence.[21] He wants to live his life undisturbed by others so that he can acquire and enjoy his possessions; and he desires an ever-increasing prosperity. And yet, it really is only living "ash heap lives," since most of these things will end up in the city dump.

For Jean Baudrillard, in a consumer-oriented age individuals consume a world fabricated by others.[22] First, desires and needs are created through advertising; then, the commodities and services are provided to meet these needs. "Unlike real human needs, material needs and spectacles are artificial as capitalism endlessly multiplies needs for the latest gadget or product line while creating a fantasy world of imagined self-realization and happiness."[23]

But even more is promoted in a society of the spectacle[24] because in our personal consumption[25] a person buys a Mercedes for its automotive value but also because the Mercedes serves as a sign[26] of the consumer's prestige, rank, and social standing. Thus we display what we buy in order to differentiate ourselves socially. And yet you can't just buy one object in order to enter a social level, you need to buy into an entire system of objects.[27]

WELFARE STATE AND CIVIL RELIGION

The Welfare State

In the nineteenth century the state came to be the central institution that was ultimately responsible for the well-being of its citizens. Responsibilities for education, healing, and public welfare, which had formerly rested with the Church, became more and more the responsibility of the nation-state.

This rise of the nation-state is one of the key factors of the post-Enlightenment Western world. As nature has taken the place of God as the ultimate reality with which we have to deal, observed Lesslie Newbigin, "the nation-state has taken the place of God as the source to which we look for happiness, health and welfare."[28]

According to Newbigin, the Enlightenment gave birth to a new conception of politics, namely, that happiness can be provided by a political system[29] and that the goal of politics is happiness.[30] The state is responsible to help each person in his or her right to life, liberty, and the pursuit of happiness.[31] Since the pursuit of happiness is endless, the demands upon the state are limitless as well. For many, especially during an election year, the measure of a politician is not his character but if he can "get things done" and make "things better for his constituents," that is, if he can make them happy and more prosperous.

Civil Religion

Within our society there is what sociologists call "civil religion." Civil religion is a commonly-held religious ideology that is both shaped by and helps to shape a nation's collective consciousness, and which serves the interests of the state by promoting public morality, encouraging citizens to do their duty, and legitimizing the state and its laws.[32]

Jean Jacques Rousseau declared that at the head of every political society stands a god. Rousseau used the term "civil religion" to describe a minimalist religion that would meet the needs of the state.[33] Civil religion possesses four dogmas: "the existence of a powerful, wise, and benevolent deity, who foresees and provides for the life to come; the happiness of the just; the punishment of the wicked; and the sanctity of the social contract and the laws."[34]

In addition to Rousseau's four dogmas that define civil religion, two additions have been added in America: the notion of America's manifest destiny and the anonymity of God. "From very early in our nation's history, people of faith in America have cultivated a sense of the unique, divinely appointed role of America in the world." It is a "city set upon a hill" and "a chosen nation."[35]

Second, for the vast majority of America's history, when the term "god" was used in public discourse, most Americans would have understood that the God being spoken about was the god who revealed Himself in the Old and New Testaments, either the Jewish god or the Christian God. Even though the common American public consciousness is still largely shaped by the Judeo-Christian concept of monothesism, the meaning of "god" has been broadened to mean a single spirit-being, malleable enough to accommodate any and all religious conceptions. In other words, god is anonymous. He has no name. God is simply god. When he is called, no one is offended because the definition is anonymous enough to allow each person to define god according to his own religious understanding, and yet "it preserves the First Amendment by showing no favoritism."[36]

The Diachronic, Cultural Order of Modernity

The way we understand life depends on what conception we have of the human story. In our contemporary culture, the dominant story that is publicly taught is the big bang theory of the origin of the universe. This theory discusses an impersonal beginning and the view that all living things evolved by a gradual, natural process, from nonliving matter to simple micro-organisms, leading eventually to man.

The Modern Story

Ever since the early 1920s, following the publication of the ideas by Albert Einstein, the majority of scientists have accepted the view that the universe started with a big bang explosion of some dense particle and has been expanding ever since. The idea of the big bang theory is that fifteen billion years ago all the matter of the universe was concentrated in a single mass. Then that very dense mass exploded with a big bang and all of the parts of the universe have been expanding into space ever since that explosion. As the initial radiation spread outward, temperatures slowly cooled enough for hydrogen and helium atoms to form. Some time later, the first stars began to form from the cooling gas in the young universe. This star-forming process eventually gave rise to the Milky Way Galaxy.

According to the evolution model, life came through change, time, and a large number of fortuitous events. Evolutionary naturalism teaches that life began by the random collusion of enough atoms to form complex molecules. These molecules eventually formed into cells and, over billions of years, evolved into all life extant today. The key to this molecule-to-human evolution was mutations (genetic copy errors) and natural selection (the selection of favorable mutations that alter the animal or plant so that they are more apt to survive). According to this story of origins, modern humans evolved from more primitive bipedal hominids. Human beings, then, are the end products of changes in living things that occurred through vertebrate ancestry to some invertebrate forms, and after spontaneous generation of first life occurred on the earth from inanimate matter.

Thus the modern story is told that the present universe did not get here because a supernatural God created it, but that its present form happened as a result of chance events. It assumes that the matter that makes up the universe was never created but has always existed. It is a view that everything began with an impersonal beginning—the impersonality of the singularity—and then everything, including the life of man, comes forth by chance from that.

In the evolutionary scheme of things, man is just a chance parade from the impersonal energy particle to man. Man is a cosmic accident, emerging from the slim by chance—a grown-up germ. Man, as he looks upon this immense universe, understands himself as a zero, dwelling on a minor planet in a minor solar system. This is our cultural story, it is our cultural song that we sing all day long.

The Biblical Story

The other story is the one embodied in the Scriptures, the story of creation and fall, of the calling of God's people out of the world in order that they might live with God forever and, until that day, proclaim the Good News of God's grace and mercy revealed in the person and work of Jesus Christ.

The story begins in a lovely garden that God provided for our first parents, Adam and Eve. From the beginning, the Creator ordained that humankind, on the Sabbath day, should reflect on the works of God and bestow honor on God with the praises that He deserved. It was also God's design that the tree of the knowledge of good and evil be the place where Adam and Eve (and their future descendants) would yield to God the obedience they owed, and call upon God for aid against temptation. Thus God's command regarding this tree was to be "an outward form of worship and an outward work of obedience toward God."[37] This tree was not deadly by nature but became so only by the Word of God and man's disobedience.

The story of humankind is the story of man's effort to live without God, to live independently and in revolt against God. Yet God, in loving response to man's disobedience, promised a Savior, a Blessed Seed who would be born of a woman and who would be born of Abraham's seed. Thus through Abraham, the Blessed Seed was linked to a certain race, this Savior was meant not only for the descendants of Abraham but all the families of the earth (Genesis 12). This promise given to Abraham was also given to Isaac (Genesis 26:4) and to Jacob (Genesis 28:14).

After the calling of Moses and the dramatic deliverance from Egypt, Israel's understanding of its covenant relationship with God as His chosen people was more fully developed and strengthened. Through Moses at Mount Sinai a covenant was made with Israel, an election not only to privilege but also to service, to further God's purposes for the nations. God did not choose Israel because they were more worthy than other nations or because He had no interest in the others; He chose Israel because He had a concern for "all the earth." Israel was appointed to be "a kingdom of priests and a holy nation," that is, a people set apart to represent God to the needy world. Their responsibility was to trust God and obey Him and be His instrument to serve the world.[38]

However, as time passed Israel broke the covenant. They did not act like God's people; they failed to trust in God and obey Him. The voices of the prophets reminded them of their high calling, pleaded with the "chosen ones" to be faithful in their covenant relation with their God, and warned "the elect" of the impending wrath of God's judgment. But for the most part, Israel remained faithless and disobedient.[39] The corruption of Israel became so complete that Jeremiah was forced to exclaim, "Can the Ethiopian change his skin or the leopard his spots?" (13:23). Jeremiah was not even permitted to intercede for Israel anymore. The end had come!

God's plan now called for a new start, a new people, and an establishment of a new covenant. Thus God exposed the false presuppositions that most of the Israelites had fostered. He demonstrated that He was not confined to any city, such as Zion, or any symbol, such as the ark or the temple. He was not bound to any nation, such as the Jews, or to any specific political or social system. He was, above all, a God of righteousness.[40]

The new beginning was an act of sheer grace, like a potter taking the rejected pieces of clay to start afresh (Jeremiah 18). From the fragments of Israel, God began to build His kingdom with new and richer promises of grace. With the coming of the Christ, the suffering servant of Isaiah 53, He established a new covenant in His blood, shed for the remission of sins. The righteousness that the Law sought to create was fulfilled through the sacrificial obedience of the Servant. He announced that the kingdom of God had come into the world, and He summoned men to that kingdom. He called His disciples to be the nucleus of a new Israel.[41]

Though the call of God was addressed primarily to "the lost sheep of Israel," it was God's purpose that the movement of "making disciples" should reach out toward all nations and peoples. So the secret and mystery of God's saving plan is revealed. God has acted in Christ and men are being led into a new reality; the living body of Christ on earth. They become participants in Christ's own life and mission. God has made us what we are. He has laid His redemptive claims on us. He wills to work out His plan in and through those who believe.[42] Each believer is a living organism indwelt by the Holy Spirit and joined to Christ, the Head of the body. Each member of the body is a member of every other, and all are givers of Christ's life to the world. Just as the Father sent Jesus into the world, so Jesus sends out His disciples to go with the Gospel to make disciples of all nations.

The mature Christian will see his membership in the Church as involving him not only in a fellowship privilege and blessing but also in a fellowship of responsibility. In his *Treatise on Christian Liberty* Luther emphasizes the responsibility of the Christian as a priest of God and states that to teach, to intercede, and to sacrifice is the whole life of a Christian in relation to his neighbor. The service of the Christian in God's plan is to be directed also to the world. The mystery of God's power and love, hidden for the ages, is to be made known openly so that all men may see what the plan is and be restored and reconciled in Christ to God. "Christians are to call to the world, 'Be reconciled to God and take your place in the reconciled community.' "[43] Acknowledge that you are a sinner and that your ways of life are filled with sin and death. Then, fall into the gracious and loving arms of the living God so that you may find the abundant life and a living hope in the Person of Jesus Christ.

The believer responds to the love of God and plunges himself into the world as the proper place for the activity of faith. By faith, man is able to surrender all of life to the will of God and bring every aspect of his life into trustful obedience to the lordship of Christ. In family duties and relationships, in friendship situations, in gainful occupations, in the activities of citizenship, and in the Christian congregation, the Christian lives out his calling with faith and love. The Christian refuses to concede that any sphere of God's creation is "secular" or "profane," and because all of life is God's, he sets out to live his faith in service to others where God has placed him. Luther states that every Christian is called by God to obey His commands in relationship to the things and people that have been allotted to him.[44] "What is God's will for me?" is answered by asking, "What are my neighbor's needs of me?"

The Cultural Order of Postmodernity

As we enter the twenty-first century, a new way of viewing the world has emerged.[45] The modern way of thinking that dominated the nineteenth and twentieth centuries has become obsolete, and this century will be ultimately characterized by an emerging postmodernism. We live in a "post" era. It has been described as postcritical (Michael Polanyi) and postmodern, postFordist,[46] postindustrial, post-metaphysical (Jurgen Habermas), post-Eurocentric, postcolonial, post imperial, postsocialist, post-patriarchal, postideological, and postconfessional (Hans Kung).

In order to understand the "post" of postmodern, we must first briefly examine the modern condition.

The Modern Era

The modern world began roughly in the seventeenth century with the emergence of new scientific and philosophical understandings about the world. "Through a series of revolutions—geographic (colonialism), intellectual (the Renaissance, modern science and the Enlightenment), economic (capitalism), political (bourgeois democracy), technological (the Industrial Revolution), and artistic (modernism)—the world of Newton, Kant, and Marx became fundamentally different from the premodern world of Dante, Aquinas, and Augustine."[47]

The Philosophical Foundation

The French philosopher René Descartes laid the philosophical foundation for the modern edifice with his focus on doubt. This led him to conclude that the thinking self is the first truth that doubt could not deny. In so doing, "Descartes defined human nature as a thinking substance and the human person as an autonomous rational subject."[48] Devoted to Rationalism, Descartes insisted upon absolute philosophical certainty. There must be a way of knowing things beyond any doubt, Descartes insisted, and therefore he sought a foundation for grounding all human knowledge. That foundation was universal reason.

The Scientific Foundation

The British physicist Isaac Newton later provided the scientific framework for modernity. He pictured the physical world as a machine whose laws and regularity could be discerned by the human mind. The modern human, therefore, is "Descartes' autonomous, rational substance encountering Newton's mechanistic world."[49]

The Enlightenment Project

"The postulates of the thinking self and the mechanistic universe opened the way for the explosion of knowledge under the banner" of the "Enlightenment project." The goal of the human intellectual quest became that of unlocking "the secrets of the universe in order to master nature for human benefit and to create a better world."[50]

The intellectual foundation of the Enlightenment project are certain epistemological[51] assumptions: that knowledge is certain, objective, and good and that such knowledge is obtainable; that knowledge is objective and that a person is able to view the world as it really is; that knowledge is good and that, as knowledge is discovered, progress is inevitable; and that the modern self is autonomous and free from the controlling influences of tradition and community.

Three Major Components of Modernity

At the heart of modernity are three major components: intellectual, technological, and sociological.

Intellectual Components

The modernists were committed to the quest for truth and believed that man could discover certain truth. The method for discovering truth was either through reason (rationalism) or through empirical investigation and analysis (empiricism). Armed with this knowledge about the world and human nature, progress was probable, even inevitable.

Technological Components

The modern age was ushered in to a significant degree by the Industrial Revolution in which new scientific understandings were harnessed in the production and distribution of material goods. This new bold spirit embraces the idea that humankind can consciously change the character of society and the condition of our lives. It is committed to the idea that we can make the future and not be dependent upon any transcendent being.

Sociological Components

One of the primary sociological realities is the growing numbers of people from varying nations, religions, and ethnic groups that now live together in a "global village." In the midst of this sociological pluralism, there has often developed a pluralism of ideas especially about the nature of truth and ethics. Religion does not disappear in a pluralistic society, but it is encouraged to become privatized for the sake of public peace and order. Religion is relegated to the private sphere of personal relationships, family, and inner-self and does not play a significant role in the public square.

The Movement from Modernity to Postmodernity

This movement from modernity to postmodernity involves a number of significant shifts in a great variety of fields. One encounters new experiences, ideas, and ways of life that contest accepted modes of thought and behavior and provide new ways of seeing, writing, and living. It is global, encompassing almost the whole world, "percolating from academic and avant-garde cultural circles to media culture and everyday life so as to become a defining, albeit highly contested, aspect of the present era."[52]

The Emergence of the "Post"

During the 1960s, a group of radical intellectuals and activists, who became the first major postmodern theorists, experienced what they believed to be a decisive break with modern society and culture. This dissolution of old paradigms[53] was joined by spectacular political upheaval[54] and "struggle throughout the world, along with the emergence of new forms of thought, culture, technology, and life, which would produce the matrix for the postmodern turn."[55]

"Thinkers like Foucault, Derrida, Lyotard, and Deleuze were turning to Nietzsche and Heidegger and appropriating their critical discourses against modern theory and modernity itself" with emphases on relativism, perspectivalism, difference, and particularity.[56]

Social and Political Blows to Modernity

World War I marks an important break in history. Coming at the end of a period of relative peace and prosperity in Europe, August 1914 shattered the foundations[57] of a stable, and ever progressing, European society. The first significant use of the term "postmodernism" was by Arnold Toynbee who, in 1939, suggested that the modern era had ended in 1914 and that the historical period that emerged out of the ruins of World War I should be described as post-modern.

The war and its horrors brought an end to modernity's promise of inevitable progress and determined optimism. The most cultured and enlightened part of the world, twentieth century Europe, had just experienced four years of intense death and destruction.

Philosophical Blows to Modernity

By the 1880s, Nietzsche had diagnosed nihilism as the sickness of the times. Kierkegaard had already explored the feelings of dread, anxiety, and sickness unto death that shook his soul. Heidegger would soon emphasize finitude and contingency as the essence of our being as we struggle to live an authentic and genuine life in a standardized mass society. Others have noted that existentialism arose as the product of a European modernity in crisis, "as the main values of civilization and of the Enlightenment were being called into question by both philosophical and historical events."[58]

Existentialist Themes

The ultimate meaning of existentialism initially exploded on the global scene on July 16, 1945, with the first successful testing of the atomic bomb.[59] "The bomb reveals the dreadful and total contingency of human existence. Existentialism is the philosophy of the atomic age."[60]

Situational Ethics

Most philosophers since Plato have expounded that the highest ethical good is the same for everyone. Existentialism, on the other hand, believes that one must choose one's own way without the aid of universal, objective standards. Against the traditional view that moral choice involves an objective judgment of right and wrong, existentialists have argued that no objective, rational base can be found for moral decisions.

Existence Before Essence

Man exists and encounters himself in the world and then defines himself afterward. Man is nothing else but that which he makes of himself; the sum of his actions. In other words, human beings do not have a fixed nature, or essence, but each human being makes choices that create his or her own nature: existence precedes essence.

Choice is therefore central to human existence and it is inescapable. Man makes himself by the choice of his morality. Because individuals are "condemned to be free" they must accept the risk and responsibility of following their commitment wherever it leads.

A DANA Existence: Dread, Anxiety, Nausea, Anguish

Man lives with *dread*, that is, a fear of specific objects and also a feeling of general apprehension. For Kierkegaard, dread was God's way of calling each individual to make a commitment to a personally valid way of life. This valid way was Christianity, which alone could save an individual from despair. In contrast to Kierkegaard, Nietzsche proclaimed "the death of God" and went on to reject the entire Judeo-Christian moral tradition in favor of a heroic pagan ideal.

The word *anxiety* has a similar role for man today. Anxiety leads to the individual's confrontation with his impending nothingness and with the impossibility of finding ultimate justification for the choices he must make. Human beings can never hope to understand why they are here; instead, each individual must choose a goal and follow it with passionate conviction, aware of the uncertainty of death and the ultimate meaning-lessness of one's life.

In the philosophy of Sartre, the word *nausea* is used for the individual's recognition of the pure contingency of the universe, and the word *anguish* is used for the recognition of the total freedom of choice that confronts the individual at every moment. Human beings require a rational basis for their lives but are unable to achieve one; thus human life is a "futile passion."

SCIENTIFIC BLOWS TO MODERNITY

The most devastating internal challenge to modernity came from physics, the discipline that had provided the firmest foundation. First, Einstein's theory of relativity showed an interaction and a dependency between matter and energy that questioned long held assumptions about the modern world. Then, Heisenberg's uncertainty principle showed a limit on our knowledge about the smallest particles, for

> we can determine with certainty either the position of the subatomic particle or its momentum, but we cannot determine both these characteristics for any given particle at any given time. Certainty evaporates at the subatomic level, leaving us with probabilities and paradoxes.[61]

At the same time, Heisenberg established that there is an essential indeterminacy about all phenomena that no kind or amount of observation can overcome.[62]

CORROBORATIVE EVIDENCE THAT A CULTURAL SHIFT HAS OCCURRED

Francis Schaeffer observed that modern music is both an avenue for creative expression and the means through which modern man is exposed to new views of perceived reality. Schaeffer also believed that music is the dominant media form for analyzing culture since philosophy and the graphic arts are not the medium of the masses. Music can provide a window into the soul of the recording artist and the target audience because they are ethnographic in nature and describe everyday life or, in our case, postmodern life.

One of the most insightful recording artists of our day is British rocker Sting. In the song "All This Time," Sting describes postmodern society from the perspective of a postmodern man. Sting, from the vantage point of a dechristianized Europe, describes the death of Christianity. In the song, he relates that only the river that flows into the sea is constant and eternal. The church steeple in the distance serves only as the dwelling place of birds because of its antiquated and irrelevant message. As he surveys daily life events, he is unable to see God or experience His presence. Thus his question is, "If the Father and Jesus exist, then how come they never live here?"

Not only has Sting lost his faith in God but he also has lost his faith in Enlightened and Modern Man. In his song "If I Ever Lose My Faith in You," Sting observes that the main themes of modernity such as science, progress, ideological dogma, politicians, and military solutions have all failed in their quest toward utopia; instead, we have been going "from a blessing to a curse." Since both God and human beings are incapable of giving us a perfect world, Sting advises postmodern man in his song "Fields of Gold" that humankind's orientation should be to forget God, find a lover, walk and lie in the fields, watch children run in the fields, and be remembered by your lover and children when death comes.

This lyrical assessment by Sting that the modern world has entered a postmodern period agrees with the writings of Christian philosophers Diogenes Allen and Thomas Oden. According to Allen, the "foundations of the modern world are collapsing, and we are entering a postmodern world. The principles forged during the Enlightenment which formed the foundations of the modern mentality, are crumbling."[63] For Oden, we "are already through the funeral of the four key assumptions of modernity (autonomous individualism, narcissistic hedonism, reductive naturalism and absolute moral relativism), although it may take time to realize just how unresponsive are the corpses."[64]

Introduction to Postmodernity

The decline of modernity occurred because the grand narratives that legitimated modern society began losing their power. Simply put, people began to doubt the metanarratives.[65] In fact, Jean-Francois Lyotard defined postmodernism as "incredulity toward metanarratives."[66] Lyotard argued that no one set of rules, no one story, no condition accurately explains reality.

As early as the end of the nineteenth century, when the writings of Friedrich Nietzsche proclaimed the death of God, one is confronted with the reality that Western civilization is no longer influenced by the Judeo-Christian religious tradition as it once had been. Instead, Nietzsche proclaimed that man is the creator of the new cultural forms rather than the preserver of the old cultural forms.

General Characteristics of the Postmodern Condition

Postmodernism is a broad concept that covers the movements and shifts that have occurred in the humanities (art, history, architecture, literature, political science, economics, theology, and philosophy) since World War II, and that reflect a significant change in Western sensibility and attitudes.

What Is Truth? Truth Is What You Make It

Postmodernism challenges the fundamental epistemological assumption of modern philosophy and science—the possibility of discovering the truth about anything.

Classical philosophy, and even modern philosophy, "always assumed that there was a single target at which everyone was aiming."[67] The epistemology of modernity had its own skepticisms, but it regarded its obstacles as challenges to be overcome. Gradually, it became clear that modernity had arrived at no absolute truth and the quest was abandoned.

In other words, the modern condition was an age of metanarratives[68] in which men sought to explain ultimate and external realities, along with the nature and destiny of man, through a grand narrative. The postmodern condition maintains that there is no grand narrative and that there are only mininarratives that operate and are promoted among different reality-defining communities. Truth is not discovered, it is constructed. All that remains is little stories. All the grand narratives of modernity (the unified theory in science, Hegel's dialecticism in philosophy, Christianity in theology) are broken down into fragmented mininarratives that function as language games.

One Postmodern Example from Architecture

Architecture is actually the area in which postmodernism began, and was a reaction against modernism, especially against the architecture connected with the Bauhaus School in Weimar, Germany. The Bauhaus

School believed that buildings should be functional. They also developed what came to be known as the International Style, a style that used new materials from the modern period, such as steel and reinforced concrete, and produced a design that consisted of a series of rectangular buildings joined together at perpendicular angles. The design was uniform, geometrically precise, devoid of ornamental detail, and completely standardized.

In direct opposition to the Bauhaus School and its rejection of history, postmodern architecture mines history for its rich symbolic and stylistic sources. Moreover, rather than one style dominating and giving meaning to the entire building, postmodern architecture creates a double coding by putting together two styles of two different periods, thereby creating ambiguity, contradiction, and paradox. The architecture of the Las Vegas strip is an excellent example of postmodern architecture where the design of the Aladdin complex is Tudor with a Moorish façade, and the design of Caesar's Palace incorporates early Christian, Roman, Neo-classical, Motel Moderne, Etruscan and Miesian.

This concern for the inclusion of plural meanings illustrates the postmodern attack on universals; it rejects the homogenization of the International Style and favors the differences of regional styles and local cultures. Unlike modern architecture that sought to embody fixed principles and a universal style, postmodern architecture supports the relativism of values in which no code is inherently better than any other.

The Discourse of the Postmodern

There are two quite different types of postmodern theory: extreme postmodern theory and a modest mode of postmodern discourse. The extreme postmodern theory of Jean Baudrillard and his followers advocates that a radical rupture has taken place between modernity and postmodernity, and "that the foundationalist, universalist and totalizing practices of modernity must be renounced and give way to a wholly new mode of postmodern theory, ethics and politics."[69]

The postmodern discourse articulated by Lyotard, Foucault, Harvey, and Rorty suggests that a fundamental break with modernity has not occurred. They "interpret the postmodern merely as a mutation of the modern, as a significant shift within modernity." These authors "combine modern and postmodern discourses and interpret the postmodern

175

primarily as a modality of the modern rather than as its radical other."[70] In other words, "the postmodern is a radicalization of the modern, which intensifies modern phenomena like commodification, massification, technology, and the media to a degree that generates genuine discontinuities and novelties from the modern world."[71]

The Synchronic, Cultural Order of Postmodernity

Deconstructionism

Deconstruction arose in response to a theory in literature called "structuralism." Structuralists theorized that cultures develop literary documents in an attempt to provide meaning by which people can make sense out of the meaninglessness of their experiences.

The deconstructionists, Jacques Derrida in particular, rejected the tenets of structuralism. Meaning is not inherent in a text[72] itself, they argued, but "emerges only as the interpreter enters into dialogue with the text. Consequently, the meaning of a text is dependent on the perspective of the one who enters into dialogue with it; there are as many interpretations of a text as readers."[73]

Michel Foucault added a moral twist to Derrida's work. He argued that every interpretation is made by those in power because to name something is to exercise power. According to Foucault, social institutions and groups impose their own understanding on the centerless flux of experience. Consequently, "Foucault claimed that every assertion of knowledge is an act of power"[74] and one must employ a "hermeneutic of suspicion" and of mistrust toward every form of interpretation.

Fragmentation

For several centuries, all Western thought was based on the idea of a center—a truth, an ideal form, a God—that guaranteed all meaning. The postmodern critique is that there is no one center that is sufficient to encompass the experiences of all people. We can never see or experience the whole of things; we can only speak parochially from our own historical and cultural-bound perspectives. Thus "the truth is shaped and understood by each individual and the community of which he or she is a part."[75] The world has no center, only differing viewpoints and perspectives. In the end, the postmodern world becomes an arena of dueling texts and a never ending struggle among competing interpretations.

Mind over Matter and the Deification of Self

The basic postmodern condition is that the mind creates the realities we know, and it leads to the view that all belief systems are social constructions.

The subjectivity of the person in the construction of reality can be illustrated by three baseball umpires who are discussing their philosophy of calling balls and strikes:

Umpire #1: There are balls and there are strikes; I call 'em the way they are!

Umpire #2: There are balls and there are strikes; I call 'em like I see them!

Umpire #3: There are balls and there are strikes; but they ain't nothing till I call 'em!

Increasingly, our postmodern world identifies with umpire #3. All reality is subjectively construed and postmodern man is the one to call them; there is no other creature that is to deny him his autonomy. In so doing, he has taken the place of God by calling things the way he wants to call them without regard to God's Word.

Therapeutic Self

A third theme of postmodernity is a stress on therapy and health toward self-realization, an ethos characterized by an almost obsessive concern with psychic and physical health. This search for health is a reaction to modernity with its depersonalization of human beings.

Increasingly, people today seek to order their lives in accordance with a commitment to psychological self-affirmation and emotional well-being. This therapeutic attitude liberates individuals by helping them get in touch with their own wants and interests and free themselves from the artificial constraints of social roles and the guilt-inducing demands of others.

If religion is sought out, it becomes merely a mechanism for self-actualization so that a person can obtain desired emotional feelings and experience the absence of inner conflict. In the postmodern world the therapist[76] has replaced the preacher. This shift to therapy and healing has led to a decline in theological concepts such as sin and salvation. People are not rebels against God but victims of society. They need health, defined primarily in terms of feelings, not an objective reconciliation with God.

Relativism

Relativism is the result of deconstructionism and pluralism within society. In a world of relativism, one can no longer speak of objective truth. In the postmodern condition, men have given up the hope of absolutes and universals.

Jerry Lee Lewis, through the use of a dance metaphor in his hit song "A Whole Lot of Shaking Going On," provided the American culture with an insight into the emerging relativistic revolution of the 1960s. Francis Schaeffer observed that a great revolution took place in twentieth century American culture, "in the short span from the twenties to the sixties,"[77] in terms of its assault upon God's ordered powers of church, state, and the home. Or, as Ken Myers suggests, "hell had been waiting in the wings for over a century; it finally broke loose in the 1960s."[78]

Modern man, in the absence of a moral imperative, has no categories beyond pragmatic ones. Not having absolutes, the modern concept is sociological. One assesses the statistics of public opinion on right and wrong and a majority determines moral questions. Or an elite, like the Supreme Court, tells the people what is right and wrong. Usually, the final value is what makes the individual or society happy or feel good at that moment.

While morality is relative and truth is subjective, there is one moral absolute—tolerance. There appears to be a great conspiracy in America, observed James Hitchcock, to extend tolerance to all forms of questionable behavior as a way of insuring tolerance for one's own views. Homosexuality is one example, because a society that approves of homosexuality will not disapprove of very many things.

In a pluralistic world in which truth is an impossible idea, tolerance of all beliefs must reign. This is especially true when coupled with the postmodern assertion that every interpretation of reality is an assertion of power over others.

CONCLUDING REMARKS

We live in a "post-era"[79] and we have entered into an epoch fundamentally at variance with anything we have yet experienced. It is a permissive society, without norms, models, and traditions. Ours is a post-Christendom world in which Christianity, not only in the number of Christians, but in cultural emphasis and cultural result, is no longer the consensus or ethos of society.

The Christian message has to be proclaimed within this context. What might such an encounter look like? According to Lesslie Newbigin, the answer to this question is the great challenge that missiological endeavors and labors face in the twenty-first century.

7

Observations and Strategies

This chapter begins with a brief descriptive summary of our post-Christian, Western culture, and then responds to Lesslie Newbigin's missiological question of our age: "What would be involved in a genuinely missionary encounter" between God's Word and this modern Western culture?"[1]

The chapter will first turn to the Scriptures for examples of the modern and postmodern condition because, as King Solomon observed centuries ago, there is nothing new under the sun. Not only do we find examples of the diseased condition, but we also are able to receive God's corrective cure through the ordered power and blessings of the home, Christian community, and good government. The final two sections explore historical and modern evangelical insights toward worldview construction and change from the writings of Dr. Martin Luther, Francis Schaeffer, Loren Mead, Lesslie Newbigin, Os Guinness, John Stott, and Carl Henry.

A Post-Christian World

In *Twilight of a Great Civilization*, Carl Henry warns that the barbarians are coming and that they threaten to undermine the foundation of Western civilization. This new barbarianism grows out of a humanistic rejection of God and the Judeo-Christian foundation of Western culture that has caused us to embrace a new mentality: "There is no fixed truth, no final good, no ultimate meaning and purpose, and that the living God is a primitive illusion."[2] It is a kind of worldly wisdom that leaves God and His revelation out of the picture and thereby ends up on the eve of destruction with a completely distorted conception of reality.

> Bent on the pursuit of autonomous freedom—freedom from any restraint, and especially from God's truth and moral absolutes—our culture has set itself on the course of self-destruction.[3]

The world spirit[4] of our age rolls on and on, claiming to be autonomous and crushing all that we cherish. Seventy years ago could we have imagined that

> unborn children would be killed by the millions here in our country? Or that we would have no freedom of speech when it comes to speaking of God and biblical truth in our public schools? Or that every form of sexual perversion would be promoted by the entertainment media? Or that marriage, raising children, and family life would be objects of attack?[5]

Due to the cultural, scientific, and philosophical revolutions of the past three centuries, we have a significantly reinterpreted Western worldview that has caused a great change to take place. It appears that everything is being questioned and the old formulas that in the past have defined our moral and epistemic boundaries are breaking away, allowing a new *Zeitgeist* (spirit of the times) and *Weltanschauung* (worldview) to take over.

> All of this gives us today an almost monolithic consensus, an almost unified voice shouting at us a fragmented concept[6] of the universe and of life. And as it comes to us from every side and with many voices, it is difficult not to be infiltrated by it.[7]

Thus we are engaged in a conflict that takes two forms. The first form has to do with the way we think—the ideas we have and the way we view the world. The second has to do with the way we live and act. Both of these conflicts—in the area of ideas and in the area of actions—are important, and in both areas Bible-believing Christians find themselves battling with the surrounding culture of our day.[8]

In this de-created world, how is the Church to proclaim Him so that the world might know Him and know what is real and true and right? In the estimation of Lesslie Newbigin, there is no higher priority for the research work of missiologists than to ask: What would be involved in a genuinely missionary encounter between God's Word and this modern Western culture?[9]

Biblical Examples toward Worldview Understanding

There Is Nothing New Under the Sun

As pointed out earlier, King Solomon observed that "there is nothing new under the sun." Even in his day people had "been there, done that." Based upon Solomon's judgment, it should be possible for us to examine the Scriptures and find biblical examples that illustrate the modern and postmodern condition.

Adam and Eve were the First Humanists

In the story of Adam and Eve in Genesis 3, Eve seeks to displace God and His revelation and make judgments autonomous from God. As the first humanists, Eve and Adam believed that they could stand alongside God as an independent power; instead, they were no longer ridden by God but by the evil one.[10]

The Generation of Noah and a Distant, Spectator God

A condition of humankind before the flood meant that every imagination of man's heart was evil continually. Instead of clinging to God's Word as proclaimed through the word of Noah (Genesis 6; Hebrews 11:7; 2 Peter 2:5), humankind was advocating a naturalistic, closed-system view of the universe. There is no way, the ancients assured themselves, that God could intervene and send a flood as Noah had proclaimed. Moreover, God is not near, His judgments are not a controlling factor in history, and He is but a mere spectator to the affairs of everyday life.

Humankind's Self-Glorification at Babel

There is the post-flood generation of Genesis 11 in which humankind, collectively, rejects the *Missio Dei* of filling the world with His Name and living a life that brings glory to God by grace through faith in Christ. Instead, the people of that time used their unity in language to engage in the worship of autonomous self as they made a name for themselves and marginalized His name in their personal and collective lives.

What is Truth?

There is Pilate's questioning of Jesus and his skepticism regarding the possibility of knowing truth. As a result, he rejects Jesus' interpretation of truth and history, namely, that Christ is truth itself and the meaning of history.

Everyone Did What Was Right in His Own Eyes

There is the condition of Israel at the time of the Judges in which, morally, every person did what was right in his own eyes. Apparently man lived for the moment and constructed his own values devoid of transcendent, moral referents.

Ancient Worldliness

There is the time of Moses, as he spoke his final words to the people of Israel before his death, when he warned them of the dangers concerning prosperity and worldliness. As the people of God are blessed, they will be tempted to follow after the foreign gods among them and forget the Lord in their thinking and in their behaviors. They may keep the form of religion, but the normative authority of God's Word would be replaced with the pagan allegiances, beliefs, and practices of the nations that came into contact with Israel. To counter this temptation, Moses encouraged the people with the words of Deuteronomy 6.

A Marginalized Faith

Finally, there is the powerful story of God's people during the time of Hosea and Amos. They frequented the house of God but they had marginalized the faith in their lives. God came to them and called them to repentance with these words:

> For I desire mercy, not sacrifice, and acknowledgement of God rather than burnt offerings. He has showed you, O man, what is good. And what does the Lord require of you? To act justly and to love mercy and to walk humbly with your God. (Micah 6:8)

In other words, the Christian life is to be lived out in a comprehensive manner since all of life is lived out *coram Deo* and *coram hominibus*; that is, God wants our faith and our neighbor needs our justice, love, and acts of mercy.

Biblical Insights toward
Worldview Construction and Change

The Christian Home as the Center of Discipleship Formation

The most important place for instilling a biblical view of reality and life is the Christian family. A biblical worldview is communicated through the teachings of the parents and through the loving, forgiving socialization of the faith that takes place in the Christian home (Deuteronomy 6:6–9).

It remains part of God's design that the Christian home be *the* place where family members learn and acquire a biblical worldview. They hear God's revealed truth about ultimate and external reality, about the nature and orientation of man, about truth and ethics, about the comprehensive nature of the Christian faith, and about the proper interpretation of history.

The Centrality of the Christian Community Within Society

According to David Wells, one of the first things the Puritans did when building a new town was to establish their colonial church building in a position of prominence, often at the center of the community. In doing so, they saw the town's church as both the place where God addresses His people through the preached Word and as the knot that bound society together. It was their hope and intention that the Christian faith permeated the lives of all who lived there.[11]

It is Loren Mead's conviction that religious congregations are the most important carriers of meaning, purpose, direction, and human community that we have, with one exception—the nuclear and extended family. Throughout history, congregations have been "an anchor, a place of stability, holding up a transcendent vision of the meaning of life."[12]

Government as an Agent of Order in a World of Chaos

One of the core elements of the modern and postmodern worldview is the postulate of human autonomy and a rage against order. For the committed modernist, the crucial insistence is that *experience* is to have no boundaries to its cravings—that there is nothing sacred.

However, man is not autonomous. There are boundaries that have been ordered by the Creator that are to define and govern our existence *coram Deo, coram hominibus,* and *coram mundo.* The Church has the responsibility before God and before our neighbor to remind and challenge temporal authority to remain faithful to its divine purpose of defining, and to uphold the boundaries for both Christian believers and unregenerate humankind.

Historical Insights toward Worldview Construction and Change

Scripture Alone

If our existence is to have meaning, we must have absolutes and a solid epistemology since morals, values, and the basis of knowledge are all derived from ultimate reality and absolutes. Because the Reformers did not mix humanism with the formal principle of Scripture alone,[13] they had no problem in deriving meaning for the particulars of reality, truth, morals, and the social location of religion.[14]

An Axiom Foundational for Christian Theology

In general, Christian theology is recognizable by the fact that it is based on the great fundamental axiom: God has revealed Himself in the world of space and time. However, this axiom cannot be demonstrated but can only be received by faith; therefore, plain and simple unbelief is the only reason for rejecting it and throwing it aside.[15]

Furthermore, only regenerate people can truly understand divine truths, for Christian theology is the theology of the regenerate. It is God's people who are His possession and instruments here in this world and that are called to uphold, affirm, confirm, and spread His truth.

Luther's Model for a Biblical and Evangelical Understanding and Application

Dr. Martin Luther understood the great challenge and necessity of translating the mental stuff that we have received through the teaching office of the Church and home and then applying these truth-claims to the experiences of daily living.

For Luther, his evangelical ministry was one of understanding and application. He learned of God through the activity of the Holy Spirit as he studied the Scriptures so that he might acquire a view of reality[16] that was in conformity with God's revealed will. In other words, Luther sought to understand *what does this mean* as derived from the authoritative and normative truth-claims of Scripture—so that he could interpret, explain, and communicate *what does this mean* for meaningful application within every area of human life.

This missiological theory and practice of Dr. Martin Luther is the missiological model that must be employed by God's people in this post-Constantinian age. In order to accomplish this, we need to understand our own worldview, "but also that of other people, so that we can first understand and then genuinely communicate with others in a pluralistic society."[17]

Thus the most important step for Christians is to be informed about the biblical worldview. Then, as Christians, "we are not only to know the right worldview, the worldview that tells us the truth of what is, but consciously to act upon that worldview so as to influence society in all its parts and facets across the whole spectrum of life."[18]

The Symbol of Our Time

At the time of the Reformation, the Reformers wrote "the symbol of our time" when they wrote the first and unaltered Augsburg Confession. They were clear in explaining that "Holy Scripture remains the only judge, rule, and norm." The Augsburg Confession, like other symbols, was "merely [a witness and exposition] of the faith, setting forth how at various times the Holy Scriptures were understood by contemporaries in the church of God with reference to controverted articles, and how contrary teachings were rejected and condemned."[19]

During the construction of their symbol, the Reformers stated the issue at hand and then proceeded to present affirmative theses and contrary antitheses. Those who read the symbol were not left in doubt, based upon the normative truth-claims of Scripture, as to what the Reformers were stating to be true concerning the issues at hand.

One of the benefits of constructing a "symbol of our time" is that such a symbol would affirm and model a proper way of theological and public discourse in an age whose epistemological method is one of synthesis. Moreover, such a symbol would also give to God's people solid and biblical answers to the issues of our day so that a relevant message might be communicated and lived out in the public domain.

At this time in the Church's history, if we were to write "the symbol of our time," what would be the issues confronting our society and our Church? What affirmative theses and corresponding antitheses could be formulated concerning these issues based upon a comprehensive exposition of Scripture?

Modern, Evangelical Insights toward Worldview Construction and Change

Let Us Be More than a Popular, Folk Religion

According to Os Guinness, "secularization makes the Christian faith seem less real, privatization makes it seem merely a private preference, and pluralization makes it seem just one among many."[20] Unless Christianity is able to break these three chains, it may never be more than a harmless, if popular, folk religion.[21]

How can Christianity overcome the losses of comprehensiveness, certainty, and compelling power? A Reformational position would begin by examining the Person and work of the Holy Spirit who is no Skeptic but who: (1) speaks existent realities (certainty), (2) brings order to chaos and universals to the particulars of human experience (comprehensiveness), and (3) grants power and purpose for daily living through one's vocation and through His abiding presence as Comforter and Counselor (compelling power).

God Is Not Silent but Has Spoken Unified Truth concerning Himself and the Universe

Due to the dialectical thinking of Hegel and the existential thinking of Sartre and Camus, modern man has difficulty making sense of the particulars of things. Where is one to find universals that grant meaning and coherence to the particulars of life?

For the Christian believer God has spoken, in a linguistic propositional form, truth concerning Himself and truth concerning man, history, and the universe. Because this is so, there is unity over the whole field of knowledge. Therefore, "on the basis of the Scriptures, while we do not have exhaustive knowledge, we have true and unified knowledge" and can "know something of both universals and particulars and this includes the meaning and proper use of the particulars."[22]

Christian Apologetics

Francis Schaeffer offers two purposes for Christian apologetics: (1) the defense of the Christian faith because in every age historic Christianity will be under attack, and (2) the responsibility to communicate the Gospel in our generation. Moreover, such a Christian apologetic "should be thought out and practiced in the rough and tumble of living in contact with the present generation so that one is conversant with the reality of the questions being asked by his own and the next generation."[23] Why? Because the goal of apologetics is "the communication of the Gospel to the present generation in terms[24] that they can understand."[25]

Unmasking the Powers

For Lesslie Newbigin, our Christian witness today requires the unmasking of the powers. "It calls for a new kind of enlightenment, namely the opening up of the underlying assumptions of a pagan society, the asking of the unasked questions, the probing of unrecognized presuppositions."[26]

It is plain, writes Newbigin, "that we do not defend the Christian message by domesticating it within the reigning plausibility structure;"[27] instead, it is the business of Christianity to "challenge the plausibility structure in light of God's revelation of the real meaning of history."[28] Furthermore, it is through its message and communal life that His people give rise to a new plausibility structure and

> a radically different vision of things from those who shape all human cultures apart from the Gospel. The Church, therefore, as the bearer of the Gospel, inhibits a plausibility structure which is at variance with, and which calls into question, those that govern all human cultures without exception.[29]

The model for our labors of unmasking the powers in our age is based upon the ministry of our Lord who, "in His earthly ministry unmasked the powers and so drew their hostility on Himself."[30] In a similar manner, "the Spirit working through the life and witness of the missionary church will overturn the world's most fundamental beliefs,[31] proving the world wrong in respect to sin, of righteousness, and of judgment."[32]

Removing the Roof

Every person has a set of presuppositions; the basic way an individual looks at life, his worldview, and the grid through which he sees the world. These presuppositions rest upon what a person considers to be the truth. These presuppositions also provide the basis for their values and decisions.

Yet no matter what a person may believe, he cannot change the reality of what actually is.[33] Thus every man, irrespective of his philosophical system, is caught. Man cannot make his own universe and then live in it; somewhere there is a point, or a series of points, of inconsistency.[34]

In other words, every man has built a roof over his head to shield himself at the point of tension—the point where a man has reached the end of his presuppositions. The roof is built as a protection against the blows of the real world, both internal and external. The Christian, lovingly, must remove the shelter and allow the truth of the external world and what man actually is to beat upon him.[35]

When the roof is off, each man must stand naked and wounded before the truth.[36] This is what shows him his need, and then the Scriptures can show him the real nature of his loss and the answer. He must realize that his system of presuppositions has no answer to the crucial questions of life. He must come to know that his roof is false protection against the storm of what is; then he can consider the storm of the judgment of God.[37]

When modern man feels dead, he is experiencing what the Word of God tells him he is. He is not able to define his deadness or how to solve it, but he knows he is dead. We are to tell him that his death is a moral and spiritual death and of God's remedy.[38]

An Invitation to Dogma in a World Constructed on Skepticism and Doubt

In the Christian era, "dogma" was a good word. It stood for the blessed gift of certainty and of an assured truth. "Doubt," on the other hand, stood for something evil and harmful. The Enlightenment reversed the roles of the two words. "Doubt" was elevated to a position of honor as the first principle of knowledge. The readiness to question all accepted opinions was the prime condition for arriving at the truth. "Dogma" became a bad word, standing for all that shackles the free exercise of human reason.

Yet doubt does not come out of a vacant mind. That is, "one must examine the dogma which undergirds this rejection of dogma" for "when we undertake to doubt any statement, we do so on the basis of beliefs—in the act of doubting, we do not doubt."[39] In other words, I can only doubt the truth of a statement on the grounds of other things that I believe to be true.[40] Consequently, we must now recognize belief once more as the source of all knowledge and that no intelligence, however critical or original, can operate outside such a fiduciary framework.

Therefore the Church, founded and based on the foundational tenets of faith and Scripture alone, invites the modern and postmodern man to recover a proper acknowledgement of the role of dogma. It is an invitation to the Church to be bold in offering to

> men and women of our culture a way of understanding which makes no claim to be demonstrable in the terms of "modern" thought, which is not "scientific" in the popular sense of that word, which is based unashamedly on the revelation of God made in Jesus Christ and attested in Scripture and the tradition of the Church, and which is offered as a fresh starting point for the exploration of the mystery of human existence and for coping with its practical tasks not only in the private and domestic life of the believers but also in the public life of the citizen.[41]

A Solid Epistemology Based upon Antithesis

Rational thought as antithesis is rooted in reality since antithesis fits the reality of His existence and the reality of His creation.[42] Moreover, God made our minds to think in the category of antithesis. However, instead of antithesis, we have the modern man's approach to truth, which is synthesis and subjectivism. Consequently, the post-Christian era is one in which there is a lack of absolutes and antithesis, leading to pragmatic relativism.[43]

Historic Christianity stands on the basis of thesis and antithesis. Moreover, Christianity must cling to the methodology of antithesis—if one thing is true, the opposite is not true; if a thing is right, the opposite is wrong.[44]

Morality Is Based Upon God's Character and Will

Modern man, in the absence of absolutes, has made moral standards completely hedonistic and relativistic. As a result, every situation is judged subjectively with no absolute to which to appeal. Yet there must be an absolute if there is to be morals and values, for one can never have real values without absolutes.[45]

Moral absolutes rest upon God's transcendent Law and are a concrete expression of His character and will. In verbalized, propositional form God has spoken and told us what His character is, and His character is the opposite of what is relativistic, for He is the same yesterday, today, and forever.

TWO STORIES AND TELLING THE TRUE STORY

The way we understand human life depends on what conception we have of the human story. In our contemporary Western culture, two quite different stories are told.

One story is that of evolution, which describes both the development of species through the survival of the strong and the story of the rise of our type of civilization, onto its success in giving humankind a mastery of nature.

The other story is the one embodied in the Bible, the story of creation and the fall, of God's election of a people[46] to be the bearers of His purpose for humankind, and of the coming of One in whom that purpose is to be fulfilled. The Bible

> sets before us a vision of cosmic history from the creation of the world to its consummation, of the nations which make up the one human family, and—of course—of one nation chosen to be the bearer of the meaning of history for the sake of all, and of the one man called to be the bearer of that meaning for that nation.[47]

As His people, we are sent to tell this story. First, though, we must study the story ourselves and know it well enough to faithfully and meaningfully share it. Second, those who believe it must stake their lives on their belief. Third, followers believe that the story describes "what is true and is therefore *true for everyone* and *for all time.*" It is, therefore, the truth about the meaning of the whole human story. Consequently, this belief has universal intent and "the proof of this is that I seek to share it with all human beings in all times and places, and to test it against every situation that confronts me; only if I am so committed is it genuine belief."[48]

Thus missions is a test of our faith and an expression of our hope and of our love. Missions is an acted out doxology and its purpose is that God may be glorified as the One who saves the lost, and that the lost might be saved through our caring proclamation and witness.

Missions as Bridge-Building

In *Between Two Worlds*, John Stott defines the proclamatory and missionary endeavors of the Church through the metaphor of bridge-building.

> Now a bridge is a means of communication between two places which would otherwise be cut off from one another by a river or a ravine. It makes possible a flow of traffic which without it would be impossible.[49]

The modern Church follows in a long succession of bridge-builders since "throughout the history of the Church Christians have tried to relate the biblical message to their particular cultures."[50] In the construction of these missiological bridges, God's people, as instruments of *Missio Dei*, have been called and enlightened by the Holy Spirit to relate God's unchanging Word to our ever-changing world.

The missionary's task is to "faithfully translate the Word of God into modern language and thought categories and to make it present in our day."[51] And yet, if we are to build bridges into the real world, and seek to relate the Word of God to the major themes of life and the major themes of the day, then

> we have to take seriously both the biblical text and the contemporary scene . . . only then shall we discern the connections between them and be able to speak the divine Word to the human situation with any degree of sensitivity and accuracy."[52]

Stott's model presents a powerful, short summary of what would be involved in an evangelical encounter between the Word of God and modern Western culture. In order to accomplish this, it demands that God's people commit themselves to a lifetime of studying God's Word, studying one's target culture, and discerning and constructing missiological bridges that communicate the apostolic message into the receptors' hearts and minds because *faith comes from what is heard, and what is heard comes by the preaching of Christ.* (Romans 10:17).

Christian Believers as Agents of Substantial Healing

Because of the fall, man has experienced four major separations: (1) separation from God, (2) separation from self, (3) separation from others, and (4) separation from nature. On the basis of the work of Christ, Christianity "has in it the possibility of substantial healings now in every area where there are divisions[53] because of the Fall." The Christian community should be a living exhibition of substantial healings and a witness to a fragmented world.

The Church ought to be a pilot plant where mankind can see in our congregations and missions a substantial healing of all the divisions; the alienations that man's rebellion has produced. Indeed, believed Schaeffer, "unless something like this happens, I do not believe the world will listen to what we have to say."[54]

THE CONCEPT OF CULTURAL FRAMING

There is one missiological concept that has enormous significance for the evangelistic outreach of God's people—the concept of cultural framing. According to Paul Hiebert, a cultural frame is a social setting that has its own subculture. In simple tribal societies, there are only a few cultural frames and the differences between them are minimal. In modern cities, on the other hand, there are many frames and the differences between them are great.

God's people in the modern and postmodern world, both ordained pastors and consecrated laity, walk in many different cultural frames.[55] Missiologically speaking, how can the body of Christ mutually equip every member in the missionary method of culture learning so that they can discern the contours of the cultural context and communicate a biblical message? Stated in a different way, cultural framing can permit the believer to understand the context. Once it has been understood and evaluated, cultural framing permits a more conscious and intentional communication of the Christian message by the Christian believer.

Moreover, it would seem that the chief categories of worldview (God, external reality, history, man, truth, and ethics) would be a manageable framework in which to know the Christian faith and from which to analyze the contexts. Once the Christian believer has discerned the ground of the mission context, he can winsomely and evangelically communicate the biblical texts to the context through confessional, hermeneutical, and Law-Gospel understandings and applications.

REINVENTING THE CONGREGATION
FOR A NEW MISSION FRONTIER

In this post-Constantinian age, the Church's mission needs to be clarified and sharpened, the passivity of God's people must be awakened to a renewed commitment in every sector of the human community, and both congregational and denominational structures must be reinvented for the emerging age if the Church is to be His servants.

Loren Mead asks two penetrating questions regarding the reinvention of the congregation for the new mission frontier. How do we build religious institutions within which we can live out our calling to serve the world? How do we form ourselves for mission in the emerging age?[56] For Mead, it means calling the Church out into a secularized world where its mission and its life must once again be defined.

The local congregation's ministry entails committing to serve and strengthen the fabric of the community and society, nurturing an intensity of faith-commitment, engaging in a lifestyle imitative of Jesus, bringing the stranger into a life-giving relationship to the Gospel and to the nurturing community,[57] and being a faith community that stands for something (confessional) and yet is able to provide wide entry points so that the lost might be included and healed (evangelical).

Formation of the Laity and Clergy

In order for God's people to accomplish His mission in the world, every believer must be deployed on the front line of the mission frontier, for the laity will be the primary missionaries.

Second, because many believers, and prospective believers, have a very low level of biblical knowledge and comprehension, strong entry processes must be developed that are able to teach, nurture, and edify believers into mature disciples. This will require an experienced, theologically-solid laity.

Third, the clergy, if they are to be effective servants, must be engaged in continuing education so that they, and God's people through their teaching and modeling ministry, might always be prepared to give an answer for the hope that lies within them.

Formation of Regional and National Leadership

The regional overseers must be flexible in terms of their roles, learn new ways to work together, and be able to provide timely, relevant materials regarding institutional and contextual factors. Those individuals who possess national leadership positions must be engaged in developing training systems and conducting research that prepare God's people for today and tomorrow.

195

Gathering and Healing the Fragmented People of Our Time

In this world of disorder and confusion, where no one religion is looked at with authority, we have the great opportunity to share the Good News of Jesus Christ. Through the friendship and belief system of the Christian community, the Church is called to bind up the fragmented people of our age and give them a solid foundation for faith and daily living. It is imperative that the Church provides and communicates biblical points of reference to a world now based on relativism and being swept away by the winds of every idea and passion.

Moreover, it will be through the medium of believers who, by their dynamic faith and lifestyle, will bear witness to the reality that they have been saved and healed by Jesus Christ. This kind of community possesses great power as it counters the danger of subjectivism by grounding the believers in objective truth and reality. It also counters the danger of individualism by calling for relationships grounded in the "one another" admonitions[58] of Scripture.

THE SEARCH FOR MEANING AND PURPOSE

A restive search is going on today, and almost everyone is engaged in it. The search is for the meaning of life, for significance, for purpose. Captured by a meaningless job and caged inside four walls with a TV set for companionship, modern man feels trapped. We need not extend the picture except to suggest that an anguish takes possession of people when they suddenly realize that life is empty and sterile, completely lacking in meaning for them.[59]

One single devastating question keeps begging for an answer: Why live? The author of Ecclesiastes struggled with this question long ago and wrote: "I have seen everything that is done under the sun; and behold, all is vanity and a striving after the wind . . . So I turned about and gave my heart up to despair" (Ecclesiastes 1:14; 2:20).

It is not unrealistic to say that the scientific view of the world and of human existence aggravates the meaninglessness of the existence of natural man. Science shows us only phenomena, a universal and unfeeling chain of facts and events without beginning and without end, without origin or goal. Whether it rains or the sun shines, whether we are miserable or happy, whether we are sick or well—these are only matters of physical, chemical, or psychological reactions that unfold entirely without significance.[60]

Standing in opposition to this "accidental" view of man and the world is the Christian view that this is God's world and that all of life is His gift. The Christian believes that God's intervention in human history gives present and eternal significance to every circumstance of life. He knows that without God's intervention, history has no final purpose. Because of God's intervention, nothing can be neutral for any man, and his actions, at every moment, either help forward God's purpose or work against it.[61]

Therefore, the search for meaning in life must begin with what God has done and is still doing. It is His purpose that all people come to a saving knowledge of Jesus Christ as their Savior; therefore, humankind is our business.

HEILSGESCHICHTE THEOLOGY

Throughout the nineteenth century in Germany, it was generally assumed by theologians that the Christian faith could be defended only by interpreting it as an expression or symbol of the religious experience of Christians, and not upon the historical Christ revealed in Gospel history. In response, Heilsgeschichte theology understands the apostolic witness as the actual testimony to the acts of God in history for the sake of us and for our salvation.[62]

> The Heilsgeschichte theology takes the biblical proclamation of God's action in history, not as mythology, not as pre-scientific way of announcing existential truth, but as ultimate and factual truth. This truth, of course, is not verifiable by the techniques of scientific historical investigation, since the action of God, precisely because it is God's action, is not accessible to man's scientific enquiry. God cannot be made an object of scientific investigation, as if he were one factor amongst many within the universe; he cannot be detected by telescopes and microscopes, or yet by critical historiography.[63]

The Heilsgeschichte theology does not claim to be able to demonstrate the historicity of the resurrection of Jesus by means of scientific historical research. It is well aware that belief in God's action in Christ requires faith and will never become a scientific explanation. Yet it is not mere credulity, since the resurrection of Christ does not lack reputable historical attestation[64] but is based historically upon the witness of those who claimed to have seen the incarnate, crucified, risen and ascended Lord.

The difficulty about accepting the revelation of God in Christ is not created by modern science or by modern historiography, for it was just as difficult for the men at the time of Jesus to believe in Him as it is for the people of today. It was a scandal to the Jews, and foolishness to the educated Greeks of His time, to believe that the life, death, resurrection and ascension of Jesus Christ was the very center of history.

The Heilsgeschichte theology emphasizes the reality of God's actions in the events of world history. History points to faith, and faith points to history, as the place of God's acts of salvation and as the place of His revelation to humankind through the prophetic and apostolic witness of the Holy Scriptures.

STEREO CATECHESIS

In *A New Era of Religious Communication*,[65] Pierre Babin argues that the Church must acknowledge that our past way of religious education, based upon the Gutenberg printing press, is now incomplete. Faith must be framed not just by the printed medium, but also by the aural sense and through the affective. Moreover, this symbolic way of images must be given priority since it is the language of our time.

Those who understand and work within this new paradigm will be able to communicate religious truth to the mind (catechetical) and to the heart (symbolic). Hence, the Church must become bilingual, speaking the language of Gutenberg and the language of symbolism. The Church must also become more diverse in its worship forms and styles, utilizing all four channels of communication: verbal, visual, pictorial, and aural.

Lutheran history should encourage us to seize this paradigm shift opportunity as our forefathers did five centuries ago. The Reformers were quick to make use of the Gutenberg press to communicate the evangelical faith and to translate the Scriptures into the heart language of the people. Likewise, we should seek to communicate this same evangelical faith into the receptor's heart language of today's global community so that people might be confronted with, and come into contact with, the living and incarnate Christ.

WORLDVIEW AXIOMS

Every theology, philosophy, or science has a starting point or touchstone thesis through which it attempts to unify and explain human existence.

Axioms are the ruling principles with which any system of thought begins. They are never deduced or inferred from other principles, but are simply presupposed.

As Carl Henry has positively affirmed, the primary ontological axiom for the Christian is the one, living, triune God. The primary epistemological axiom is divine revelation. All core beliefs of biblical theism depend on these basic axioms.[66] Therefore, the Christian believer knows assuredly that his truth-claims are not conjecturally grounded, but are anchored in the triune God's self-existence and self-disclosure. Moreover, these axioms are fundamental to all thought and being since they are basic to human intellect, and are grounded ultimately and eternally in the Logos of God.

Apostolic Contextualization

This final missiological strategy reviews some of the basic biblical and anthropological premises involved in apostolic contextualization. The following definition, and corresponding footnotes and Bible verses, is my attempt at understanding what aspects of Gospel communication are most fundamental to the missiological enterprise.

Apostolic contextualization[67] is the grounding of God's Word[68] in such a way that the Gospel comes alive[69] through the Spirit's power and activity[70] in a particular context.[71] It is communicated in the language and communication patterns[72] of the receptor's frame of reference,[73] and it is clothed in symbols[74] that are meaningful and significant[75] for the formation of Triune-God-Centered pilgrims; priests who are the incarnate temples and living letters[76] of the Holy Spirit. We can practice apostolic contextualization by

- Being devoted "To the apostles' teaching, to fellowship, to the breaking of bread, to prayers" and to having all things in common and distributing to all as any have need (Acts 2:42–47)
- Presenting one's body as a living sacrifice and being transformed by the renewal of one's mind (Romans 12:1–2)
- Becoming all things to all people that I might win some, doing it all for the sake of the Gospel (1 Corinthians 9:19–23a)
- Being His living letters, "written not with ink but the Spirit of the living God" (2 Corinthians 3:3)
- Having this treasure in earthen vessels, to show that the transcendent power belongs to God and not to us (2 Corinthians 4:7)

- "Always carrying in the body the death of Jesus, so that the life of Jesus may also be manifested in our bodies" (2 Corinthians 4:10)
- Having the love of Christ controlling us (2 Corinthians 5:14)
- Being convinced that One has died for all (2 Corinthians 5:14)
- Living no longer for ourselves but for "Him who for their sake died and was raised" (2 Corinthians 5:15)
- Being His ambassadors, making His appeal through us (2 Corinthians 5:20)
- Being crucified with Christ so that the life I now live in the flesh I live by faith in the Son of God (Galatians 2:20)
- Walking in the same way in which He walked (1 John 2:6)

8

The True and False Church

Jesus, as He began His ministry in the city of Capernaum, fulfilled an ancient Messianic prophecy: "The land of Zebulun and the land of Naphtali, toward the sea, across the Jordan, Galilee of the Gentiles—the people who sat in darkness have seen a great light, and for those who sat in the region and shadow of death light has dawned" (Matthew 4:15–16). This Jesus, the apostle John wrote, "was life and the life was the light of men. The light shines in the darkness and the darkness has not overcome it" (John 1:4–5).

From the very beginning of history, the Good News of this Light has been revealed. For example, "When Adam and Eve fell into sin, the knowledge of grace was at once divulged to them in the promise of Christ. They were told that the woman's Seed would crush the serpent's head, which means that Adam should be saved through this grace which the promised Seed would bring to the world."[1] Thus from Adam to Abel, down to our day, there is but one way to salvation, for the promise of Christ and of the Christian faith began with the promise of the woman's Seed. The Old Testament saints of God were saved by grace through faith in Christ who was to come and we, His New Testaments saints, are saved by grace through faith in the Christ who has come and who will come again on the Last Day.

But the news and promise of this Light has not been the only light that has been shining in the world. It has always been the world's misfortune, writes Luther, that there have been many "self-styled lights who explore their own way to heaven and presume to be the lights of the world, to teach it, and lead it to God."[2] Yet "the only way, ladder, and bridge for ascending into heaven is Christ, the Son of Man, who is the only one ever to ascend into heaven. Any other way, ladder, or bridge is invented and dreamed up [and, in the end,] useless and vain."[3] Satan is the source of these many false lights, as he is the great deceiver of humankind and that ancient serpent whom the woman's Seed crushed when Christ died and rose victorious from the grave. Thus, there have always been two churches.

From the very beginning, God ordained that humankind be busy with the Word and "with the other forms of worship established by Him, so that we might give first thought to the fact that this nature was created chiefly for acknowledging and glorifying God."[4]

> On the Sabbath day [Adam] would have taught his children; through public preaching he would have bestowed honor on God with the praises which He deserved; and through reflection on the works of God he would have incited himself and others to expressions of thanks.[5]

It was God's design that the tree of the knowledge of good and evil be the place where Adam was "to yield to God the obedience he owed, give recognition to the Word and will of God, give thanks to God, and call upon God for aid against temptation."[6] Adam "would have admonished his descendants to live a holy and sinless life, to work faithfully in the garden, to watch it carefully, and to beware" of the forbidden tree.[7]

Thus God's command regarding this tree was to be "an outward form of worship and an outward work of obedience toward God."[8] This tree was not deadly by nature but became so only through the Word of God and man's disobedience.

> It was God's intention that this command should provide man with an opportunity for obedience and outward worship, and that this tree should be a sort of sign by which man would give evidence that he was obeying God.[9]

Satan tempted Eve by making it his business "to prove from the prohibition of the tree[10] that God's will toward man is not good."[11] "Satan spoke in order to lead [Adam and Eve] away from what God had said; and after he had taken away the Word, he made corrupt [man's perfect will] so that he became a rebel. [Satan also] corrupted the intellect so that it doubted the will of God. The eventual result was a rebellious hand, extended against the will of God, to pick the fruit."[12]

It was a very great measure of grace that after Adam's sin, God did not remain silent but spoke "in order to show signs of His fatherly disposition."[13] In loving response to Adam's disobedience, God, in His mercy, enveloped Himself in a gentle breeze so that He might reveal Himself to Adam under a cover and bring to Adam and Eve a fatherly reprimand. The question, "where are you?" reveals God's love, for God sought out Adam so that they could talk, and so that Adam might receive mercy.[14] "It was a great comfort for Adam that, after he had lost Paradise, the tree of life . . . [God gave him] another sign of grace, namely, the sacrifices." [In this sign Adam could know] that he had not been cast off by God but was still the object of God's concern and regard."[15]

At that time, in response to God's promise of the Blessed Seed, humankind began to call upon the name of the Lord. Shem, Seth, and Enos exhorted their descendants to wait for their redemption and to believe that promise concerning the Blessed Seed, for the true Church trusts in God's mercy and hopes in the promised Christ. Therefore this

> doctrine of the Gospel has been in the world ever since our first parents fell, and by various signs God confirmed this promise to the fathers. The earlier times knew nothing of the rainbow, circumcision, and other things that were ordained later on. But all ages had the knowledge of the Blessed Seed.[16]

"Adam's temple, or church, was some tree or some small hill beneath the open sky, where they used to come together to hear the Word of God and to bring sacrifices, for which they had erected altars."[17] Alongside this Good News of the Blessed Seed, the sacrifices provided an outward and visible sign of God's grace. This sign reminded humankind of His mercy and kindness, and provided the proper form for the worship of God.

> Abel and Cain had been accustomed by their father to sacrifice, which at that time was the proper form for the worship of God; and they continued to offer sacrifices. In the same manner Shem had meetings, sermons, forms of worship, sacrifices, and other ceremonies, which continued in existence up to the time of Abraham.[18]

It is in the sacrifices of Abel and Cain that we begin to differentiate between the true and false church. God rejects Cain, not because his sacrifice was inferior, but because his person was evil, without faith, and full of pride and conceit. Cain appears to be godly, but he is wicked and does not believe the divine promise. Cain "comes without faith, without any confession of sin, without any supplication for grace, without trust in God's mercy, without any prayer for the forgiveness of his sins." In Cain's contempt for and rejection of the Word, he left the true Church to form a special church without God's command. Abel, on the other hand, is godly and believes solely in the mercy of Christ. "[Abel] did not rely on his own worthiness, his sacrifices, or his work, but on the plain promise which had been given about the woman's Seed."[19] Thus "the brothers Abel and Cain bring sacrifices. For Abel the sacrifice is a seal of righteousness, because he believes. For Cain, however, it is not a seal of righteousness, because he does not believe but retains the bare work without faith."[20]

Here, in the story of Cain and Abel, we also have another "distinction between the two churches, the one being the righteous one, which has the promises of the future life but in this life is afflicted and poor, the other one being the ungodly one, which prospers in this life and is rich"[21] and which troubles and persecutes the true Church. Yet "Whenever God permits His own to be oppressed by the might and treachery of the devil and of the world, He always in turn comforts them and gives them prophets and godly teachers to restore the wavering church and for some time to hold Satan's raging in check."[22]

Just as Abel and Cain formed two churches, so also Ham, after the flood, left the godly church of his father Noah and established a false church. It is Ham's descendants, especially his grandson Nimrod, who seek to build a name for themselves and to persecute the true Church spiritually, "by means of false doctrine and ungodly forms of worship, and physically, by means of the sword and tyranny."[23] Yet God has always counteracted the false church with a people who would cling to His Word and the forms of worship instituted by Him. They would be "the guardian of religion and of sound doctrine in the world, lest everything degenerate into ungodliness and there be no knowledge of God among men."[24]

Thus when Abraham was nearly swallowed up by the false church of Nimrod and its Babylonian religion, God called Abraham out through the ministry of Shem[25] and directed him to separate from the ungodly race[26] and seek a new dwelling place. Abraham is seized through the Word and formed into a new being. Of himself, Abraham is nothing but an idolater, but through God's mercy "is freed from sin, death, and damnation through Christ, the Blessed Seed."[27] Abraham permits himself to be reproved, acknowledges that he is an idolater and an ungodly man, and sets out without knowing where he is going.

Later, in the home of Laban, both the sons of God and sons of the evil one are found. The same happened in the homes of Adam [Cain and Abel], Abraham [Ishmael and Isaac], and Isaac [Esau and Jacob]. When Jacob was near death, as he was blessing his sons, he foresaw that his descendants would continue to form two churches. The true Church would be saved because of faith in the promise concerning the Savior who was to descend from his flesh. The false church would "consist of the carnal Israelites, who would boast that they were the seed of Abraham and of the fathers," but they would have neither His Word nor the signs ordained by Him.[28] So, from the very beginning of Genesis we have seen two generations of human beings; those who are righteous, who by grace through faith believe in the Promised Seed and are the true Church, and those who are unrighteous, who do not believe, and who belong to "the school of Satan."[29]

The Word Constitutes the House of God, the Gate of Heaven, and the Church on Earth

Wherever the Word is heard, there is the Church, for it is God's Word that establishes the Church. The Church is not confined to a place or persons, but it will be and exist wherever the Word is, for He is the Lord over all places. "For the church exists only where the Word is and where there are people who believe the Word."[30]

> Wherever the Word is heard, where Baptism, the Sacrament of the Altar, and absolution are administered, there you must determine and conclude with certainty: "This is surely God's house; here heaven has been opened." But just as the Word is not bound to any place, so the church is not bound to any place.[31]

Therefore, "Direct your step to the place where the Word resounds and the sacraments are administered, and there write the title 'the gate of God.'"[32] As we gather at these external places to hear a sermon delivered through a human voice, and gather at temples built of stones and wood to receive the Sacraments, we must always remember that "here is the house of God and the gate of heaven;[33] for God Himself is speaking."[34]

I hear a man's voice. I see human gestures. The bread and the wine in the Supper are physical things. At ordination the hands of carnal men are imposed. In Baptism water is water. For the flesh judges in no other way concerning all these matters. But if you look at that addition with spiritual eyes, namely, at whose Word it is that is spoken and heard there, not indeed the word of a man—for if it is the word of a man, then the devil is speaking—but the Word of God, then you will understand that it is THE HOUSE OF GOD and THE GATE OF HEAVEN.[35]

The great danger for the church is our sleeping eyes and dull ears whereby we slight these "faces of God." This is what happened to the carnal descendants of Abraham who despised the Word and signs of grace, which had been given by God, and they began to run after the desires of their hearts and became carnal Israelites. They forgot His commandments and ceremonies and, after despising the tabernacle and temple, they brought their sacrifices under trees and groves and even sacrificed their own children.[36] Instead of taking hold of God in the sign, "Everyone devised his own way of worshiping God and followed it to his own certain destruction."[37]

The Bed is Too Narrow

In this Church nothing should be heard or seen except what God does. However, wherever the Word is, there Satan is active and seeks to spread false teaching by corrupting the Word of God in such a way that humankind doubts the goodness of God.[38] Satan, through false teaching, seeks to rob humankind of God as he fabricates a new god who exists nowhere. In addition, Satan fills the world with various kinds of sects in which the proper forms of worship are kept but emptied of their meaning and promise. For example,

> there is no doubt that our first parents worshiped God early in the morning, when the sun was rising, by marveling at the Creator in the creature or, to express myself more clearly, because they were urged on by the creature. Their descendants continued the custom, but without understanding. Thus this practice turned into idolatry.[39]

Therefore, it is important that the Church maintains and remains firm in its adherence to pure doctrine. If we want to have and be the Church, it must not be polluted and commingled with any satanic doctrine. The bed is too narrow for Christ and Belial to remain together. "Consequently, one of the two falls out, and the short cloak cannot cover them both."[40]

Christ Alone is the Ladder and the Way

In His goodness, God satisfied our desire to know and see Him by showing us a visible sign. God can be touched and seen in the incarnate Son. It was for this very reason that, when Scripture spoke about God as if He were a human being and attributed to Him all human qualities, He was foretelling the mystery of His future incarnation and providing "a definite pattern for recognizing and taking hold of God."[41]

Unregenerate man, led and guided by unregenerate reason, cannot see that the crucified Christ is God. Moreover, the devil seeks to fight against the mystery of Christ's incarnation by setting into motion all sorts of heresies in order that humankind might be diverted from the true knowledge of Christ. The chief attack of Satan, and of all heresies, is to deny His incarnation, to rob men of God and His Word, and to create a new god. This is the way Satan goes to work.

> He attacks Christ with three storm-columns. One will not suffer Him to be God; the other will not suffer Him to be man; the third denies that He has merited salvation for us. Each of the three endeavors to destroy Christ. . . . Surely all three parts must be believed, namely, that He is God, also, that He is man, and that He became such a man for us . . . If one small part if lacking, then all parts are lacking.[42]

Larvae Dei and the Harlot at the Gate

Humankind cannot ascend to God. Therefore God, in His mercy, ordained to put before us an image (Incarnation of the Son, the Word, Baptism, the Lord's Supper) of Himself so that He can be grasped. In these signs, He deals with us within the range of our comprehension. "In these images we see and meet a God whom we can bear, one who comforts us, lifts us up into hope, and saves us."[43]

These signs are the common and public appearances for all Christians, and God Himself is present in these *Larvae Dei*. Those who "believe the promise and make use of these signs become the people of God and are saved."[44] These signs are also given so that the ungodly might be attracted to Him and obtain salvation to those who make use of them in faith.

In contrast to these fatherly appearances of God, the harlot at the gate[45] looks for more attractive externals that appeal to unregenerate reason and the human eye.[46] Satan "ignites many new lights, all of whom boldly presume to show the people the right way to heaven."[47] In other words, "Satan continually strives to remove the true signs from our sight and to set up false signs." In this way, Satan and his servants "strive to divert us from those divinely appointed visible forms [Baptism, Eucharist, spoken Word, and the Incarnate Word born of Mary] to their own forms."[48]

For wherever Christ builds a temple and gathers a church, "Satan invariably has the habit of imitating Him like an ape and inventing idolatrous forms of worship and idolatrous traditions similar to the true doctrine and the true forms of worship." "For it is the devil's rule to build a chapel next to a church and temple of Christ."[49]

Because His presence is concealed, unregenerate reason and the flesh reject these signs of grace and devise new ones. It is only by faith, acquired through the Word and the gracious workings of the Holy Spirit, that a person is able to force his way through the darkness and see the Light.[50]

> We shall be safe from these dangers if we follow that visible form or those signs which God Himself has set before us. In the New Testament we have as a visible form the Son of God on the lap of His mother Mary. He suffered and died for us, as the Creed teaches. Besides, we have other visible forms: Baptism, the Eucharist, and the spoken Word itself. Therefore we cannot complain of having been forsaken.[51]

THE MARKS OF THE CHURCH

"[T]hank God," Luther wrote in the Smalcald Articles, "a seven-year-old child knows what the church is, namely, holy believers and sheep who hear the voice of their Shepherd. So children pray, 'I believe in one holy Christian Church.' Its holiness does not consist of surplices, tonsures, albs, or other ceremonies of theirs which they have invented over and above the Holy Scriptures, but it consists of the Word of God and true faith."[52]

Luther was wrongly accused by Johann Eck, and others, of radical individualism in his attack and reform of the Church. However, Luther urged reform on the basis of who and what the Church really is, namely, "Where the Word is, there is the faith; and where faith is, there is the true church."[53] The Church is a holy Christian people and is both a hidden community of faith and a visible fellowship gathered around the marks of the Church.

The certain mark of a Christian Church is wherever the pure Gospel is being preached.[54] If the Gospel is present, there must be Christians. Hence, the primary distinction between the true and false church is that the true, ancient, apostolic,[55] evangelical Church is built upon grace whereas the false church is built upon works.[56] The true marks whereby a person can find the church are: (1) the Word of God, (2) Baptism, (3) the Lord's Supper, (4) the Keys, (5) called ministers, (6) prayer and worship, and (7) the sacred cross.[57]

Man Does Not Live by Bread Alone but by Every Word That Proceeds from the Lord's Mouth

The cause of Israel's rejection as God's people was her refusal to be led and governed by God. Israel wanted to live, not by faith in the promise, but by what was actually present. On the other hand, God wanted her to rely on faith in His promises and leading. Sadly, if they did not get what they sought, they looked for another god.[58]

> The Jews tempted Him. When God did not immediately supply them with everything according to their liking and prescription, they quickly ran after strange gods . . . Therefore they chose other forms of worship and sought such gods as Ashtaroth and Baal, to give them help on the spot and forthwith, without faith in a promise, so that they could feel the help and take hold of it with their hands.[59]

Israel's history reveals that our sinful nature seeks to flee from the worship and fear of the true God and, instead, to devise its own forms of worship. Therefore God, in order to deal with these sinful tendencies, offers promises to His people, but at the same time "He also tests and exercises them in faith and teaches them that they should live more by the Word than by bread."[60]

> One must be careful to hold fast to the fact that God makes promises and defers the things promised, and that He tries us with a scarcity of available things in order to instruct us in faith in the promise and in order that this faith may be strengthened and may learn to believe God not only in prosperous times, when things are available, but also in adversity, when things are lacking.[61]

"If bread is lacking, a strange god should not be called upon . . . the heart should be strengthened by faith in the Word."[62] In all things, "God wants His threats to be feared and His promises to be awaited. But this is impossible except by faith."[63] Therefore, it is the nature of faith to

> believe and fear things that are invisible, just as Noah fears the punishment of the flood, which he does not see, and hopes for a liberation, which is not in sight. We believe in Christ the Lord, whom we do not see, and we believe that He will come on the Last Day and raise us from the dead and glorify us, as Phil. 3:20–21 says, but that He will inflict punishments on the ungodly, who do not know God and do not obey the Gospel. . . . Thus *the godly fear the threats and trust the promises*. But the ungodly do not fear, do not believe, do not hope, and do not care about God.[64]

ADAM'S WHY AND ABRAHAM'S FAITH

Simply defined, original sin is "to become a god."[65] Adam put himself in the position of God as Creator[66] when he wondered why God commanded and made a prohibition concerning the tree. He was not satisfied to accept God's command on faith, but instead, sought to learn the reason why God ordered him to stay away. He ultimately passed judgment upon God Himself. Therefore, it became ruinous for Adam to think about the why and it caused him great harm.[67]

In contrast, Abraham obeyed God's command without hesitation. When God commanded Abraham to be circumcised,[68] or when God asked Abraham to go to Mt. Moriah and offer up his son Isaac as a burnt sacrifice, Abraham obeyed Him at once. "He does not debate with himself why God has given this command but goes immediately to the designated place."[69]

Abraham considered who was speaking and "simply cuts the throat of this baneful *why* and tears it out of his heart by the roots."[70] He understood that it was God's will that his curiosity be restrained and that he remain within the definite bounds placed upon him by God in His Word.

> He takes reason captive and finds satisfaction in the one fact that He who gives the command is just, good, and wise; therefore He cannot command anything but what is just, good, and wise, no matter what the opinion of reason is, and no matter if reason does not understand.[71]

After Abraham had received the order, he saw nothing else than God's will. He mortifies the head of the serpent, which is his unregenerate reason, and acts on what God has declared him to do.[72] "Therefore let no one add this detestable and fatal little word 'why' to God's commands. . . . [L]et it be enough for us that we hear the Word and understand what it commands, even though we do not understand the reason for the command."[73]

FAITH AND THE PROMISES OF GOD: THE RIGHTEOUSNESS OF ABRAHAM

Faith consists in giving assent to the promises of God and concluding that they are true. God speaks to Abraham, and Abraham believes what God is saying. "Faith alone lays hold of the promise, believes God when He gives the promises, stretches out its hand when God offers something, and accepts what He offers." Thus the only faith that justifies and makes one righteous is "the faith that deals with God in His promises and accepts them."[74]

Love is concerned with another matter; it does not lay hold of the promise but "it carries out the commands and obeys God."[75] Thus one cannot attribute righteousness to one's love or works, for they are always unclean, imperfect, and polluted. Instead, attribute your righteousness to mercy alone, to the promise concerning Christ alone; the promise that faith accepts. For Abraham is righteous prior to the Law and prior to the works of Law solely because Abraham believed God who gave the promise.[76]

FAITH AND THE PROMISES OF GOD: THE LIFE OF JACOB

For Luther, Christianity represented a very simple relationship: on the one hand, God's promises; on the other hand, man's faith.[77] Where faith is mentioned there must always be a promise on which to lay hold, and where we speak of a promise, faith is always demanded.

One of the great examples of faith in the face of adversity was the life of Jacob. For Luther, the story of Jacob recorded in Genesis 32 reveals that by his faith, Jacob was able to conquer God just as the Canaanite woman[78] was able to cling to Christ when Jesus opposed her in Matthew 15. After the wrestling with Jacob had ended, Christ laid aside His mask and spoke life-giving words to him. Christ revealed Himself as the One who rewards those who seek Him and cling to Him in faith.[79] He is the Man who exercises Jacob in their wrestling until his faith shows itself. As evidence of his faith, Jacob's name is changed to Israel by God Himself "because you have struggled with God and with men and have overcome" (Genesis 32:28). In this test and in the changing of Jacob's name, Jesus sought not to destroy him but to confirm and strengthen him in the promises of God that he might conquer.

Yet, reminds Luther, the believers have not conquered God in such a way that He is subjected to us, but that His wrath and judgment are conquered by us through praying, seeking, and knocking. He no longer is an angry judge, as He seemed to be, but He becomes a most loving Father, and therefore, your faith has saved you.

Thus Jacob is a wanderer all of his life, yet he is a patriarch and a saint. In his sojourns he suffers[80] much, especially with the incest of Reuben, the defilement of Dinah, the death of Rachel, and the enslavement of Joseph. Yet God allowed these things to happen so that faith might be exercised and that Jacob could learn to depend on God's Word and promises alone despite the visible things perceptible to the senses.

> For the things which are discerned by the eyes are deceiving and transient, but the things which are promised and not seen are sure and steadfast. But delay and postponement are to be awaited in faith and borne with equanimity, for the invisible things will appear at the right time.[81]

In the picture of Jacob's struggle, we also see the struggle of the Church of God, observed Luther. The Church appears to have nothing but the Word and the Sacraments, yet it has an infinite number of adversaries. To the understanding of the flesh, it appears that the Church is rejected by God and that He is hiding from us. In our daily struggles, it appears that God has turned His face away from us and shows us only His back so that our conscience is troubled and we wonder how we stand before God. But when He addresses us in the Word and the Sacraments, we see His goodwill toward us by His words and deeds and gracious face.[82]

Luther advises that in the darkness of the cross, and of the trial, we must cling to the Word of God. Yet this knowledge of God does not come without practice and experience as we understand that these struggles are indications of His great love and goodness, and not of His wrath and anger.[83] These things are done by God so that we might learn what is the good, acceptable, and perfect will of God and be equipped to comfort others in their trials.

The worst form of punishment that God can bring upon a people is to not punish them. In contrast, the most blessed kind of life is when God does not close His eyes to our faults but immediately seeks to correct us with His rods and crosses.[84] As He seeks to correct us, "God uses powerful and bitter remedies to make [our sin] manifest and to cleanse it. If He is to sweep out the evil, He must take a broom and sharp sand, and He must scrub until blood flows."[85]

Therefore, we must learn to live with our eyes shut and to trust simply in His promises even though He sometimes seems to exercise no care for us. In the midst of these trials and afflictions, we are in need of His wisdom by which we are reminded that we have been baptized, absolved, fed in His Supper, and possess His Word and promise despite the present circumstances.

THE CROSS AND HIS WAY OF GOVERNING HIS PEOPLE: THE LIFE OF JOSEPH

According to Luther, it is faith that takes hold of the promises of God and fixes the heart on that which is altogether absurd, impossible, and contained in the Word and God's promise. This simply was the life of Joseph, the man of exceptional faith.

Joseph, through his faith, conquered all. First, the devil assailed him with all sorts of troubles while he was in exile away from his parents and family.

> For [Joseph] was a youth 17 years of age, and there is no reason for us to suppose that he was a blockhead or a log without any sensation of such great evils, since he was being hurled into these atrocious trials of despair, indignation, and hatred against God, of lust, and, in the end, of the harshest slavery, where he, betrayed and cast aside by his blood brothers, was compelled to serve unknown foreigners like the vilest slave.[86]

Next, the devil assailed him again with the allurements of the flesh such as lust and pleasure, especially when he was tempted by Potiphar's wife to commit adultery. This is especially the more difficult trial because of Joseph's youth. Joseph felt all of these temptations in the flesh, but he was able to overcome them because he had the Word in his heart. Joseph's faith overcomes the temptations of the evil one as he takes hold of the Word spoken by his father Jacob and clings to it.

> Nevertheless, the Word spoken by his father reigns in his heart. This he retains with the utmost firmness. "My father has taught me. No matter

how long God wants to forsake me, I will hold out. My father has taught me to believe and to wait patiently for God's help, no matter how long He postpones or delays."[87]

For we see that through the Holy Spirit, Joseph listened to and retained the teachings of his father with the greatest faithfulness and diligence. The rest of his brothers did not listen with the same care and results, though their training and the Word were the same since Jacob undoubtedly impressed this Word on all of them. Joseph alone takes hold of the Word spoken by his father and clings fast to them. As a result, he does not allow Satan to rob him of his promise.[88] The Holy Spirit was present with Joseph so that the Word planted in his heart would become an immovable rock against the devil.

> For Joseph had the entire Psalter in his heart, in actuality and in effect he does everything taught in the Psalms about faith, patience, and waiting. He waits, and he sustains himself with the divine promises which he heard from his father. He does not despair; nor does he murmur against God.[89]

Joseph was well taught in the faith by his father, who experienced many crosses[90] and joys, his mother Rachel, and his nurse Deborah. It is especially Deborah that Luther commends, who was like a grandmother to Joseph and who still had a fresh memory of the patriarchs such as Noah, Shem, and Eber. Isaac, too, was still alive and he also carefully impressed the Word upon Joseph as he recounted the histories of the patriarchs. It was with this teaching, and the Lord's presence, that Joseph was kept in the faith while he served the Lord in exile for

> that Wisdom, that is, God's Son, did not leave the righteous man when he was sold but went down with him into the pit and prison. Joseph had Him as a Teacher who gave the increase, so that he kept the Word which he had heard firmly fixed in his heart. He had the punishment of the Flood before his eyes, the burning of the Sodomites, and other disasters, then also the various liberations of godly men recounted by his father. From this source the fear of God, faith, hope, and other virtues grew and were strengthened in him, so that his heart could not be made to totter by any commotions.[91]

Joseph was content with his lot and bore his poverty with great courage. He retained his patience and his trust in God and was liberal and kind toward the tyrant Potiphar by managing the house with great diligence and trustworthiness. Joseph was the model of a perfect human being and was the most precious treasure, yet this treasure was unknown to the world. Though all seemed hopeless for Joseph, and though he was alone in his trials and afflictions, Christ, "the Bishop of souls," saw Joseph and cared for him.[92] Christ rejoiced in the life of Joseph, and that such a beautiful sacrifice was being offered to Him.

The life of Joseph is an excellent illustration of the manner in which God governs His saints. When He works, He turns His face away at first and shows only His back as He fashions and refashions you according to His good pleasure.[93] Joseph patiently beheld His back and trustingly waited until God would reveal His salvation.[94]

Because Joseph waits patiently upon the Lord, he becomes a savior of the world. God uses all of Egypt to restore Joseph and deliver him from his imprisonment. Pharaoh and the entire nation are moved by God to serve His purpose and to deliver Joseph from his cross.[95] Joseph learned that a man does not live by bread alone but by every Word that proceeds from the Lord's mouth. For if Joseph did not have the Word with him,

> if the Holy Spirit and God's Son had not gone down with him into the pit and had not sustained him with the Word which he had learned from his father, he would not have been able to bear and conquer the assaults of Satan.[96]

These examples of Jacob and Joseph "are set before us to instruct and strengthen us, in order that we may learn faith and hope in the Lord. But it is not a faith in things that are seen. No, it is a faith in things that are invisible."[97] For the believer simply clings to the promise and is prepared to endure great evils, even though according to the spirit he desires to be freed from the difficult trial. Because he sees that it is God's will, he rests content with God's good pleasure and mortifies the flesh.

> When there is affliction, we see God from behind; that is, we conclude that God has turned away from us. . . . This is the view from behind, when we feel nothing but affliction and doubts; but later, when the trial has passed, it becomes clear that by the very fact that God has showed Himself to us from behind He has showed us His face, that He did not forsake us but turned away His eyes just a little.[98]

The purpose of the cross is so that God can crucify, mortify, and reduce the old man to nothing so that the flesh is humbled and does not rebel and exercise dominion over the spirit. Yet "This does not come about except through suffering and the cross; for then you are upholding the work of God, who forms you, planes you, and cuts off the rough branches. With ax, saw, and mattock He cuts down everything that hinders the eternal building."[99] In the cross, He seeks to form you according to His plan; and we cannot be sanctified unless the flesh and the body of sin is mortified with all its adulteries and lusts. Therefore, God "judges, chastises, and scourges until we learn what is the good and acceptable and perfect will of God."[100]

The life of Joseph shows us that "Faith must precede, and then the waiting must follow."[101] We must learn that God hides Himself under the form of the cross so that, to those who wait, He will come and save them. The life of a Christian should teach him that the goodness, mercy, and power of God cannot be grasped by speculation, but must be understood on the basis of experience and confident reliance on the Word of God.

Just endure and wait for the Lord. Be content with His Word and cling to His promises. This is how God exercises, exalts, and plays with His people. "For in reality God does not play this way with the ungodly; but, as Job 21:13 says, 'they spend their days in prosperity, and in peace they go down to Sheol.' He did not play this way with Sodom and Gomorrah, where there was ease, pride, abundance, and bread in plenty. But Lot and Abraham were harshly troubled."[102]

It is out of His great love for us that He governs us in this manner. Because He is a loving Father, He must discipline us. To God, these crosses and trials are a game, but to us, they are death since original sin necessitates the rod of discipline.[103] Paternal love demands that blows and stripes be administered in order that His children may be improved.

> This, then, is a holy, blessed, and safe kind of life, when God does not close His eyes to our faults and forbidden pursuits but immediately corrects and chastises us with His rods, troubles, and crosses of every kind or through men who by their admonitions lead us back to the right path so that our foolish lusts are curbed.[104]

This Christian life of the cross began for every believer in Baptism, for we receive in our Baptism not only the forgiveness of sins but also the purging away of sin. Forgiveness is free due to the merits of Christ. Yet this forgiveness is followed by distress, tribulation, and mortification. Like a skillful physician, God proceeds with purging, burning, and cutting, even though this is not done without pain. The cross and trials become "the medicines with which God purges away sin."[105] God does this lest we are apathetic through life and perish in our sins.

God, in His goodness, alternates our times of trial and comfort, just as night follows day, so that "in this way the word of promise and faith are put to use."[106] For one should look for comfort after tribulation, for this alternation is continuous in the life of the godly. Just as misfortunes drive one "to prayer and faith, so, when the saints are delivered, they are impelled to give thanks and to praise God's mercy."[107]

On the other hand, affliction follows comfort so "that the body of sin may be mortified and that it may not be exalted by pride, and then that the spirit may not be devoured by sorrow and exhausted by terrors."[108] For affliction without an end or reprieve would shatter the spirit and drive it to despair. Therefore God, in His wonderful goodness, tempers the afflictions with His mercy and alternates tribulation with consolation.

Thus the wonderful government of God presents us with a paradox; He keeps His promises but "in such a way that everything seems contradictory and far different from the Word."[109] We are His people, loved by Him, and yet daily He confronts us with the cross and trials so that we are doubtful, perplexed, and filled with despair. This is what it means for Him to love those whom He chastises. Nevertheless, He has mercy on His faithful children, for we know that He is faithful to us, and will keep His promise.

> This love must be learned from experience, nor should chastisement be avoided and shunned. The story is told of a peasant who, when he heard this consolation from his pastor, that the afflictions and troubles by which God afflicts us are signs of His love, replied: "Ah, how I would like Him to love others and not me!"[110]

Therefore, of all the sacrifices that one can make the one most acceptable to God is this: to kill sin, to live in righteousness, holiness, obedience, and mortification of the flesh. This is indeed painful and difficult for us, but one must accustom oneself to what is the good and acceptable will of God. God "does not test in order that we may fear and hate Him like a tyrant but to the end that He may exercise and stir up faith and love in us."[111]

There Is Only One True Church

We have learned in this short history, from the Book of Genesis, of the true and false church, and that the certain mark of the true Church is the

Gospel that a person is saved by grace through faith in Jesus Christ. For Luther, there is only one definition of the true Church, that is, those who believe in Christ and hear His Word.[112] It is there that

> God's Word is preached and believed purely and ardently; there children are accepted into the kingdom of God through Baptism; there hearts assailed by sin and temptation find solace and strength in Holy Communion; there sinners unburden their conscience in confession; there ministers are commissioned in orderly fashion for preaching the Word, for administering the Sacraments, and for other pastoral ministrations; there a prayerful Christian people are opposed and persecuted for the sake of Christ, and there they must bear the cross[113] of their Master.[114]

We have examined the true and false church, and explored how Christianity is becoming absorbed into the pluralistic nature of our day. With this knowledge we can prayerfully remain grounded in the true saving formula of Christ and His salvation.

Conclusion

SAVING FORMULAS OF
World Religions
and the True Saving Formula

Introduction

Religion is universal because man himself is inherently religious. There is a law of creation that compels man to have and to make gods,[1] for it is the basic situation that man must have something upon which to rely, to trust, and to believe. Thus the question is not whether man ought to believe, for man is always and ever a believer, but whether faith is filled by the work of our Lord Jesus Christ or by an idol.

Consequently, every person and every nation must produce some concept of a god. However, as long as he is under the devil's dominion, he must create gods in the image of his own desires. For example, the idols of the ancient unbelievers were brought forth by man's desire for fortune in war, fertility, health, and beauty.

The heart of false religion is man's belief that if he acts a certain way, God will be well disposed toward him. And, because God is the God of the law, unregenerate humankind assumes that He must deal with them on a legal basis of merit and reward. The orientation of unregenerate reason is such that man must change God's attitude by the gift of a sacrifice or by humankind's own holiness. Hence, they seek to gain His approval by performing what they devise as good works. Thus idolatry[2] and works-righteousness[3] go hand-in-hand.

Religions of the Law

Some religions fall outside the Gospel, and believe that man must bring something to God, that he dare not trust in God's unconditional mercy and grace. In these religions, the direction of the order of salvation is from earth upward, with the law being made into a way that leads to God. This form of religion seeks to ascend into heaven by the ladders of moralism, mysticism, and speculation, or a combination of the three.

Moralism

Moralism is the ladder by which communion with God may be attained by the fulfillment of ethical duties. It is the struggle to gain personal righteousness by way of the law. Examples of this struggle can be seen in the moral discipline of the teachings of Confucius; the self-discipline of Stoic morals; the efforts of the Buddhist monk to destroy all enjoyment of sin; the Pharisee; and the lodge brother who by moral effort out of the raw material of his human nature makes himself free.

All these attempts have one common trait: they do not regard the human will as evil, or as something that separates us from God, which is a deadly offense against His holiness. They see it as something that is weak and imperfect, whose defects must continually be overcome through disciplined, moral behavior. All alike are sure that communion with God may be attained by the fulfillment of ethical duties.[4] It is, simply, the struggle to gain personal righteousness by the law.

> The primary idea is that by the aid of renewed, self-interest and discipline man will finally be able to liberate his spirit from the prison of a base sensuality and, thanks to his personal efforts to gain holiness, he will be able at last to appear just before God.[5]

Mysticism

Mysticism is the ladder by which the attempt is made to construct a bridge to God by the power of the human will. Mysticism lives on the assurance that hidden springs of divinity flow in the depths of the soul. If we only penetrate deeply enough into the innermost being of the soul, we will come at last to a place untouched by sin where the hidden, inner, pure essence rests in God.

The most complete development of the teaching[6] of the essential unity of the human soul with its divine source has taken place in India. For within Hinduism, salvation consists of the recognition of the unity of atman, the basis of the soul, with Brahman, the basis of the world,[7] and the immediate union of the soul's essence with the divine essence. This is accomplished through

> contemplative exercises, by an ascetic liberation from created things and by the greatest possible intensification of the strength gained by spiritual experiences, the ego, liberated from the burden of the earth, is continually to raise itself upward to an ultimate penetration of the universal ego.[8]

Speculation

Speculation is the ladder by which autonomous reason is able to evolve the ultimate metaphysical truths out of itself. It is the Greek who seeks wisdom to reach God. There is room in this quest for a teacher who can assist, through dialectic conversation, in the discovery of the divine truth hidden in the student, but the teacher cannot produce the truth. For it is only the act of thinking that a direct contact is established between the human and divine spirit.[9]

The Saving Formulas
of the Major World Religions

The Saving Formula of Tribalism

A man's primary duty is to preserve and strengthen the "vital force" of the tribe. So the gifts, sacrifices, and libations are regarded as absolutely necessary to ward off evil and calamity, and to preserve the life-force of both the living and the dead; and in this preservation lies their conception of salvation.[10]

The Saving Formula of Buddhism

As with Hinduism, the basic emphasis of Buddhism is on man working out his own salvation. Salvation is granted by a knowledge of the Four Noble Truths and practicing the eightfold moral discipline of the Middle Way, which is the path of nirvana.[11]

The Saving Formula of Confucianism

Confucius was an agnostic, believing that humankind cannot know things beyond this world. Because of his lack of knowledge about God, he chose to remain silent. Instead, Confucius focused his attention upon man and his relationship to other human beings. The destiny of man is to lead a life on this earth that will embody harmony. What lies beyond the grave is hidden from us and we must leave it in the hands of heaven.

The Saving Formula of Hinduism

For the Hindu, salvation means moksha, or liberation, not from moral guilt but from the human condition of being subject to the migratory samsara process. Salvation is release from space, time, and the ever-repeated reincarnations that the karma or actions of the past entail, and this can be achieved in one of several ways:

* by fulfilling not only the temporal dharma, or duty, of one's caste but also the eternal dharma

* by practicing the rigorous discipline of the Yoga technique and teaching

* by realizing that individuality and all duality is an illusion and that there is in fact only One without any second, the One Brahman-Atman, which is Absolute Being, Consciousness, and Bliss

* by attaining, after liberation, a state of unification with a personal God

So salvation is attained, though very rarely, by way of righteousness (dharma); much more frequently by means of asceticism and yoga disciplines (tapas); by knowledge (jnana) attained through the practice of virtue, piety, and meditation; and by devotion (bhakti) to some god or gods. Any of these are means by which union with Brahman may ultimately be achieved.[12]

The Saving Formula of Islam

If Muslims recite the Muslim creed from their hearts, and if they make some attempt to fulfill their obligations in keeping the five pillars, they may have to taste the fire of judgment for a time but will eventually be saved and admitted to paradise.

The Religion of the Gospel

It is the nature of all outside of the Christian faith and Gospel to trust in their own righteousness in order to pacify the wrath of God by their own will,[13] worship, and voluntary[14] religion. The source of these false religions is the devil who sends out false apostles[15] and who seeks to bewitch people to believe that they are justified by the works of the law. Unregenerate reason judges that God is not merciful and gracious but that He is an angry judge who must be pacified by works of personal holiness. These false apostles, and their false gospel, find a ready audience in the world's population since it is the general opinion of man that righteousness is achieved through the works of the law, and yet they do not understand the righteousness of faith.

Yet it is a horrible blasphemy to imagine that there is any work whereby someone should presume to pacify God except for the death and blood of the Son of God. That is, to abolish sin, to destroy death, to take away the curse of God and to give righteousness are the works of the Divine Majesty. The truth of the Gospel is that our righteousness and salvation comes by faith in Jesus Christ. The direction of salvation is from heaven downward, with the Gospel being the only way that leads to God and eternal life.

The Saving Formula
of the Christian Faith

The Law

The first use of the Law is civil and these laws are given to punish civic transgressions and to bridle wickedness in the public square. Therefore, God has ordained judges, parents, pastors, and all civic laws so that the devil's hands may be bound and that his followers are not able to rage after their own lusts. Thus the civil use of the law restrains those who are carnal and rebellious. Just as a mad or wild beast is bound lest it should destroy, so the law does bridle a mad and furious man so that he may not sin after his own lust. In this way, the first use of the law restrains sin and makes a man righteous, not because he does these civic laws willingly or for the love of virtue (even though there are many men and women who live a life filled with many commendable civic virtues), but for fear of prison and the public executioner. Thus through the words, threats, and penalties of the civil law God is able to defend and fortify the life of all humankind with a wall against the force and violence of the wicked. But this civic form of righteousness, even though it does bridle a man's wickedness and constrain him to do good, does not deliver from sin or prepare a way to get to heaven.

The second use of the Law is given to increase transgressions in the sight of God. It is a light that is given, not to justify and quiet afflicted consciences, but rather to increase sin, terrify the conscience, and to engender the wrath and judgment of God. The Law can do nothing except cause the conscience to know sin, death, and the judgment and wrath of God. In this way it reveals to the sinner his blindness in believing that he can offer works and merits sufficient to warrant salvation before God, his misery in the midst of one's guilt and alienations, his iniquity expressed in a lifetime of sins against God and against others, his ignorance of the way to salvation by grace through faith in Jesus Christ, and the deserved wrath and condemnation of God. This use of the Law accuses and terrifies the sinner so that he may be humbled, bruised, and broken, and this ultimately means to be driven to seek comfort in Christ, the Blessed Seed.

The Gospel

There is Good News for all of humankind and this Good News is the announcement from God that a person's salvation is found, not in the works of the Law, but by the grace of God. The troubled and afflicted conscience has only one remedy against the wrath and judgment of God upon sin, and that is the forgiveness of sins by grace, freely offered in Christ Jesus. For Christ came into this world by the Father's will and took our nature[16] upon Himself that He might be made a sacrifice[17] for the sins of all humankind, and ultimately to reconcile[18] the Father to us.

In other words, Christ became a curse[19] for us. For Christ is innocent concerning His own person because He is the unspotted and undefiled Lamb of God. Because He bears the sins of the world, His innocence is burdened with the sins and guilt of the whole world. God laid our sins not upon us, but upon Christ His Son that He, bearing its punishment, might be our peace[20] and that by His life we might be saved.

Therefore, because all sins have been imputed to Him, Christ is the greatest sinner[21] that ever lived. For example, He carried the sins of Paul, a blasphemer of God and persecutor of God's people. He carried the sins of Peter who denied Him several times. He carried the sins of David, an adulterer and murderer. Thus Christ bore the sins of all people in His body, not that He is guilty of any sin, but that He received them, being committed and done by us, and laid them upon His own body that He might make satisfaction for them with His own blood.

The Saving Formula of Christianity

The first part of Christianity is that a person must be taught by the Law to know himself as a sinner so that he may learn to say "all have sinned and fall short of the glory of God and are justified by His grace as a gift, through the redemption[22] that is in Christ Jesus whom, God put forward as a propitiation[23] by His blood, to be received by faith" (Romans 3:23–25a) and "the wages of sin is death, but the free gift of God is eternal life in Christ Jesus our Lord" (Romans 6:23). Now when a man is humbled by the Law and brought to a knowledge of himself as a sinner, he deserves God's wrath and judgment. He then follows true repentance and he sees himself to be so great a sinner that he can find no means how he can be delivered from his sins by his own strength, works, or merits. For he, being thus terrified by the Law and utterly despairing of his own strength, looks about and sighs for the help of another; of a mediator[24] and savior.[25]

The second part of Christianity is that if you would be saved, you must not seek salvation by works, for God sent Jesus Christ into the world that we might live eternally through Him. The Good News is to believe that Jesus Christ was crucified for your sins. We are delivered from sin and justified in the presence of God, not for our works, but by faith that lays hold upon Christ. This salvation by grace, through faith in Jesus Christ, has been the hope of God's people since the fall of humankind into sin recorded in Genesis 3. The Old Testament people of God[26] were saved by faith in the Christ to come, but we are saved by faith in the Christ who has come and who has brought us grace and peace. A true and steadfast faith must lay hold of nothing but Christ alone. For the promise of salvation is not apprehended by working, but by believing.

It is not that we are free from sin, because sin is always in us, but it is covered and is not imputed to us for Christ's sake. But when Christ and faith are not present, there is no remission and covering of sins, but imputation of sins and eternal condemnation. Through faith in Christ, therefore, all things are given to us—grace, peace, forgiveness of sins, salvation, and everlasting life.

When he has heard and believed this Good News about Jesus as his mediator and savior, he gives thanks to God with a joyful and glad heart and exercises himself in good works expressed in loving God and loving one's neighbor. For the believing man has the Holy Spirit and where the Holy Spirit dwells He will not permit a man to be idle but will stir him up to all works of godliness—love of God, patient suffering of afflictions, prayer, thanksgiving, and works of charity toward all people. For where the Spirit is, it renews the believer and works in him so that he seeks not his own glory, but the glory of God.

Therefore, the whole life of a Christian consists inwardly of faith toward God, and His promises of grace and salvation in Jesus Christ, and outwardly in charity and good works toward one's neighbor.

Epilogue

Missiologists speak of the importance of revitalization in a culture that is experiencing demoralization due to acculturation. In order for a revitalizing movement to occur, often it requires a reformation or innovation so that a new steady state might be achieved. It is my hope that God's people might experience such a reformation by the power of His Spirit and boldly, yet winsomely, fulfill its mission in this modern and postmodern age.

May we be good soldiers, then, not flinching at the point of battle but lovingly, joyfully, and evangelically being engaged in scattering the seed of His Law and Gospel, as given in the Word realizing that "faith comes by preaching, and preaching by the Word of God."[27]

May we be good communicators, always being grounded in the Word of God and seeking to construct relevant and meaningful bridges into the hearts and minds of the regenerate and the lost.

May the Lord bless us in our storytelling. This concept of storytelling lends itself well to the audiovisual age. May we use both the medium of Gutenberg and of the audiovisual age in stereo catechesis to tell the story to the hearts and minds of this generation so that they might hear and believe. May we also use the music form in creative ways so that the only true story might be heard and sung into the hearts of those who listen.

May we construct, by the Spirit's power and guidance, caring Christian communities where people are drawn to Jesus Christ as their Savior, nurtured in the Christian faith through the apostles' teaching, fellowship, and prayer, and equipped for works of Christian service on the mission frontier.

May we, as did Luther, always realize that the sovereign Lord is working in His world according to His timing. As modern men and women struggle *coram Deo*, may we be sensitive to the Lord's working, like Philip did with the Ethiopian eunuch, so that a timely interpretation of life might be shared that permits the receptor to repent and make sense of his relationship to God and to man.

Finally, may we be bearers of Good News to an age that has experienced the loss of certainty, comprehensiveness, and compelling power. May the Lord bless us in this task of laying solid Christological foundations and grant us wisdom as we are called to build relevant, missiological bridges into this fragmented and sinfully dark world. May the one who believes in a false gospel find meaning and salvation in the way, the truth, and the life: our Lord Jesus Christ alone.

Bibliography

Adams, David L. *The Challenges of American Civil Religion for the Church* in *Witness and Worship in Pluralistic America*. John F. Johnson, editor. St. Louis: Concordia Seminary, 2003.

Allen, Diogenes. *Christian Belief in a Postmodern World*. Louisville: John Knox Press, 1989.

Althaus, Paul. *The Theology of Martin Luther*. Translated by Robert C. Schulz. Philadephia: Fortress Press, 1966.

Anderson, Norman. *Christianity and World Religions: The Challenge of Pluralism*. Downers Grove: InterVarsity, 1984.

Babin, Pierre. *The New Era in Religious Communication*. Minneapolis: Fortress Press, 1991.

Barrett, William. *Irrational Man*. Garden City, NY: Doubleday, 1962.

Bebbington, David. *Patterns in History*. Grand Rapids: Baker, 1979.

Bellah, Robert. *Habits of the Heart: Individualism and Commitment in American Life*. Berkeley: Regents of the University of California, 1985.

Bente, F. *Historical Introductions to the Book of Concord*. St. Louis: Concordia, 1965.

Berger, Peter. *The Homeless Mind*. New York: Vintage Books, 1974.

———. *The Sacred Canopy*. Garden City: Doubleday, 1967.

———. *The Social Reality of Religion*. London: Faber, 1969.

Best, Steven, and Douglas Kellner. *The Postmodern Turn*. New York: Guilford Press, 1997.

Bornkamm, Heinrich. *Luther and the Old Testament*. Translated by Eric W. and Ruth C. Gritsch. Philadelphia: Fortress Press, 1969.

———. *Luther's World of Thought*. Translated by Martin H. Bertram. St. Louis: Concordia, 1958.

Burke, T. Patrick. *The Major Religions: An Introduction with Texts*. Malden, MA: Blackwell, 1996.

Coiner, Harry. "The Secret of God's Plan." St. Louis: Concordia Theological Monthly, May 1963.

Cox, Harvey. *The Secular City*. New York: The Macmillan Company, 1965.

Demarest, Bruce and Gordon R. Lewis, ed. *Challenges to Inerrancy*. Chicago: Moody Press, 1984.

Dockery, David S., ed. *The Challenge of Postmodernism*. Grand Rapids: Baker, 1995.

Ebeling, Gerhard. *Luther: An Introduction to His Thought*. Philadelphia: Fortress Press, 1970.

Forell, George Wolfgang. *Ethics of Decision*. Philadelphia: Fortress Press, 1955.

———. *Faith Active in Love: An Investigation of the Principles Underlying Luther's Social Ethics*. New York: American Press, 1954.

———. *The Proclamation of the Gospel in a Pluralistic World*. Philadelphia: Fortress Press, 1973.

Glover, Willis. *Biblical Origins of Modern Secular Culture*. Macon: Mercer University Press, 1984.

Grenz, Stanley. *A Primer on Postmodernism*. Grand Rapids: Eerdmans, 1996.

Guinness, Os. *The Gravedigger File: Papers on the Subversion of the Modern Church*. Downers Grove: InterVarsity, 1983.

Headley, John. *Luther's View of Church History*. New Haven: Yale University Press, 1963.

Henry, Carl F. H. *Toward a Recovery of Christian Belief*. Wheaton: Crossway, 1990.

———. *Twilight of a Great Civilization: The Drift Toward Neo-Paganism*. Wheaton: Crossway, 1988.

Hiebert, Paul G. *Anthropological Insights for Missionaries*. Grand Rapids: Baker Book House, 1985.

Hunsberger, George R., and Craig Van Gelder. *The Church Between Gospel and Culture*. Grand Rapids: Eerdmans, 1996.

Hunter, George. *How to Reach Secular People*. Nashville: Abingdon, 1992.

Kang, C. H., and Ethel R. Nelson. *The Discovery of Genesis*. St. Louis: Concordia, 1979.

Kaufmann, Walter, ed. *The Portable Nietzsche*. New York: Penguin, 1976.

Köberle, Adolf. *The Quest for Holiness*. Translated by John C. Mattes. Minneapolis: Augsburg, 1938. Reprinted in the *Concordia Heritage Series*, Concordia: St. Louis, 1982.

Löwith, Karl. *Meaning in History*. Chicago: University of Chicago Press, 1949.

Luther, Martin. *Luther's Works*. American Edition. General editors Jaroslav Pelikan and Helmut T. Lehmann. 56 vols. St. Louis: Concordia, and Philadelphia: Muhlenberg and Fortress, 1955–1986.

———. *Works of Martin Luther: The Philadelphia Edition*. 6 vols. Philadelphia: Muhlenberg Press, 1943.

Lyotard, Jean Francois. *The Postmodern Condition*. Minneapolis: University of Minnesota Press, 1984.

Mbiti, John S. *Introduction to African Religion*. Nairobi: East African Educational Publishers, 1992.

Mead, Loren. *The Once and Future Church*. New York: Alban Institute, 1991.

Molloy, Michael. *Experiencing the World's Religions*. Mountain View, CA: Mayfield, 1999.

Myers, Kenneth. *All God's Children and Blue Suede Shoes*. Wheaton: Crossway, 1989.

Neusch, Marcel. *The Sources of Modern Atheism*. Translated by Matthew J. O'Connell. New York: Paulist Press, 1982.

Newbigin, Lesslie. *Foolishness to the Greeks*. Grand Rapids: Eerdmans, 1984.

———. *The Gospel in a Pluralist Society*. Grand Rapids: Eerdmans, 1989.

———. *The Other Side of 1984: Questions for the Churches*. Geneva: World Council of Churches, 1983.

———. *Truth to Tell: The Gospel and Public Truth*. Grand Rapids: Eerdmans, 1991.

Nida, Eugene. *Religion Across Cultures*. Pasadena: William Carey Library, 1968.

Oden, Thomas. "After-Modern Evangelical Spirituality Toward a Neoclassic Critique of Criticism." St. Louis: Concordia Journal, 1994.

Pinomaa, Lennart. *Faith Victorious: An Introduction to Luther's Theology*. Translated by Walter Kukkonen. Philadelphia: Fortress Press, 1963.

Polanyi, Michael. *Personal Knowledge*. Chicago: University of Chicago Press, 1958.

Richardson, Alan. *The Bible in the Age of Science*. Philadelphia: The Westminster Press, 1961.

Schaeffer, Francis. *The God Who Is There*. Downer's Grove: InterVarsity, 1968.

———. *Escape From Reason*. Wheaton: Crossway, 1968.

———. *Pollution and the Death of Man*. Wheaton: Crossway, 1970.

———. *How Should We Then Live?* Wheaton: Crossway, 1976.

———. *Whatever Happened to the Human Race?* Wheaton: Crossway, 1979.

———. *Death in the City*. Wheaton: Crossway, 1982.

———. *The Great Evangelical Disaster*. Wheaton: Crossway, 1984.

Schilling, S. Paul. *God in an Age of Atheism*. Nashville: Abingdon, 1969.

Sire, James. *The Universe Next Door*. Downers Grove: InterVarsity, 1988.

Sproul, R. C. *Lifeviews*. Old Tappan, NJ: Fleming H. Revell, 1986.

Stott, John. *Between Two Worlds*. Grand Rapids: Eerdmans, 1982.

Tappert, Theodore G. ed. *The Book of Concord*. Philadelphia: Fortress, 1959.

Tarnas, Richard. *The Passion of the Western Mind*. New York: Harmony Books, 1991.

Vajta, Vilmos. *Luther On Worship*. Philadelphia: Muhlenberg Press, 1958.

Van Rheenen, Gailyn. *Communicating Christ in Animistic Contexts*. Grand Rapids: Baker Book House, 1991.

Vicedom, Georg F. *The Mission of God: An Introduction to a Theology of Mission*. Translated by Gilbert A. Thiele and Dennis Hilgendorf. St. Louis: Concordia, 1965.

Watson, Philip. *Let God Be God! An Interpretation of the Theology of Martin Luther*. London: Epworth Press, 1947.

Wells, David. *No Place for Truth*. Grand Rapids: Eerdmans, 1993.

Wingren, Gustaf. *Luther On Vocation*. Translated by Carl C. Rasmussen. Philadelphia: Muhlenberg Press, 1957.

Acknowledgments

Excerpts from *Pollution and the Death of Man, How Should We Then Live?, Whatever Happened to the Human Race?, Death in the City,* and *The Great Evangelical Disaster* by Francis Schaeffer, copyright © 1970, 1976, 1979, 1982, 1984. Used by permission of Crossway Books, a division of Good News Publishers, Wheaton, Illinois 60187, www.gnpcb.org.

Excerpts from *All God's Children and Blue Suede Shoes* by Kenneth Myers, copyright © 1989. Used by permission of Crossway Books, a division of Good News Publishers, Wheaton, Illinois 60187, www.gnpcp.org.

Excerpts from Watson, Philip. *Let God Be God! An Interpretation of the Theology of Martin Luther* by Philip Watson. © Epworth Press, 1947. Used by permission of Methodist Publishing House.

Excerpts from *The Sources of Modern Atheism,* by Marcel Neusch, copyright © 1982, Paulist Press, Inc., New York/Mahwah, N.J. Used with permission of Paulist Press. www.paulistpress.com.

Excerpts from *Biblical Origins of Modern Secular Culture,* by Willis Glover, reprinted by permission of Mercer University Press, 1984.

Excerpts from *God in an Age of Atheism,* by S. Paul Schilling. Nashville: Abingdon, 1969. Used by permission.

Excerpts from *How to Reach Secular People,* by George Hunter. Nashville: Abingdon, 1992. Used by permission.

Excerpts reprinted from *The Once and Future Church: Reinventing the Congregation for a New Mission Frontier* by Loren B. Mead, with permission from the Alban Institute. Copyright © 1991 by The Alban Institute, Inc. All rights reserved.

Excerpts from *Luther On Vocation,* by Gustaf Wingren. Translated by Carl C. Rasmussen. Philadelphia: Muhlenberg Press, 1957. The full text of this book can be obtained from Wipf & Stock Publishers (www.wipfandstock.com).

Notes

Preface

1. Henry, *Twilight of a Great Civilization*, ix.
2. Schaeffer, *Great Evangelical Disaster*, 317.
3. Schaeffer, *Great Evangelical Disaster*, 316.
4. Schaeffer, *Great Evangelical Disaster*, 321.
5. Schaeffer, *God Who Is There*, 11.
6. Guinness, *Gravedigger File*, 114.
7. "[T]he Bible in its totality ascribes only one intention to God: to save mankind" (Vicedom, *Mission of God*, 4). God is the protagonist in this mission, and His people are the instruments through whom God carries out His mission.
8. Sire, *Universe Next Door*, 15.
9. Stott, *Between Two Worlds*, 149.
10. Stott, *Between Two Worlds*, 180.
11. Newbigin, *Foolishness to the Greeks*, 2, 3.
12. Vicedom, *Mission of God*, 5.
13. Vicedom, *Mission of God*, 45.
14. Vicedom, *Mission of God*, 52.
15. Vicedom, *Mission of God*, 28.
16. Vicedom, *Mission of God*, 103.
17. Vicedom, *Mission of God*, 107–08.
18. Vicedom, *Mission of God*, 65.
19. Cognitive assumptions "shape the mental categories people use for thinking; they play a vital role in determining the kinds of authority people trust and the types of logic they use. Taken together these assumptions give order and meaning to life and reality" (Hiebert, *Anthropological Insights*, 46).
20. "Affective assumptions underlie the notions of beauty, style, and aesthetics found in a culture. They influence people's tastes in music, art, dress, food, and architecture as well as the ways they feel towards each other and about life in general" (Hiebert, *Anthropological Insights*, 46).
21. "Evaluative assumptions provide the standards people use to make judgments, including their criteria for determining truth and error, likes and dislikes, and right and wrong. . . . Evaluative assumptions also determine the priorities of a culture, and thereby shape the desires and allegiances of the people" (Hiebert, *Anthropological Insights*, 46–47).
22. Hiebert, *Anthropological Insights*, 47–48.
23. Hiebert, *Anthropological Insights*, 48.

Chapter One

1. The Border Sacrifice was a ceremony conducted in unbroken sequence from the first dynastic rule, which began in 2205 BC, until the rite ended in AD 1911.
2. Kang and Nelson, *Discovery of Genesis*, 14.

3. "The god Rudra brought winds. Varuna was the god of sky and justice; Vishnu was a god of cosmic order, and Surya was the major sun god" (Molloy, *Experiencing the World's Religions*, 65, used with permission of The McGraw-Hill Companies).

4. Indra, the god associated with storms, thunder, and lightning, brought rain to the crops and herds. Also, as the god of power, Indra is the god of battles and warriors who leads the people to victory. Agni is the god of fire. As the sacrifices were offered with fire, Agni is the god of the Brahmin caste. As each home centers around the hearth, Agni is also the god of the household.

5. "Brahma represents the creative force that made the universe. He is considered the personal aspect of Brahman. . . . He has four faces, each looking in one of the four directions, and eight arms, each holding symbols of power. His companion animal is a white goose" (Molloy, *Experiencing the World's Religions*, 81).

6. "Vishnu represents the force of preservation in the universe. In the Vedas he is a god associated with the sun." Today Vishnu is the major god of Hinduism and "almost always has four arms that hold symbols of power. His companion animal is a great eagle-like bird, Garuda, on whom he flies through the universe" (Molloy, *Experiencing the World's Religions*, 82). Because Vishnu is connected with loving-kindness, it is understood that he can appear on earth at different times and in various physical forms to help those in need. It is believed that there are ten avatars of Vishnu. Of these ten, nine have already appeared. The tenth avatar, yet to come, is said to be that of Kalki, a savior riding on a white horse and coming to save the righteous and destroy the wicked. The previous nine avatars, when Vishnu took on an earthly form to save the world when its destruction by evil forces was threatened, are Matsya (fish), Kurma (tortoise), Varaha (boar), Narasimha (man-lion), Vamana (dwarf), Rama of the Axe, Rama, king of Ayodhya, Krishna, Buddha, and Kalki. Of these nine, only Rama, Krishna, and Buddha have followings today.

7. Shiva is the god linked with destruction. Destruction does not have the negative connotation with Hinduism as it does for many in the West because destruction must occur so that new forms may appear.

8. Muslims explain that the word *Allah* is not the name of God but simply means God. Instead, it is said that Allah has ninety-nine names such as "the Merciful," "the Just," and "the Compassionate."

9. The Ka'ba marks the place where Adam discovered the stone. However, during the time of the flood, the stone was lost. Much later Abraham, while visiting Ishmael in Mecca, built a temple to Allah with his son. As they completed the Ka'ba, an angel unburied the stone and brought it to Abraham to put in the temple. By the time of Muhammad, the shrine was officially dedicated to Hubal, and there were 360 deities inside the structure, probably representing the 360 days of the lunar year.

10. "According to Phil Parshall, 70 percent of all Islamic people are folk Muslims and only 30 percent are orthodox" (Van Rheenan, *Communicating Christ*, 27).

11. There are remnants of animism among many who claim to be Christians. For example, animistic tendencies are expressed in such behaviors as turning back if a black cat crosses one's path, never walking under a ladder, not staying on the thirteenth floor of a hotel, carrying a rabbit's foot when there is something important to be decided, having an image of St. Christopher on the dashboard to guard against accidents, or reading the daily horoscopes to understand the best times to engage in certain actions and to make certain decisions.

12. There was a Triune God who existed, and He had revealed Himself through nature, through His Word and Sacraments, and through the incarnation of the Son. The universe was created out of nothing in seven, twenty-four hour days, and human beings were His special creation.

13. Sire, *Universe Next Door*, 24.

14. Glover, *Biblical Origins of Modern Secular Culture*, 10.

15. Glover, *Biblical Origins of Modern Secular Culture*, 12.

16. Demarest, *Challenges to Inerrancy*, 11.

17. Naturalism is the rejection of the supernaturalist worldview that understands God as the ultimate source of all existence and value.

18. Reuben Abel traces the origin of modern anthropocentric thought to an assertion by Protagoras that man is the measure of all things. (See Reuben Abel, *Man is the Measure*, New York: Free Press, 1997.)

19. For many people, science is the measure of what exists and of what does not exist. Since the Enlightenment period, the Christian truth-claims have had diminishing effectiveness for many people, partly because they have seemed inconsistent with the understanding of the world in modern science.

20. Glover, *Biblical Origins of Modern Secular Culture*, 109.

21. Schaeffer, *Great Evangelical Disaster*, 315.

22. For further reading, consult Neusch, *Sources of Modern Atheism*, 31–56 and Schilling, *God in an Age of Atheism*, 23–25.

23. Neusch, *Sources of Modern Atheism*, 35.

24. For further reading, consult Neusch, *Sources of Modern Atheism*, 57–88 and Schilling, *God in an Age of Atheism*, 26–28.

25. Neusch, *Sources of Modern Atheism*, 67.

26. Neusch, *Sources of Modern Atheism*, 67.

27. For further reading, consult Neusch, *Sources of Modern Atheism*, 110–133 and Schilling, *God in an Age of Atheism*, 33–39.

28. Zarathustra, age 30, comes down from his meditative mountain to preach to the crowd. Of the many memorable thoughts spoken by Zarathustra in Nietzsche's *Thus Spoke Zarathustra,* is that "God is dead" and that man is to be "the overman," that is, a person who remains faithful to the earth and who does not believe those who speak of otherworldly hopes.

29. Kaufmann, *Portable Nietzsche*, 125.

30. For further reading, consult Neusch, *Sources of Modern Atheism*, 89–109 and Schilling, *God in an Age of Atheism*, 40–51.

31. The Oedipus conflict is the hatred that a child possesses in the Oedipal stage of infancy; he desires his father's death, though he must yield and submit to the father's more powerful will.

32. For further reading, consult Neusch, *Sources of Modern Atheism*, 134–156 and Schilling, *God in an Age of Atheism*, 65–69.

33. Neusch, *Sources of Modern Atheism*, 134.

34. Schilling, *God in an Age of Atheism*, 66.

35. For further reading, consult Schilling, *God in an Age of Atheism*, 69–74.

36. Bebbington, *Patterns in History*, 23.

37. Bebbington, *Patterns in History*, 43.

38. "Asiatic, ancient, feudal, and bourgeois phases have already emerged" (Bebbington, *Patterns in History*, 123).

39. Until the deist understanding of a clockwork universe, it was believed that God provided for his created world in an active and ever-present fashion, and that without him nothing would exist and nothing would happen.

40. For example, Turgot understood that "the course of history is directed by the simple and single principle of a one-dimensional progression, though interrupted by periods of temporary decay" (Löwith, *Meaning in History*, 100).

41. At the theological stage, human and national events are immaturely explained by appealing to the will of the gods or of God.

42. At the metaphysical stage, all phenomena are explained by appealing to abstract philosophical categories; for example, within the civic realm, fundamental philosophic categories would involve concepts of social contract and the equality of persons.

43. At the scientific stage, the quest for absolute explanations of metaphysical causes is abandoned and a scientific approach to social and political organization is adopted.

44. For Auguste Comte, history is the progression of man in three stages: from the theological stage to the metaphysical stage to the positive stage. The chief purpose and meaning of history is the improvement of the condition of man (Löwith, *Meaning in History*, 69).

45. For Voltaire, history is the progressive development of economics and skills, morals and laws, and commerce and industry, with the two great obstacles to progress being religions and wars.

46. Bebbington, *Patterns in History*, 114.

47. A people's worldview is the integrated system of beliefs, feelings, and values that make up the cultural order of society. They contain the fundamental, unquestioned assumptions that we make about the nature of things. They are our mental maps of the world that define reality for us, and they are also the maps for guiding our lives; that is, they explain why things are the way they are and prescribe how things should be.

48. LC, "The Ten Commandments," (Tappert, 365).

49. AC I (Tappert, 27).

50. LC, "The Creed," (Tappert, 411).

51. LC, "The Creed," (Tappert, 419).

52. The unregenerate human nature has become so misshapen through sin that it cannot recognize God's nature without a covering. "It is for this reason that God lowers Himself to the level of our weak comprehension and presents Himself to us . . . in coverings" (LW 2:45).

53. LW 3:108–09.

54. LW 4:61.

55. LW 23:125–26.

56. LW 5:220–21.

57. LW 5:228–29.

58. "And there she was made pregnant by the most shameful act of incest, and the flesh from which Christ was to be born was poured from the loins of Judah and was propagated, carried about, and contaminated with sin right up to the conception of Christ. This is how our Lord God treats our Savior. God allows Him to be conceived in most disgraceful incest, in order that He may assume the truest flesh, just as our flesh is poured forth, conceived, and nourished in sins. But later, when the time for assuming the flesh in the womb of the Virgin came, it was purified and sanctified by the power of the Holy Spirit" (LW 7:31).

59. LW 7:15.

60. "Christ was truly born from true and natural flesh and human blood which was corrupted by original sin in Adam, but in such a way that it could be healed . . . in the moment of the Virgin's conception the Holy Spirit purged and sanctified the sinful mass and wiped out the

poison of . . . sin. . . . Therefore it is truly human nature no different from what it is in us. And Christ is the Son of Adam and of his seed and flesh, but . . . with the Holy Spirit over-shadowing it, active in it, and purging it, in order that it might be fit for this most innocent conception and the pure and holy birth by which we were to be purged and freed from sin" (LW 7:12–13).

61. LW 23:195.

62. "Therefore you must hear Him; for He came from the Father, and He was with the Father from eternity. He knows how to reveal Him" (LW 23:93).

63. LW 22:329–30.

64. LW 3:80.

65. LW 33:189.

66. Headley, *Luther's View of Church History*, 10.

67. LW 33:41.

68. LW 33:37–38.

69. LW 3:273.

70. LW 3:274.

71. LW 33:287.

72. LW 1:259.

73. Ebeling, *Luther*, 179.

74. Bornkamm, *Luther's World of Thought*, 209.

75. The Old Testament, when describing the beginning, course, and end of a society, never assesses them as being on the rise or decline, but history is filled with God's judgment upon idolatry and the account of God giving kingdoms to the nations and fixing their bound-aries.

76. Luther, *Works of Martin Luther*, 3:183.

77. LW 2:4–5.

78. "[U]ngodly governments are like God's swine. He fattens them; He gives them wealth, power, honors, and the obedience of their subjects. Therefore they are not molested, but they themselves molest and oppress others. They do not suffer violence; they inflict it on others. They do not give, but they take away from others until the hour comes when they are slaughtered like swine that have been fattened for a long time" (LW 2:35–36).

79. "God's acts of judgments are preceded by a period of silence. [That is, before the judgment,] while man supposes all is going well and becomes arrogant, God pursues a policy of angry silence" (Bornkamm, *Luther's World of Thought*, 210).

80. Luther, *Works of Martin Luther*, 3:179.

81. LW 2:12.

82. That one ruler should be victorious and supplant another does not mean that he is neces-sarily right, but rather that he is the instrument of the hidden activity of God.

83. For example, Luther refers to such great men as Hannibal and Alexander the Great, who were able to conquer and change history through their courage and greater gifts. However, they are only masks under God's control, employed by Him to either strengthen or overturn governments according to His purpose.

84. Forell, *Faith Active in Love*, 136.

85. LW 5:314–15, author's emphasis.

86. God "also has regard for the proud and the great men in the world. But they have no need of His grace and mercy; they despise His regard. Therefore He must disregard them" (LW 5:316).

87. Headley, *Luther's View of Church History*, 4.

88. Richardson, *Bible in the Age of Science*, 127.

89. Richardson, *Bible in the Age of Science*, 127.

Chapter Two

1. The twelve links in the chain of dependent causation are (1) ignorance or avidya, from which arise (2) volitional activities, which in turn produce (3) consciousness linked to existence, (4) mind and matter, and, hence, physical existence, (5) the six senses, (6) impressions, (7) feeling, (8) craving, (9) attachment, (10) the process of becoming, (11) rebirth, and (12) old age and death. However, if the first link can be broken, namely, ignorance, then the rest of the chain of causation can be undone.

2. See chapter 1, note 1.

3. Burke, *Major Religions*, 113.

4. Veda means "knowledge". The Rig Veda is a collection of more than a thousand hymn chants to the Aryan gods. These hymns were handed down by word of mouth over many centuries.

5. Creation is attributed to the sacrifice by Purusha of himself; by the dismemberment of his own body. From his head sprang the Brahmins, from his shoulders the warriors, from his thighs the merchant class, and from his feet the servile shudras, thus fixing the functions and rank of the four estates.

6. Samsara is the belief that the soul repeatedly dies and is reborn, embodied in a new organism.

7. According to Hindu belief, atman is a person's inner self, the spiritual essence of every individual.

8. Burke, *Major Religions*, 30.

9. Molloy, *Experiencing the World's Religions*, 408.

10. In many tribal stories it is told that at one time the heavens and the earth were united as one. This is depicted in art as the earth and heavens touching each other or of a ladder joining the heaven and earth. However, due to the error or fault of man, the two parts of the universe were separated.

11. Nature spirits are those spirits that people associate with natural objects and forces such as the sun, the moon, stars, rainbows, rain, storms, wind, thunder, and lightning, and which occupy and control them. Just as there are spirits associated with the things and forces of the sky, so there are those associated with the things and forces of the earth, hills, mountains, rocks, trees, metals, water, different animals and insects, and various diseases such as smallpox.

12. Mbiti, *Introduction to African Religion*, 77–78.

13. In our culture it is widely believed that the final reality is some form of energy or mass, shaped into its present form by pure chance.

14. Richardson, *Bible in an Age of Science*, 36.

15. "The sciences, both natural and human, have been so successful in uncovering the cause and effect links which lie behind all happenings that there seems to be no crack or cranny through which divine action could enter and influence them. . . . The door seems to be

firmly shut against any intervention from outside the closed system" (Newbigin, *Gospel in a Pluralist Society*, 69).

16. Richardson, *Bible in an Age of Science*, 33.

17. Newbigin, *Foolishness to the Greeks*, 24.

18. Berger, *Sacred Canopy*, 112.

19. Nida, *Religion Across Cultures*, 53.

20. Berger, *Sacred Canopy*, 45.

21. LC, "The Creed," (Tappert, 412).

22. LW 1:18, 19.

23. "The Father creates heaven and earth out of nothing through the Son, whom Moses calls the Word. Over these the Holy Spirit broods . . . on the waters to bring to life those substances which were to be quickened and adorned. For it is the office of the Holy Spirit to make alive" (LW 1:9).

24. "Christ is true God, who is with the Father from eternity, before the world was made, and that through Him, who is the wisdom and the Word of the Father, the Father made everything" (LW 1:17). "God reveals Himself to us as the Speaker who has with Him the uncreated Word, through whom He created the world and all things with the greatest ease, namely, by speaking" (LW 1:22).

25. LW 1:19.

26. Althaus, *Theology of Martin Luther*, 105.

27. Althaus, *Theology of Martin Luther*, 106.

28. LW 22:27.

29. LW 4:5.

30. LW 4:90.

31. "Therefore these words, 'God said: "Let there be, grow, multiply," ' established the creatures as they are now and as they will be to the end of the world" (LW 1:76).

32. LW 1:47.

33. Thus "In Adam the human race had its beginning; in the earth the animal race . . . had its beginning through the Word; and in the sea that of the fish and of the birds had its beginning" (LW 1:75).

34. In the words "Grow and multiply . . . the power and effectiveness of the Word which thus preserves and governs the entire creation" (LW 1:75).

35. LW 1:75–76.

36. "Just as at that time He filled the sea with fish, the heaven with flying things, and the earth with cattle, so these are complete, remain to the present time, and are preserved" (LW 1:76).

37. LW 1:39.

38. LW 1:92.

39. LW 1:110.

40. LW 1:94–95.

41. LW 1:94.

42. LW 1:96.

43. LW 1:64.

44. LW 1:207.

45. LW 1:205.

46. "[B]efore sin no part of the earth was barren and inferior, but all of it was amazingly fertile and productive. Now the earth is not only barren in many places; but even the fertile areas are defaced by darnel, weeds, thorns, and thistles" (LW 1:205).

47. LW 1:205.

48. LW 6:173.

49. Bornkamm, *Luther's World of Thought*, 183–84.

50. LW 4:7–8.

51. Pinomaa, *Faith Victorious*, 7.

52. Watson, *Let God Be God*, 80.

53. Bornkamm, *Luther and the Old Testament*, 63.

54. LW 7:191.

55. The rainbow "also gives comfort, that we may have the conviction that God is kindly inclined toward us again and will never again make use of so horrible a punishment. Thus it teaches the *fear of God* and *faith* at the same time" (LW 2:148, author's emphasis).

56. LW 1:221.

57. LW 1:208.

58. LW 1:209.

59. "This life is profitably divided into three orders: (1) life in the home; (2) life in the state; (3) life in the church" (LW 3:217).

60. Althaus, *Theology of Martin Luther*, 108.

61. LW 3:279.

62. LW 4:249.

63. LW 3:279.

64. LW 4:222.

65. "For if you have the gift of being able to abstain from [marriage] and to avoid it without sin, abstain from it by all means, if you can do so without sin. But if you cannot avoid being joined to a woman without sinning, use the remedy shown by God. And if you do not seek the function of bringing children into being, at least seek the remedy against sin, in order that fornication and adultery may be avoided as well as pollutions and promiscuous lusts" (LW 5:190).

66. LW 4:244.

67. LW 4:221.

68. LW 5:189.

69. "If you judge in accordance with reason and outward appearance, marital intercourse differs in no respect from harlotry. Yet the former is chaste and honorable under the forgiveness of sin and under the blessing, and is pleasing to God; the latter is shameful and condemned under the wrath of God" (LW 4:232).

70. "[M]any have no desire for children. The only thing they look for is the pleasure of the flesh. Later on, therefore, when they have had their fill, they begin to loathe, hate, and detest that union" (LW 4:299).

71. LW 3:48.

72. LW 1:103–04.

73. "Wherever that Word is heard, where Baptism, the Sacrament of the Altar, and absolution are administered, there you must determine and conclude with certainty: 'This is surely God's house; here heaven has been opened.' But just as the Word is not bound to any place, so the church is not bound to any place" (LW 5:244).

74. LW 4:31.

75. LW 4:53.

76. LW 5:247.

77. LW 8:54.

78. This is the purpose of the sacraments being "administered and the Word is taught in order that we may be led into the kingdom of heaven and through the church may enter heaven" (LW 5:250).

79. LW 2:51.

80. LW 2:287.

81. LW 1:103.

82. LW 4:291.

83. LW 4:304.

84. LW 1:247.

85. LW 1:115.

86. LW 1:104.

87. Forell, *Ethics of Decision*, 85–87.

88. "Under God's law society has a responsibility to protect the family, to protect life, to protect property from wanton destruction, to protect against each other and against themselves" (Forell, *Ethics of Decision*, 90).

89. LW 2:140.

90. For "human beings have the power to kill only when we are guilty before the world and when the crime has been established. For this reason courts have been established and a definite method of procedure has been prescribed. Thus a crime may be investigated and proved before the death sentence is imposed" (LW 2:140).

91. Whosoever sheds the blood of man, by man shall his blood be shed. "[T]he life of one who does not want to show respect for the image of God in man but wants to yield to his anger . . . this life God turns over to government, in order that his blood, too, may be shed" (LW 2:141).

92. LW 2:366.

93. "They say that as often as Emperor Maximilian passed a place of public execution, he uncovered his head and saluted it with these words: 'Hail, holy justice!' For if there were no punishments and executions, we would achieve nothing with our sermons and the forgiveness of sins, and the populace would abuse the doctrine of the mercy of God for boundless license to sin" (LW 8:205).

94. "God allots kingdoms and governments even to reprobate and evil men, not because of their merit . . . but for the sake of the church, which alone in the world prays for kings and governments, in order that they may be able to have a quiet lodging place in this life and to propagate the Word of God in peace" (LW 4:35).

95. LW 3:279.

96. LW 7:181.

97. LW 8:205.

98. LW 5:122–24.

99. LW 8:94–95.

100. In our work, God "wants to remain concealed and do all things. . . . Govern, and let Him give His blessing. Fight, and let Him win the victory. Preach, and let Him win hearts. Take a husband or a wife, and let Him produce the children. Eat and drink, and let Him nourish and strengthen you. And so on. In all our doings He is to work through us, and He alone shall have the glory for it" (LW 14:114–15).

101. LW 6:173.

102. LW 6:89.

103. LW 4:265.

104. "[Satan] stirs up storms, hurls thunderbolts. . . . He sends enemies; he even infects the body and covers it with boils. Therefore the good angels are busy in order that the fierce enemy may not inflict harm. Neither medicine nor other means would be effective by themselves if the angels were not present" (LW 3:270–71).

105. "For if God were not to govern the world through His angels even for one day, the devil would certainly strike down the whole human race all of a sudden, plunder it, and drive it off, destroying it with famine, plague, wars, and fires" (LW 6:92).

106. LW 3:270.

107. LW 4:256, author's emphasis.

108. LW 4:253–54.

Chapter Three

1. Hinduism teaches that each person has an individual soul, named jiva, but the Upanishads teach that all human beings share the same atman; thus, beneath the surface differences among individuals, all human beings share the same divine spirit.

2. "Often the term Brahman refers to the experience of the sacred and divine reality within nature and the external universe, while Atman refers to the experience of the sacred within oneself" (Molloy, *Experiencing the World's Religions*, 69).

3. Burke, *Major Religions*, 21.

4. On the subhuman level, the transmigration is virtually automatic until a human body is attained.

5. Traditionally, females and lower-caste males were not given this type of religious education. Females in the learning stage of life remained at home and were trained in domestic work.

6. Molloy, *Experiencing the World's Religions*, 76.

7. Hinduism began as a polytheistic and ritualistic religion. The head of the household in his home first performed the rituals. As the centuries passed, however, these rituals became increasingly complex. As a result, it became necessary to create a priestly class and to train those priests to perform the rituals correctly. During this time, the Vedas were written to give the priests instructions as to how to perform the rituals. As a result of the cultural emphasis on the rituals, the priests became the sole means by which the people could approach and appease the gods. Because of their position as mediators with the gods, the priests gained an increasing amount of power and control over the lives of the people.

8. Punishment for an infraction is graded according to one's caste position, with the higher castes receiving the greater punishment.

9. For example, the straight path involves how to be ritually pure for the five daily prayers, what food to eat, what clothes to wear, what the proper roles of males and females are in marriage, how is one to treat a Muslim neighbor and a neighbor who is not a Muslim, how to engage in proper business practices, what the fundamental standards are for governing a society, and what the proper conditions and justifications are for waging war.

10. Mbiti, *Introduction to African Religion*, 108.

11. Mbiti, *Introduction to African Religion*, 87.

12. Mbiti, *Introduction to African Religion*, 90–91.

13. Forell, *Proclamation of the Gospel*, 45.

14. Instead of seeing him as something significant, man is seen in his essence only as an intrinsically competitive animal that has no other basic operating principle than natural selection brought about by the strongest and the fittest ending up on top. Tribalism sees man as acting in this way both individually and collectively as society.

15. Forell, *Proclamation of the Gospel*, 44–45.

16. Schaeffer, *How Should We Then Live*, 102.

17. Schaeffer, *How Should We Then Live*, 173–44.

18. Sproul, *Lifeviews*, 43.

19. Schaeffer, *How Should We Then Live*, 229–36.

20. Francis Crick, co-discoverer of the DNA structure, believed that "man can be essentially reduced to the chemical and physical properties that go to make up his DNA template" (Schaeffer, *How Should We Then Live*, 232). Man is basically reduced to being an electro-chemical machine.

21. It was the thesis of B. F. Skinner that "all that people are can be explained by the way their environment has conditioned him" (Schaeffer, *How Should We Then Live*, 230).

22. Tarnas, *Passion of the Western Mind*, 319.

23. Schaeffer, *Death in the City*, 270.

24. Myers, *All God's Children*, 61.

25. Cox, *Secular City*, 60–61.

26. Television is the most significant shared reality in our entire society. What is presented on television and the way it is presented are, for many people, the equivalent of what is real. Television, by determining what ideas will be discussed in public, also determines which ideas are to be considered respectable, rational, and true.

27. Wells, *No Place for Truth*, 157.

28. Guinness, *Gravedigger File*, 151.

29. Schaeffer, *How Should We Then Live*, 211.

30. Schaeffer, *How Should We Then Live*, 211.

31. LC, "The Creed," (Tappert, 412).

32. LW 1:58.

33. " 'Let Us make' and 'He made,' [is] in the plural and [is] in the singular; thereby Moses clearly and forcibly shows us that within and in the very Godhead and the Creating Essence there is one inseparable and eternal plurality. . . . 'Let Us make' [is a] sure indication of the

Trinity, that in one divine essence there are three Persons: the Father, the Son, and the Holy Spirit" (LW 1:58).

34. "The beasts greatly resemble man. They dwell together; they are fed together; they eat together; they receive their nourishment from the same materials; they sleep and rest among us. Therefore if you take into account their way of life, their food, and their support, the similarity is great" and yet there is "an outstanding difference between these living beings and man [in that] man was created by the *special plan* and *providence of God*. This indicates that man is a creature far superior to the rest of the living beings that live a physical life . . ." (LW 1:56, author's emphasis).

35. Adam "lived among the creatures of God in peace, without fear of death, and without any fear of sickness" (LW 1:113).

36. LW 1:62–63.

37. LW 1:165.

38. LW 1:65.

39. LW 1:63.

40. LW 1:119.

41. LW 1:66.

42. LW 1:83.

43. LW 1:91.

44. LW 1:102.

45. LW 1:113.

46. "On the Sabbath day he would have taught his children; through public preaching he would have bestowed honor on God with the praises which He deserved; and through reflection on the works of God he would have incited himself and others to expressions of thanks. On the other days he would have worked, either tilling his field or hunting" (LW 1:82).

47. LW 1:80.

48. LW 1:141.

49. LW 1:63.

50. Fallen, unregenerate man does not know "what God is, what grace is, what righteousness is, and finally what sin itself is" (LW 1:141). Thus, "unless the severity of [this blindness and disease] is correctly recognized, the cure is also not known or desired. The more you minimize sin, the more will grace decline in value" (LW 1:142).

51. LW 1:114.

52. "We are born from unclean seed and that from the very nature of the seed we acquire ignorance of God, smugness, unbelief, hatred against God, disobedience, impatience, and similar grave faults" (LW 1:166).

53. LW 1:165.

54. LW 1:64.

55. Luther, *Works of Martin Luther*, 3:132.

56. Luther, *Works of Martin Luther*, 3:132–33.

57. Luther, *Works of Martin Luther*, 3:133.

58. LW 2:5.

59. LW 33:65.

60. LW 33:64.

61. Forell, *Ethics of Decision*, 73.

62. LW 1:141.

63. Forell, *Ethics of Decision*, 71.

64. LW 33:115.

65. LW 33:176–77.

66. LW 33:174.

67. LW 33:176.

68. LW 33:176.

69. LW 1:85.

70. LW 33:119.

71. LW 33:70.

72. LW 2:350.

73. LW 4:146.

74. LW 1:85.

75. LW 3:139.

76. "Every man sets up as his god that from which he hopes to obtain good, help and comfort" (Watson, *Let God Be God*, 89).

77. "As long as he is under the devil's dominion he must create his gods in the image of his own desires" (Vajta, *Luther On Worship*, 9). "Since the fall, man has become a maker of gods who worships the figments of his own making" (Vajta, *Luther On Worship*, 13).

78. LW 1:249.

79. Forell, *Ethics of Decision*, 77.

80. LW 21:309–11.

81. It is easy to love God and to appreciate His love when life is going well, but it is not so easy to love Him and remain close to Him when life is difficult. Jesus, in the parable of the Sower (Matthew 13:3–9), talked about those who received the Gospel with great joy but who, when tribulation or persecution arose on account of the Word, fell away.

82. Althaus, *Theology of Martin Luther*, 146.

83. LW 21:311.

84. LW 4:29.

85. LW 4:206.

86. LW 2:379–80.

87. LW 6:42–43.

88. LW 5:153–55.

89. LW 2:378.

90. LW 4:256.

91. "Pride gets no pleasure out of having something, only out of having more than the next man. We say that people are proud of being rich, or clever, or good looking, but they are not. They are proud of being richer, or cleverer, or better looking than others" (Forell, *Ethics of Decision*, 75).

92. LW 3:5.

93. LW 4:381.

94. LW 2:347.

95. LW 2:5.

96. "Without fear death is not death; it is a sleep" (LW 4:115).

97. LW 4:197.

98. LW 4:311, author's emphasis.

Chapter Four

1. Molloy, *Experiencing the World's Religions*, 113.

2. Molloy, *Experiencing the World's Religions*, 114.

3. Ahimsa is the view that because souls can wander through every form of being, life, even in its lowest form, is to be respected and preserved. There is no greater sin than the taking of life even though it may be only a gnat or a worm that perishes.

4. Molloy, *Experiencing the World's Religions*, 218.

5. Each Veda (*veda* means knowledge or sacred lore) is divided into four parts: the basic verses or hymns sung during the rituals, the explanations of the verses, the reflections on the verse's meaning, and the mystical interpretations of the verses.

6. The Sama Veda, chant knowledge, is a handbook of musical elaborations of Vedic chants.

7. The Yajur Veda, ceremonial knowledge, contains words for recitation during the sacrifices.

8. The Atharva Veda, teacher knowledge, consists of practical prayers and charms.

9. The Upanishads are a collection of about one hundred works that record insights into external and internal reality. "Primary to the Upanishads is the notion that with spiritual discipline and meditation both priests and nonpriests can experience the spiritual reality that underlies all seemingly separate realities." "The most important notions in the Upanishads are Brahman, Atman, maya, karma-samsara and moksha" (Molloy, *Experiencing the World's Religions*, 67).

10. The reality is that the wheel of samsara belongs to the world of maya, and when the veil of maya is pierced and Brahman is revealed as the sole existent Reality, release will be obtained from the wheel of samsara.

11. Muhammad is said to have doubted initially the origin of these new revelations. He thought that perhaps he had been possessed by jinn. His wife Khadijah, however, assured him that his visions were of divine origin, and she encouraged him to teach that which had been revealed to him.

12. Molloy, *Experiencing the World's Religions*, 409.

13. It is not permissible for the Qur'an to be translated into any other language.

14. Islamic tradition claims that there have been 124,000 prophets in the world, though only twenty-five are named in the Qur'an. There have also been 104 books revealed by Allah to humankind, but most of these books have either been lost or have been taken back to heaven by God.

15. For 500 years after Muhammad, there was allowance in Islam for personal interpretation in how to answer a situation that was not already defined in Islamic law. However, since AD 1100, it has been decided that all important questions have been addressed and the time for personal interpretation closed. Thus there is to be no innovation within Islam. Avoid novelties, spoke Muhammad, for every novelty is an innovation and every innovation is error.

16. The Qur'an is the highest and infallible authority.

17. The sunna of Muhammad are second in authority and are recorded in the hadiths. The hadiths are descriptions of what Muhammad did in a multitude of various and often mundane situations. His behavior, his acts, and his words serve as models for the pious.

18. Even with the Qur'an and the sunna, there are still many situations in life for which a Muslim would like to receive guidance but of which there are no definitive answers in the Qur'an or the sunna. In such situations, the void is filled by the ijma', which is the unanimous, interpretive consensus of Islamic scholars or judges regarding the correctness of a certain action.

19. The qiyas is deductive reasoning by analogy, that is, an application of a fundamental ethical principle from Muhammad's life to a present day situation. It tackles the difficult and doubtful questions of doctrine and practice by comparing them with matters already settled in the Qur'an. For instance, wine, as an intoxicating substance, is forbidden in the Qur'an. On the basis of analogy, anything that intoxicates, such as drug abuse, is therefore forbidden as well.

20. Islam has traditionally listed seventeen major sins: idolatrous infidelity, constant minor sins, despair of Allah's mercy, a lack of fear of Allah's wrath, false witness, falsely accusing a Muslim of adultery, false oaths, magic, ingestion of alcohol, theft of an orphan's property, usury, adultery, unnatural sin, theft, murder, sympathy in battle against infidels, and disobedience to parents.

21. The "living dead" are those ancestors who have died physically but who are alive and active in watching over and governing their descendants; blessing those descendants who are faithful to the clan and its way of life with fruitfulness and prosperity, and punishing unfaithful descendants with hardship and suffering.

22. Nonage is the inability to use one's own understanding without another's guidance.

23. Wells, *No Place for Truth*, 118.

24. Forell, *Proclamation of the Gospel*, 2.

25. In such a pluralist society, any confident statement of ultimate belief, any claim to announce truth about God and His purpose for the world, is dismissed as ignorant, arrogant, or dogmatic. Instead, must we not accept that truth is larger, richer and more complex than can be contained in any one religion or cultural tradition?

26. Forell, *Proclamation of the Gospel*, 3.

27. Schaeffer, *God Who Is There*, 6.

28. The historical flow began with the philosophers from Rousseau, Kant, Hegel, and Kierkegaard onward who, having lost their hope of a unity of knowledge and a unity of life, presented a fragmented concept of reality. Then the artists painted human existence that way. The artists carried the idea of a fragmented reality onto the canvas and to the absurdity of all things.

29. Modern art has expressed a worldview centered in the concept of a fragmented world and fragmented man.

30. The fragmentation occurring in music is parallel to the fragmentation that occurred in art. Music became a vehicle for carrying the idea of a fragmented worldview to masses of people that the base philosophic writings would not have touched.

31. Schaeffer, *How Should We Then Live*, 195.

32. Nida, *Religion Across Cultures*, 53.

33. Forell, *Ethics of Decision*, 23.

34. Forell, *Ethics of Decision*, 27.

35. Nida, *Religion Across Cultures*, 54.

36. Forell, *Ethics of Decision*, 17.

37. Even Christians can be tempted to turn to God primarily as a means to an end; to gain pleasures in heaven and avoid the pain of hell. "We use God and the Church to achieve our own happiness. Love for one's neighbor is reduced to a means for the accumulation of merits to bring us into heaven" (Forell, *Ethics of Decision*, 23).

38. Forell, *Ethics of Decision*, 42–43.

39. Forell, *Ethics of Decision*, xi.

40. Bellah, *Habits of the Heart*, 35.

41. Bellah, *Habits of the Heart*, 99.

42. When a Christian ethic dominated our culture before the 1920s, it gave a foundation for law. In those days, a lone individual with the Bible could judge and warn society, regardless of the majority vote, because there was an absolute by which to judge. There was an absolute for both morals and law.

43. Schaeffer, *Whatever Happened to the Human Race*, 286.

44. Schaeffer, *Pollution and the Death of Man*, 53–54.

45. He eats up man and nature and exploits created things as though he has autonomous right to them. If people are not unique, as made in the image of God, the barrier is gone and there is nothing to stand in the way of inhumanity.

46. Forell, *Ethics of Decision*, 29.

47. Schaeffer, *How Should We Then Live*, 224.

48. LW 1:13.

49. LW 3:109.

50. God instituted the sacraments and absolution "to make you completely certain and to remove the disease of doubt from you heart, in order that you might not only believe with the heart but also see with your physical eyes and touch with your hands" (LW 5:45).

51. "For what benefit, then, was circumcision given? To make known that the Savior was to be born from this circumcised nation and not from the Gentiles. He who was desired by all the nations did not become incarnate among all the nations; He became incarnate among this one people" (LW 3:91). "It is the custom of Holy Scripture to add signs to promises. Thus in Baptism and in the Lord's Supper there is not only the Word of promise but also a sign or work or ceremony" (LW 3:29). "[I]t is a great praise of God's mercy that He did not let the human race walk and go astray in its own thoughts but set up for those who feared Him public signs at which they might gather" (LW 3:145).

52. LW 3:109.

53. After the fall of Adam and Eve into sin God enveloped Himself in a gentle breeze and brought them a Fatherly reprimand. "It was a great comfort for Adam that, after he had lost Paradise, the tree of life, and the other privileges which were signs of grace, there was given to him another sign of grace, namely, the sacrifices, by which he could perceive that he had not been cast off by God but was still the object of God's concern and regard" (LW 1:249).

54. LW 1:248.

55. The fanatical spirits believed that God, and His will, are to be investigated apart from the Word. But if anything beyond the Word is revealed, it must be "judged by the analogy of faith"; and "the analogy of faith is this: 'There is no other name under heaven given among men by which we must be saved' (Acts 4:12)" (LW 4:130).

56. LW 2:47.

57. "Outwardly he deals with us through the oral word of the gospel and through material signs, that is, baptism and the sacrament of the altar. Inwardly he deals with us through the Holy Spirit, faith, and other gifts. But whatever their measure or order the outward factors should and must precede. The inward experience follows and is effected by the outward. God has determined to give the inward to no one except through the outward. For he wants to give no one the Spirit or faith outside of the outward Word and sign instituted by him. . . . Observe carefully, my brother, this order, for everything depends on it" (LW 40:146).

58. "The ability to know God comes, not from our innate reason but from the Spirit of God, who enlightens our minds through the Word" (LW 2:313).

59. LW 1:122.

60. LW 1:125.

61. LW 1:131.

62. LW 32:223.

63. LW 33:24.

64. LW 1:185.

65. Althaus, *Theology of Martin Luther*, 64.

66. LW 1:130.

67. LW 2:308, 348.

68. LW 5:70.

69. LW 6:335.

70. LW 33:93.

71. LW 8:250–51.

72. LW 2:355.

73. LW 2:355, author's emphasis.

74. LW 4:38.

75. LW 1:329.

76. LW 1: 329. "[T]he fault does not lie in those things that are good and are truly gifts of God but in the human beings who possess them and make use of them" (LW 2:328). For example, it is "not evil to look at a woman, for woman is a good creature of God; but the fault is in your heart, because it desires a woman who is not yours" (LW 2:328). "Eyes, feet, and hands are gifts of God; and so, if you become inflamed when you look at a girl, it is not the fault of your eyes; your heart is to blame" (LW 2:329).

77. LW 1:258–59. "The [tax collector] calls upon God in his sins, praises Him, and fulfils the two greatest commandments, faith and the honoring of God. The Pharisee misses the mark on both. He struts about with other good works by which he praises himself, not God, and puts his trust more in himself than in God" (LW 44:41).

78. LW 1:259.

79. LW 1:257.

80. LW 2:349.

81. LW 1:257.

82. LW 1:268.

83. LW 1:258.

84. LW 3:24.

85. LW 3:22.

86. Luther, *Works of Martin Luther*, 3:239.

87. "It is love that deals with God when He gives commands; it carries out those commands and obeys God" (LW 3:24–25).

88. Wingren, *Luther On Vocation*, 120.

89. LW 3:240.

90. LW 2:299.

91. LW 2:269–70.

92. LW 3:170–71, author's emphasis.

93. LW 3:283–84.

94. LW 3:173.

95. LW 3:172–73, author's emphasis.

96. "[T]his kind of life is most pleasing to God: doing good to everybody and nevertheless enduring envy, hatred, and the injustices of the devil and of men" (LW 4:74). The Christian is to learn that in whatever state one exists, to be content. When "we are in a trial we may be strong, but when we are not in a trial we may be humble and grateful" (LW 2:370).

97. LW 22:286–87.

98. Luther, *Works of Martin Luther*, 3:239.

Chapter Five

1. "The Buddha is thought of as an ideal human being whom other human beings should imitate, and the image of him, seated in meditation, is a constant model of self-control and mindfulness" (Molloy, *Experiencing the World's Religions*, 111).

2. The dharma "means the sum total of Buddhist teachings about how to view the world and how to live properly" (Molloy, *Experiencing the World's Religions*, 111).

3. Molloy, *Experiencing the World's Religions*, 122.

4. Molloy, *Experiencing the World's Religions*, 129.

5. There are five writings that comprise the classics of Confucius: (1) the Classic of Changes, *I Ching*, book of divination; (2) the Classic of History, *Shu Ching*, which contains the Chou theology; (3) the Classic of Poetry, *Shih Ching*, a collection of three hundred poems; (4) the Classic of Ritual, *Li Chi*; and (5) the Spring and Autumn Annuals, *Ch'un Ch'iu*.

6. Kang and Nelson, *Discovery of Genesis*, 16.

7. It is recorded that Confucius sacrificed to the ancestors and spirits as if they were present. His every gesture during the sacrificial rites gave the impression that he had a deep respect for the ancestors. Yet his focus was not whether or not the ancestors and spirits enjoyed the offerings but that the duty of descendants be kept.

8. For example, when a Hindu sees an animal or insect he or she sees prehuman beings who are in their spiritual evolution toward eventually becoming a human being.

9. Molloy, *Experiencing the World's Religions*, 409–11.

10. Molloy, *Experiencing the World's Religions*, 414.

11. A Muslim is required to say seventeen cycles of prayer each day. These cycles are usually

spread over five periods of prayer per day.

12. The Ka'ba stands at the center of the great open-air mosque of Mecca. It constitutes the Qiblah, the specific point which Muslims face when performing the daily ritual prayers.

13. Ramadan is the time during which Muhammad first received his revelations that comprise the Qur'an.

14. The pilgrims start at the black stone and run three times quickly and four times slowly around the Ka'ba, stopping each time to kiss the stone or, if the crowds are too great, to touch it with a hand or stick or just look intensely at it.

15. The Lesser Pilgrimage is an imitative remembrance by the group of Hagar frantically looking for water for her suffering son Ishmael. This frantic searching takes place between two hills, and then one drinks from the well at Zamzam, which is believed to be the well that an angel showed to Hagar.

16. The Greater Pilgrimage calls for the pilgrims to move off toward Arafat in mass with some spending the night at Mina and others traveling the entire distance. The next day, when all the pilgrims have arrived, they move slowly, from noon until sunset, over the Arafat plain, absorbed in pious meditation. At sunrise they make their way back to Mina in order to cast seven pebbles at three small pillars and cry out: "In the name of God! Allah is almighty!" This ritual recalls how Abraham threw stones at a demon and drove it away, thereby overcoming temptation when he was tempted to disobey God's command to sacrifice his son.

17. The sacrifice recalls the time when God provided a substitute ram sacrifice in the place of Abraham's son. The great feast is a time where those who possess sufficient wealth offer a sacrifice of camel or sheep and then share the meat with poorer pilgrims. For three days the assembly eats, visits, and celebrates.

18. Molloy, *Experiencing the World's Religions*, 419.

19. The robe of Abraham consists of two pieces of white, seamless cloth. One piece is worn around the waist and lower body and the other piece covers the upper body and the left arm.

20. Molloy, *Experiencing the World's Religions*, 422–23.

21. Molloy, *Experiencing the World's Religions*, 44.

22. Neusch, *Sources of Modern Atheism*, 103.

23. Neusch, *Sources of Modern Atheism*, 33.

24. Neusch, *Sources of Modern Atheism*, 57.

25. Kaufmann, *Portable Nietzsche*.

26. Secularization is the process by which the social and cultural significance of religion in the central sectors of modern society, such as the worlds of science, technology, education, and politics are displaced, "making religious ideas less meaningful and religious institutions more marginal" (Guinness, *Gravedigger File*, 51). Secularization, then, marginalizes the social location of religion in two ways as it compounds secularism and constricts religion.

27. Privatization is "the process by which modernization produces a cleavage between the public world and the private spheres of life and focuses the private sphere as the special arena for the expansion of individual freedom and fulfillment" (Guinness, *Gravedigger File*, 74).

28. Pluralization is "the process by which the number of options in the private sphere of modern society rapidly multiplies at all levels, especially at the levels of worldviews, faiths, and ideologies" (Guinness, *Gravedigger File*, 93).

29. "The central sectors [science, technology, bureaucracy; most business, politics and education] are where the carriers of modernization are located" (Guinness, *Gravedigger File*, 65).

These central sectors are outside the sphere of influence of religion. Here is where you find faith most irrelevant.

30. Guinness, *Gravedigger File*, 73.

31. Berger, *Sacred Canopy*, 127.

32. Forell, *Proclamation of the Gospel*, 6.

33. Guinness, *Gravedigger File*, 26.

34. Hunter, *How to Reach Secular People*, 34.

35. Newbigin, *Truth to Tell*, 49.

36. "Darwin has convinced many that religion is an evolutionary phase, Marx that it is a sociological phenomenon, and Freud that it is a neurosis. Biblical authority for many has been undermined by biblical criticism. The comparative study of religions has tended to downgrade Christianity to one religion among many, and has encouraged the growth of syncretism. Existentialism severs our historical roots, insisting that nothing matters but the encounter and decision of the moment" (Stott, *Between Two Worlds*, 84).

37. The devil's aim is "to ensure that the church is shaped rather than shaping, reverting to the pattern of its culture rather than renewing its culture after the pattern of the Adversary [the living God]" (Guinness, *Gravedigger File*, 138).

38. Coram means "in the presence of."

39. "All the external, daily events which form the course of a man's life are guided by God and proceed from His will" (Wingren, *Luther On Vocation*, 71).

40. Althaus, *Theology of Martin Luther*, 166.

41. Althaus, *Theology of Martin Luther*, 111.

42. "[T]he Law binds not only the Jews but also the heathen, for it is the eternal and immutable decree of God concerning the worship of God and the love of one's neighbor. Moreover, God's decree has been written in the hearts of all men from the beginning of the world" (LW 3:84).

43. LW 1:164.

44. LW 1:169.

45. LW 4:52.

46. For the Law's "function and use is not only to disclose the sin and wrath of God but also to drive us to Christ" (LW 26:315).

47. LW 26:279–80.

48. LW 33:261.

49. LW 33:262.

50. LW 1:82.

51. LW 2:221–22.

52. "It happens naturally in the case of every sin that we stupidly try to escape God's wrath and yet cannot escape it. It is the utmost stupidity for us to imagine that our cure lies in the flight from God rather than in our return to God, and yet our sinful nature cannot return to God" (LW 1:173–74).

53. LW 1:173.

54. LW 1:178.

55. LW 1:277.

56. LW 1:193.

57. LW 1:193.

58. LW 1:191, author's emphasis.

59. Therefore Adam used "his wife's name as a means of finding comfort in the life which was to be restored through the promised Seed, who would crush the serpent's head and would slay the slayer himself" (LW 1:221).

60. LW 1:220.

61. LW 1:197.

62. LW 1:328.

63. LW 1:285.

64. LW 2:261.

65. LW 1:194.

66. There is a threefold progeny of Abraham revealed in the Scriptures. The first progeny is physical and is without the promise concerning Christ (Ishmael). The second is also physical, but with the promise concerning Christ (Isaac). The third is not physical, but is the offspring only of the promise who do not belong to the flesh of Abraham, but still hold fast to the faith and embrace the promise made to him that through this Promised Seed all the nations of the earth would be blessed (the nations). (See LW 4:25–28.)

67. "For we must have sure proof that He was in all truth the Son of Man, a natural man, and not a specter, not an apparition, as Manichaeus raved. Therefore we have His ancestors, who were true men. Nor can He be named without these fathers, without Abraham, Isaac, Jacob, and Adam, in order that He may have a definite lineage, a true father, a true mother, and that it may be certain that He is from a human seed and that He took upon Himself human nature, not the angels, not any other creature" (LW 5:228–29).

68. LW 2:261.

69. LW 4:160.

70. LW 4:157.

71. LW 4:171.

72. "For doing away with sin and death, blessing, and bestowing on men spiritual and eternal benefits are divine works and favors" (LW 4:173).

73. LW 4:171.

74. LW 4:173.

75. LW 5:19.

76. LW 5:219.

77. LW 5:218.

78. LW 5:220.

79. LW 7:13.

80. LW 7:15.

81. "Christ was truly born from true and natural flesh and human blood which was corrupted by original sin in Adam, but in such a way that it could be healed . . . [for] in the moment of the Virgin's conception the Holy Spirit purged and sanctified the sinful mass and wiped out the poison of . . . sin" (LW 7:12–13). "Therefore it is truly human nature no different from what it is in us. And Christ is the Son of Adam and of his seed and flesh, but . . . with the Holy Spirit overshadowing it, active in it, and purging it, in order that it might be fit for this

most innocent conception and the pure and holy birth by which we were to be purged and freed from sin" (LW 7:13).

82. LW 7:31.

83. LW 23:14.

84. "It is most certainly true that no one enters heaven but the Son of God and of Mary. He is the only one who knows the way. He does not keep this knowledge to Himself; otherwise He would have remained in heaven. No, He shows us the way by means of His dear Gospel, so that we will be born anew of water and of the Holy Spirit, adhere to His testimony, and believe in Him. And then we, too, will ascend into heaven, not by virtue of our own person but by nestling up and pressing close to Him who alone ascends into heaven" (LW 22:329–30).

85. LW 2:260–61.

86. Luther believed that Jerusalem was the very place where Adam, Abel, and Noah brought their sacrifices. Before the flood, Paradise was located in the region of Jerusalem and Adam lived there after he had been driven from Paradise. LW 5:243.

87. LW 5:252.

88. LW 5:243.

89. LW 1:180.

90. LW 1:249.

91. "For what benefit, then, was circumcision given? To make known that the Savior was to be born from this circumcised nation and not from the Gentiles. He who was desired by all the nations did not become incarnate among all nations; He became incarnate among this one people which had been commanded by God to be circumcised" (LW 3:91). "[F]or throughout all ages there had to be one definite family from which alone it would be believed Christ was to be born" (LW 3:111). In circumcision the nations would see this sign and "it would give them the opportunity to come to the knowledge of God" (LW 3:114).

92. LW 3:106–07.

93. LW 3:168.

94. LW 3:166.

95. LW 1:13.

96. LW 24:67.

97. LW 21:56.

98. "Lot lived in Sodom itself; Shem or Melchizedek lived in neighboring Jerusalem; Abraham lived in Mamre; and the others lived in other places, but those places were in the neighborhood" (LW 3:234).

99. "The heinous conduct of the people of Sodom is extraordinary, inasmuch as they departed from the natural passion and longing of the male for the female, which was implanted into nature by God, and desired what is altogether contrary to nature" (LW 3:255).

100. LW 3:238.

101. "God wants the destruction of Sodom by fire and that lake of asphalt to be conspicuous to this day and to be spoken of in sermons and made known among all posterity, in order that at least some may be reformed and may learn to fear God" (LW 3:222).

102. LW 5:39.

103. LW 30:248.

104. LW 3:125.

105. Luther limited the public preaching of the Word within the church to those who have been called by the community. "[J]ust because we are all in like manner priests, no one must put himself forward and undertake, without our consent and election, to do what is in the power of all of us. For what is common to all, no one dare take upon himself without the will and the command of the community" (Luther, *Works of Martin Luther*, 2:68).

106. Luther, *Works of Martin Luther*, 2:69.

107. Luther, *Works of Martin Luther*, 2:76.

108. LW 2:392.

109. Luther, *Works of Martin Luther*, 2:68.

110. Althaus, *Theology of Martin Luther*, 325.

111. "It is only before God, in heaven, that the individual stands alone. In the earthly realm man always stands in relation, always bound to another" (Wingren, *Luther On Vocation*, 5). "Each office represents the possibility of a channel of God's love to man" (Headley, *Luther's View of Church History*, 8).

112. Wingren, *Luther On Vocation*, 8.

113. Althaus, *Theology of Martin Luther*, 134.

114. Wingren, *Luther On Vocation*, 11.

115. Wingren, *Luther On Vocation*, 126.

116. Wingren, *Luther On Vocation*, 145.

117. Wingren, *Luther On Vocation*, 213.

118. Wingren, *Luther On Vocation*, 219.

119. "Every vocation has its setting in a particular place and deals with particular people of a definite time" (Wingren, *Luther On Vocation*, 155).

120. LW 3:128.

Chapter Six

1. Root metaphors are basic value-laden analogies used to describe worldviews. They pervade the whole culture and are expressed in social institutions, myths, and above all else, in rituals that deeply influence the beliefs, emotions, and actions of a society.

2. Hunsberger and Van Gelder, *Church Between Gospel and Culture*, 139–157.

3. Berger, *Homeless Mind*.

4. Newbigin, *Foolishness to the Greeks*, 31.

5. There are many voices in a pluralistic society that are spoken and heard that compete for societal dominance and control. Prominent in our day would be secularism, pessimistic existentialism, sentimental humanism, pragmatism, hedonism, relativism, Marxism, and Christianity.

6. The architectural styles of the modern era include Renaissance, mannerism, baroque, rococo and neo-classicism, expressionism, art nouveau, and the American industrial style.

7. Deconstruction arose in response to a theory in literature called structuralism. It rejects that structural premise that meaning is inherent in a text, but that meaning emerges only as the interpreter enters into dialogue with the text. Consequently, every interpreter is free to deconstruct the text and to refashion it according to personal preferences without anchorage in the text.

8. Newbigin, *Foolishness to the Greeks*, 16.

9. Newbigin, *Foolishness to the Greeks*, 35–36.

10. Newbigin, *Foolishness to the Greeks*, 19.

11. Newbigin, *Gospel in a Pluralist Society*, 27.

12. Newbigin, *Gospel in a Pluralist Society*, 27.

13. Polanyi, *Personal Knowledge*, 140.

14. Newbigin, *Gospel in a Pluralist Society*, 36.

15. Newbigin, *Gospel in a Pluralist Society*, 36–37.

16. One of the classic songs that has been written to express this individualistic spirit within our culture is "My Way." The builder generation had Frank Sinatra to sing it and the Baby Boomer generation had Elvis Presley to sing it. The song is about a man who is about to die, and as he faces the final curtain of human existence he gives his testimony, of which he is certain. Wherever he traveled, he planned each step and lived life his way. Even when life got difficult, when he had doubts and experienced his share of losing, he faced it all and did things his way. Another song that understands well the autonomous nature of each human being is a song by Billy Joel titled "My Life." The songwriter received a call from an old friend who left his traditional way of life and escaped to Los Angeles. He wanted his friends and family back home not to worry about him and to stop telling him to return to his past. He had established his own way of life; they were to go ahead with their own lives and leave him alone. Both songs illustrate that the only person that matters, and the only person you must answer to, is yourself.

17. Hunsberger and Van Gelder, *Church Between Gospel and Culture*, 149.

18. Newbigin, *Foolishness to the Greeks*, 28.

19. Money usurps the place of God in the modern world and is worshiped by nearly everyone.

20. Best and Kellner, *Postmodern Turn*, 47.

21. Schaeffer, *How Should We Then Live*, 211.

22. "By the 1920s, advertising had become a major social force, and films were celebrating affluence and consumer lifestyle, but the depression of the 1930s and World War II prevented the consumer society from developing. After the war, however, the consumer society took off as soldiers returned with money in their pockets to start families and to buy the new products offered and promoted on radio and television" (Best and Kellner, *Postmodern Turn*, 86).

23. Best and Kellner, *Postmodern Turn*, 89.

24. In modern society, life becomes an immense accumulation of spectacles—the consumption of images and commodities.

25. "For example, life in the suburbs was centered on consumption, and new shopping malls gathered together a diversity of department stores and specialty shops in an environment designed to promote consumption" (Best and Kellner, *Postmodern Turn*, 86).

26. In the imaginary world of sign value, one consumes the signs of power or prestige by driving a certain type of car or wearing designer clothes.

27. Therefore, when you buy a Mercedes, you also need to shop for tennis and golf clubs, an estate in an exclusive neighborhood, a good private school for your children, and a fashionable vacation spot.

28. Newbigin, *Foolishness to the Greeks*, 27.

29. National governments are widely assumed to be responsible for and capable of providing those things that former generations thought only God could provide—freedom from fear, hunger, disease, and want—in a word: happiness.

30. Newbigin, *Foolishness to the Greeks*, 117.

31. Newbigin, *Foolishness to the Greeks*, 27.

32. Adams, *Challenges of American Civil Religion*, 23.

33. In our day, "civil religion has come to serve the following four functions: (1) securing the blessings of God for the state and/or society, (2) contributing to the coherence of the society by establishing a fundamental aspect of the identity that connects the individual to the community, (3) providing the society with a unifying rallying point in times of national crisis, and (4) providing a least-common denominator for the national ideological and moral discourse" (Adams, *Challenges of American Civil Religion*, 22).

34. Adams, *Challenges of American Civil Religion*, 22.

35. Adams, *Challenges of American Civil Religion*, 22–23.

36. Adams, *Challenges of American Civil Religion*, 24.

37. LW 1:109.

38. Coiner, *Secret of God's Plan*, 263.

39. Coiner, *Secret of God's Plan*, 263.

40. Coiner, *Secret of God's Plan*, 264.

41. Coiner, *Secret of God's Plan*, 264.

42. Coiner, *Secret of God's Plan*, 265.

43. Coiner, *Secret of God's Plan*, 268.

44. Coiner, *Secret of God's Plan*, 269–70.

45. "Key postmodern theorists argue that contemporary societies, with their new technologies, novel forms of culture and experience, and striking economic, social, and political transformations, constitute a decisive rupture with previous ways of life, bringing an end to the modern era" (Best and Kellner, *Postmodern Turn*, viii).

46. "A new 'postFordist' society in which the modern, Fordist form of capitalist society, marked by mass production and consumption, state regulation of the economy, and a homogeneous mass culture, is being replaced by 'more flexible' modes of sociopolitical and economic organization" (Best and Kellner, *Postmodern Turn*, 13).

47. Best and Kellner, *Postmodern Turn*, 18.

48. Grenz, *Primer on Postmodernism*, 3.

49. Grenz, *Primer on Postmodernism*, 3.

50. Grenz, *Primer on Postmodernism*, 3.

51. Epistemology is the study of the origin, nature, methods, and limits of knowledge. Epistemological assumptions deal with those statements made about the origin and nature of knowledge that we take for granted.

52. Best and Kellner, *Postmodern Turn*, ix.

53. "The counterculture believed that it was creating an entirely new society and culture, based on a new set of values, sensibilities, consciousness, culture, and institutions, which produced a rupture with mainstream, or 'establishment,' society." Best and Kellner, *Postmodern Turn*, 5).

54. "These theorists believed that significant changes were occurring in history with the advent of new social movements opposing the Vietnam War, imperialism, racism, sexism, and capitalist societies in their entirety, demanding revolution and an entirely new social order" (Best and Kellner, *Postmodern Turn*, 4).

55. Best and Kellner, *Postmodern Turn*, 8.

56. Best and Kellner, *Postmodern Turn*, 6.

57. The foundations of national and political stability in Europe continued to weaken when the Communist revolution of 1917 took place, followed by the gradual disintegration of the British, French, Belgian, and Dutch empires.

58. Best and Kellner, *Postmodern Turn*, 7.

59. Best and Kellner, *Postmodern Turn*, 6–7.

60. William Barrett, *Irrational Man*, 65.

61. Grenz, *Primer on Postmodernism*, 52.

62. Grenz, *Primer on Postmodernism*, 53.

63. Allen, *Christian Belief in a Postmodern World*, 2.

64. Oden, *After-Modern Evangelical Spirituality*, 19.

65. A metanarrative is the big story that claims to be able to make sense of and explain all of the lesser and local narratives.

66. Lyotard, *Postmodern Condition*, xxiv.

67. Dockery, *Challenge of Postmodernism*, 132.

68. The time span of modernity is "this precise 200-year period between 1789 and 1989, between the French Revolution and the collapse of communism." Dockery, *Challenge of Postmodernism*, 23.

69. Best and Kellner, *Postmodern Turn*, 24.

70. Best and Kellner, *Postmodern Turn*, 25.

71. Best and Kellner, *Postmodern Turn*, 26.

72. A traditional reader of any given text believes that language is capable of expressing ideas that reflect reality, and that the author of a text is the source of its meaning. Derrida, in his deconstructive style of reading, challenges the idea that a text has an unchanging, unified meaning. There is no meaning in the literary texts, only the subjectivity of the reader. The goal is no longer to understand what the author is saying but rather what we readers are saying to the text. Thus there is no text; there are only readers.

73. Dockery, *Challenge of Postmodernism*, 78–79.

74. Dockery, *Challenge of Postmodernism*, 79.

75. Dockery, *Challenge of Postmodernism*, 13.

76. Therapists can help individuals become autonomous by affirming over and over again that they are worthy of acceptance just the way they are, and by teaching the client "to be independent of anyone else's standards" (Bellah, *Habits of the Heart*, 99).

77. Schaeffer, *Death in the City*, 211.

78. Myers, *All God's Children and Blue Suede Shoes*, 118.

79. Postindustrialism, postFordism, postMarxism, posthumanism, posthistory and postmodernism.

Chapter Seven

1. Newbigin, *Foolishness to the Greeks*, 3.

2. Henry, *Twilight of a Great Civilization*, ix.

3. Schaeffer, *Great Evangelical Disaster*, 315–316.

4. "Here we have world spirit of the age—autonomous man setting himself up as God, in defiance of the knowledge and the moral and spiritual truth which God has given. Here is the reason why we have a moral breakdown in every area of life" (Schaeffer, *Great Evangelical Disaster*, 309–10).

5. Schaeffer, *Great Evangelical Disaster*, 310.

6. "Modern pessimism and modern fragmentation have spread in three different ways to people of our culture and to people across the world. Geographically, it spread from the European mainland to England, after a time jumping the Atlantic to the United States. Culturally, it spread in the various disciplines from philosophy, to art, to music, to general culture, and to theology. Socially, it spread from the intellectuals to the educated and then through the mass media to everyone" (Schaeffer, *How Should We Then Live*, 195).

7. Schaeffer, *How Should We Then Live*, 204.

8. Schaeffer, *Great Evangelical Disaster*, 312.

9. Newbigin, *Foolishness to the Greeks*, 3.

10. LW 33:65.

11. Wells, *No Place for Truth*, 24.

12. Mead, *Once and Future Church*, 2.

13. "In contrast with the Renaissance humanists, the Reformers refused to accept the autonomy of human reason, which acts as though the human mind is infinite, with all knowledge within its realm. Rather, they took seriously the Bible's own claim for itself—that it is the final authority [in all matters]" (Schaeffer, *How Should We Then Live*, 121).

14. The Reformation "not only brought forth a clear preaching of the Gospel, it also gave shape to society as a whole—including government, how people viewed the world, and the full spectrum of culture" (Schaeffer, *Great Evangelical Disaster*, 309).

15. "There can be no coercive proof that those who believe are right. If there could be, revelation would be unnecessary" (Newbigin, *Gospel in a Pluralist Society*, 92).

16. Luther's method of understanding and acquiring a biblical view of reality possessed three elements: *Oratio, Meditatio, Tentatio*. See LW 34:285–86.

17. Sire, *Universe Next Door*, 15.

18. Schaeffer, *How Should We Then Live*, 254.

19. FC, Epitome, Rule and Norm (Tappert, 465).

20. Guinness, *Gravedigger File*, 161.

21. Guinness, *Gravedigger File*, 221.

22. Schaeffer, *Pollution and the Death of Man*, 22.

23. Schaeffer, *God Who Is There*, 152.

24. "If a person is to really communicate with a people, he must learn another language—that of the thought-forms of the people to whom he speaks. . . . Every generation of Christians has the problem of learning how to speak meaningfully to its own age" (Schaeffer, *Escape from Reason*, 207).

25. Schaeffer, *God Who Is There*, 153.

26. Newbigin, *Gospel in a Pluralist Society*, 220.

27. Newbigin, *Gospel in a Pluralist Society*, 10.

28. Newbigin, *Gospel in a Pluralist Society*, 96.

29. Newbigin, *Gospel in a Pluralist Society*, 9.

30. Newbigin, *Gospel in a Pluralist Society*, 107.

31. "We are called to bring our faith into the public arena, to publish it, to put it to risk in the encounter with other faiths and ideologies in open debate and argument" (Newbigin, *Truth to Tell*, 59–60).

32. Newbigin, *Gospel in a Pluralist Society*, 107.

33. Schaeffer, *God Who Is There*, 132.

34. For example, we have an ordered universe that arises out of random chance; we have spontaneous generation of life from nonlife; we have human personality from an impersonal big bang beginning.

35. Schaeffer, *God Who Is There*, 140.

36. Schaeffer, *God Who Is There*, 140.

37. Schaeffer, *God Who Is There*, 141.

38. Schaeffer, *God Who Is There*, 142.

39. Newbigin, *Gospel in a Pluralist Society*, 18–19.

40. "You cannot criticize a statement of what claims to be the truth except on the basis of some other truth-claims which you accept without criticism" (Newbigin, *Truth to Tell*, 29).

41. Newbigin, *Other Side of 1984*, 27.

42. Schaeffer, *God Who Is There*, 184.

43. Schaeffer, *God Who Is There*, 11.

44. Schaeffer, *God Who Is There*, 47.

45. Schaeffer, *Pollution and the Death of Man*, 15.

46. "The secret [of mankind's salvation and its Savior] is communicated through happenings in the course of history of one nation, Israel" (Newbigin, *Gospel in a Pluralist Society*, 93).

47. Newbigin, *Gospel in a Pluralist Society*, 89.

48. Newbigin, *Gospel in a Pluralist Society*, 92.

49. Stott, *Between Two Worlds*, 137–138.

50. Stott, *Between Two Worlds*, 139.

51. Stott, *Between Two Worlds*, 149.

52. Stott, *Between Two Worlds*, 180.

53. "First of all, my division from God is healed by justification, but then there must be the 'existential reality' of this moment by moment. Second, there is the psychological division from himself. Third, the sociological divisions of man from other men. And last, the division of man from nature, and nature from nature" (Schaeffer, *Pollution and the Death of Man*, 39).

54. Schaeffer, *Pollution and the Death of Man*, 47–48.

55. "Worlds which are only apart physically may be light years apart morally or spiritually. A person's life can therefore come to resemble a non-stop process of commuting between almost completely separate, even segregated, worlds" (Guinness, *Gravedigger File*, 80).

56. Mead, *Once and Future Church*, 29.

57. Mead, *Once and Future Church*, 44–46.

58. "Love one another with brotherly affection" (Romans 12:10). "Therefore welcome one another as Christ has accepted you, for the glory of God" (Romans 15:7). "Through love serve one another" (Galatians 5:13). "Bear each other's burdens, and so fulfill the law of

Christ" (Galatians 6:2). "With patience, bearing with one another in love" (Ephesians 4:2). "As the Lord has forgiven you, you also must forgive" (Colossians 3:13). "Therefore confess your sins to one another and pray for one another" (James 5:16). "Love one another earnestly from a pure heart" (1 Peter 1:22).

59. Coiner, *Secret of God's Plan*, 261.

60. Coiner, *Secret of God's Plan*, 261.

61. Coiner, *Secret of God's Plan*, 261.

62. Richardson, *Bible in the Age of Science*, 126–27.

63. Richardson, *Bible in the Age of Science*, 127.

64. Richardson, *Bible in the Age of Science*, 127.

65. Babin, *New Era in Religious Communication*.

66. Henry, *Toward A Recovery of Christian Belief*, 68.

67. To create communicational impact, God takes the initiative. This was evidenced in the Garden of Eden when Adam and Eve rebelled. From the biblical point of view, God always begins the conversation and He begins this conversation through His sent people. He has told us to go, and keep on going, to the nations to make disciples of the nations. As we go, He is with us to the very end of the age.

   In contextualization, the communicator takes the initiative and moves into the receptor's frame of reference. The idea of contextualization is to frame the Gospel message in language and communication forms that are appropriate and meaningful to the target culture, and to focus the message upon the crucial issues in the lives of the people.

68. The communicator knows both the biblical Word and the pagan world so that the proper bridges might be discerned and constructed from the biblical world (apostolic message) into the real world (contextualization).

   The communicator preaches two sermons. The first sermon is the preaching of the Law so that the sinner might come to a condemning and convicting knowledge of his sin. The second sermon is the preaching of the Good News of God's grace, the Gospel, so that a person is saved by grace through faith in Jesus Christ.

69. The communicator accords to the Word of God its rightful primacy, that is, its power to penetrate every culture and speak within each culture, in its own speech and symbol, the Word that is both judgment and grace.

   The communicator speaks to the heart of the receptor since the heart is the place of ultimate allegiance.

70. No one can say that Jesus is Lord except by the power of the Holy Spirit (1 Corinthians 12:3; John 3:6). As God comes to us in His Word and sacraments, He deals with us in a twofold manner: first outwardly, then inwardly. He draws us outwardly through Christ's Word and the Gospel, and inwardly through the Holy Spirit.

71. The receptor's specific culture will determine the language and manner in which the Gospel should be communicated, and also the patterns in which one's new life in Christ is nurtured and exercised. The communicator also recognizes that every human being has, anthropologically speaking, two identities—one as a member of the human race and the other as a member of a specific culture.

72. The communicator realizes that one's credibility is an integral part of the communication process; in other words, the messenger is not separable from the message. The fundamental element in culture is language. The Gospel comes to any human community in the words of a particular language.

   The communicator seeks to interpret the Word in the thought forms, spirituality, philosophy, and idioms of the receptor culture; that is, the communicator moves into the cultural and linguistic water in which we are immersed in order to make contact.

73. The communicator seeks to communicate within the receptor's frame of reference; his culture, language, space, and time. He is careful to make every effort to meet his receptors where they are and to understand, empathize, and identify with the receptor. He is primarily oriented toward getting the message into the mind and heart of the receptor.

74. The communicator seeks to reproduce, in the receptor's language, the closest natural equivalent of the source-language message, both in terms of meaning and style. He affirms that if the Gospel is to be understood, if it is to be received as something that communicates truth about the real human situation, if it is to "make sense," it has to be clothed in symbols that are meaningful to them.

75. It is the task of the communicator to so present this new message within the receptor's frame of reference so that the receptor can interact with it thoroughly enough to produce constructive new understandings within his head.

The communicator seeks to make such an impression that the receptors respond by becoming involved in those things communicated to them.

76. God continues to tabernacle the face of the earth through His "possessed people." Every believer is God's dwelling place in which His Spirit resides (1 Corinthians 3:16; 6:19). The believer has been bought with a price and has been set apart for His presence and activity alone.

His people are His instruments sent to go and walk among the nations of the world so that they might hear of Him and believe in the Word of Life. Wherever He sends us, we are to actively communicate His name and be as living letters of the Holy Spirit.

Chapter Eight

1. LW 22:154.
2. LW 22:56–57.
3. LW 22:330.
4. LW 1:80.
5. LW 1:82.
6. LW 1:95.
7. LW 1:106.
8. LW 1:109.
9. LW 1:154.
10. "It is as if Satan were saying: 'Surely you are very silly if you think that God did not want you to eat from this tree, you whom He appointed lords over all the trees of Paradise. In fact, He created the trees on your account. How can He, who favored you with all these things, be so envious as to withhold from you the fruits of this one single tree, which are so delightful and lovely?'" In this temptation, "Satan is seeking to deprive [Adam and Eve] of the Word and knowledge of God that they may reach the conclusion: 'This is not the will of God; God does not command this'" (LW 1:152).
11. LW 1:146.
12. LW 1:147.
13. LW 1:181.
14. LW 1:186.
15. LW 1:249.

16. LW 2:163–64.

17. LW 1:284.

18. LW 2:197.

19. LW 1:258–59.

20. LW 3:106.

21. LW 1:325.

22. LW 1:328.

23. LW 2:214.

24. LW 2:229.

25. In the ministry of the Word, God came to His people through the instrumentality of men and angels. When God confronted Adam with his sin, Luther was pleased with the suggestion that God spoke through an angel. Through his chronology of the Old Testament, Luther was always able to find a patriarch alive who could speak for God in His place. For example, Adam confronted Cain with the sin of killing his brother as he spoke for God. Methuselah spoke to Noah to enter the ark. Abraham was called by God through Shem to leave Ur and go to the promised land. (See LW: Companion Volume, 103–05.)

26. "[I]f you desire to be saved, abandon that land, abandon your kindred, abandon the house of your father. Go away as far as possible from those idolaters" (LW 2:250).

27. LW 2:247.

28. LW 8:217.

29. LW 3:227.

30. LW 4:31.

31. LW 5:244.

32. LW 5:247.

33. "Throughout the world the house of God and the gate of heaven is wherever there is the pure teaching of the Word together with the sacraments" (LW 5:247).

34. LW 5:248.

35. LW 5:248.

36. LW 1:249.

37. LW 3:108.

38. LW 1:147–48.

39. LW 1:15.

40. LW 5:246.

41. LW 4:133.

42. Bente, *Historical Introductions*, 14.

43. LW 2:48.

44. LW 3:110.

45. "Christ must be sought where He has manifested Himself and wants to be known, as in the Word, in Baptism, and in the Supper; there He is certainly found, for the Word cannot deceive us. But it generally happens that reason disregards those signs and turns aside to the harlot sitting at the gate" (LW 3:108).

46. LW 3:108.

47. LW 22:67.

48. LW 3:108–09.

49. LW 4:236–37.

50. LW 30:267.

51. LW 3:108–09.

52. Tappert, *The Book of Concord*, 315.

53. LW 39:xii.

54. LW 39:305.

55. This evangelical Church is the true, ancient Church because its essence is the same as the ancient, apostolic Church as evidenced in Baptism, the Lord's Supper, the Keys, Preaching office, Apostles' Creed, Lord's Prayer, temporal authority being honored, marriage being honored and praised, Christian suffering, bearing the cross, and praying for others. See LW 41:193–96.

56. LW 41:207.

57. LW 41:148.

58. LW 8:200.

59. LW 8:201.

60. LW 8:201.

61. LW 8:201.

62. LW 8:204.

63. LW 8:202.

64. LW 8:202, author's emphasis.

65. LW 3:139.

66. God "wanted us to follow His Word and command, not to inquire with inordinate diligence into the reasons for His commands. When Adam and Eve do this, they perish; for they put themselves in the place of God the Creator and forget that they are creatures" (LW 3:139).

67. LW 4:144.

68. Abraham exhibited a perfect act of obedience as he puts his faith into practice in circumcision. This example teaches that "before God we must again become children and not argue about how or why God gives us a particular command, but that we must simply hold fast to what God has commanded and obey." It is enough for Abraham to know that it pleases God to have him do this. LW 3:171.

69. LW 3:282.

70. LW 3:173.

71. LW 3:173.

72. LW 4:109.

73. LW 3:172–73.

74. LW 3:24.

75. LW 3:25.

76. LW 3:20.

77. Luther, in his definition of faith, speaks of notitia, assensus, and fiducia. First of all, there can be no faith in a vacuum. We cannot believe in things which we do not know; therefore,

faith assumes knowledge (*notitia*). Second, it is not enough for a person to know about Jesus but he must assent to the truth about who He is, why He came into the world, and what He has done to effect salvation (*assensus*). Finally, a person must believe and trust in Jesus for one's salvation; Jesus Christ is my Savior (*fiducia*).

78. "The outstanding example of [faith] is the Canaanite woman in Matt. 15:22–28, who is very well exercised in the speculative life and who presses on in such a manner that she does not allow herself to be repelled by any words, however harsh. She knocks at and pounds the door so long until Christ is compelled to yield and listen to her and to praise her faith and perseverance" (LW 6:262).

79. LW 6:139–40.

80. "For from early youth and ever since [Jacob] received the blessing, he was disciplined in various ways. He left his father's house because he feared his angry brother Esau, and he lived in exile for 20 whole years. In exile he endured the harshest servitude under his godless and greedy father-in-law Laban. Furthermore, Bilhah, his wife, and Dinah, his daughter, were ravished, and Rachel died. Finally his dearly beloved son was sold and carried off to Egypt" (LW 8:92).

81. LW 6:305.

82. "But God's winsome face must be recognized in His promises, in the sacraments, and likewise in external blessings and gifts, in a gracious prince, a neighbor, a father, and a mother. When I see that the face of my parents is gracious, I see at the same time the winsome face of God smiling at me. As Jacob had previously said that he had seen the Lord face to face, he now discerns the same face of GOD in the face of his brother Esau, for he sees the good pleasure of God's will in the goodwill and favor of his brother. In the same manner, the face of God shines forth in all His creatures because they are works of God and testimonies of God's will and presence" (LW 6:173).

83. LW 6:151.

84. LW 6:327.

85. LW 7:228.

86. LW 7:55.

87. LW 7:56.

88. LW 7:55.

89. LW 7:56.

90. "Joseph himself, in great part, was a spectator of the life of his father in Syria and later of his afflictions in connection with the defilement of Dinah, the slaughter of the Shechemites, and the incest of Reuben. He saw the tears and sobs of his father" (LW 7:125).

91. LW 7:125.

92. LW 7:100.

93. LW 7:104.

94. Jacob thought that he had lost his son "But God replies: 'He has not been lost or destroyed; but I am using him as an ambassador to Egypt for the salvation not only of his father, his brothers, and his domestics but also of the whole kingdom and of all lands, and in such a way that it is not only a physical but also a spiritual salvation, so that he may instruct the king, the princes, and the people in faith and in the knowledge of God' " (LW 8:35).

95. LW 7:136.

96. LW 7:128.

97. LW 7:105–06.
98. LW 3:71–72.
99. LW 7:133.
100. LW 6:152.
101. LW 7:174.
102. LW 7:232.
103. LW 7:233.
104. LW 6:327.
105. LW 8:7.
106. LW 5:55.
107. LW 4:73.
108. LW 6:180.
109. LW 8:79.
110. LW 6:152.
111. LW 4:132.
112. For "Wherever that Word is heard, where Baptism, the Sacrament of the Altar, and absolution are administered, there you must determine and conclude with certainty: 'There is surely God's house; here heaven has been opened.'" (LW 5:244).
113. "For he who is not a 'Crosstian,' so to speak, is not a Christian; for he is not like Christ, his Teacher" (LW 5:274).
114. Bornkamm, *Luther's World of Thought*, 145.

Conclusion

1. All men have the general knowledge that there is a God, that He created heaven and earth, that He is just, and that He punishes the wicked. But what God thinks of us, what His will is toward us, what He will give, or what He will do that we may be saved from sin and death, they do not know. Instead of the true God, they worship the dreams of their own hearts.
2. Those that trust in their own strength and righteousness do serve a god, but they serve a god that they themselves have devised and not the true God. They think of God in terms of their own reason and not in terms of the Word of God. Therefore, "all the children of Adam are idolaters, for they try by some means or another to 'take God captive' or 'to bewitch God' as if He could conform to their ideas or be subservient to their interests" (Watson, *Let God be God*, 90).
3. The sign of the false believer is that he always believes himself to be saved by his own works. He reasons that if he does this work, God will have mercy on him; if he does not, He will be angry.
4. Köberle, *Quest for Holiness*, 3.
5. Köberle, *Quest for Holiness*, 6.
6. Two other examples would be the Chinese Tao-mystic and the Persian Surfist.
7. Köberle, *Quest for Holiness*, 8.
8. Köberle, *Quest for Holiness*, 11.
9. Köberle, *Quest for Holiness*, 13.
10. Anderson, *Christianity and World Religions*, 100.

11. Anderson, *Christianity and World Religions*, 102.

12. Anderson, *Christianity and World Religions*, 101.

13. They devise their saving formula according to their unregenerate will and reason.

14. Their religious formula does not find its source in God, but in their own reasoning. In that respect, it is a voluntary religion since God does not ask for these things to be done, but they are devised by a reason that is not enlightened by the Holy Spirit or revealed as pleasing in God's sight.

15. The proper office of an apostle is to set forth the glory and benefit of Christ as the world's only mediator and savior, and to raise up and comfort troubled and afflicted consciences through the forgiveness of sins.

16. "Since therefore the children share in flesh and blood, He Himself likewise partook of the same things, that through death He might destroy the one who has the power of death, that is, the devil, and deliver all those who through fear of death were subject to lifelong slavery. For surely it is not angels that He helps, but He helps the offspring of Abraham. Therefore He had to be made like His brothers in every respect, so that He might become a merciful and faithful high priest in the service of God, to make propitiation for the sins of the people" (Hebrews 2:14–17).

17. "For it was indeed fitting that we should have such a high priest, holy, innocent, unstained, separated from sinners, and exalted above the heavens. He has no need, like those high priests, to offer sacrifices daily, first for His own sins and then for those of the people, since He did this once for all when He offered up Himself" (Hebrews 7:26–27). "But when Christ had offered for all time a single sacrifice for sins, He sat down at the right hand of God, waiting from that time until His enemies should be made a footstool for His feet. For by a single offering He had perfected for all time those who are being sanctified. . . . Where there is forgiveness of these, there is no longer any offering for sin" (Hebrews 10:12–14, 18).

18. "For in Him all the fullness of God was pleased to dwell, and through Him to reconcile to Himself all things, whether on earth or in heaven, making peace by the blood of His cross. And you, who once were alienated and hostile in mind, doing evil deeds, He has now reconciled in His body of flesh by His death, in order to present you holy and blameless and above reproach before Him" (Colossians 1:19–22).

19. "Now it is evident that no one is justified before God by the law, for 'The righteous shall live by faith.' But the law is not of faith, rather 'The one who does them shall live by them.' Christ redeemed us from the curse of the law by becoming a curse for us" (Galatians 3:11–13a).

20 "Therefore, since we have been justified by faith, we have peace with God through our Lord Jesus Christ" (Romans 5:1). "But now in Christ Jesus you who once were far off have been brought near by the blood of Christ. For He Himself is our peace, who has made us both one and has broken down in His flesh the dividing wall of hostility by abolishing the law of commandments and ordinances, that He might create in Himself one new man in place of the two, so making peace, and might reconcile us both to God in one body through the cross, thereby killing the hostility. And He came and preached peace to you who were far off and peace to those who were near. For through Him we both have access in one Spirit to the Father. So then you are no longer strangers and aliens, but you are fellow citizens with the saints and members of the household of God, built on the foundation of the apostles and prophets, Christ Jesus Himself being the cornerstone, in whom the whole structure, being joined together, grows into a holy temple in the Lord. In Him you also are being built together into a dwelling place for God by the Spirit" (Ephesians 2:13–22).

21. "For our sake He made Him to be sin who knew no sin, so that in Him we might become the righteousness of God" (2 Corinthians 5:21).

22. "But when the fullness of time had come, God sent forth His Son, born of woman, born under the law, to redeem those who were under the law, so that we might receive adoption as sons" (Galatians 4:4–5).

23. "My little children, I am writing these things to you so that you may not sin. But if anyone does sin, we have an advocate with the Father, Jesus Christ the righteous. He is the propitiation for our sins, and not for ours only but also for the sins of the whole world" (1 John 2:1–2).

24. It is the work of a mediator to pacify the party that is offended and to reconcile God to those who have offended Him because of their sins and unbelief. That mediator is Jesus Christ, who did not change the Law, but who set Himself against the wrath of the Law and took it away and satisfied it in His own body. We, every person who has ever lived, are the offenders and God is the One who is offended. God cannot pardon these offenses and neither can we make satisfaction for them. Therefore, there is separation and discord between God and us. God cannot revoke the Law but He will have it observed. We, who have transgressed the Law, cannot fly from the presence of God, so God, in His mercy, sent Christ as mediator between He and us and accomplished our reconciliation.

25. It is the saving work of Christ to pacify God, to make intercession for sinners, to offer up Himself as a sacrifice for the sins of the whole world, and to redeem, instruct, and comfort sinners.

26. They believed in Christ who should be revealed as we believe in Christ who is revealed, and they were saved by Him, as we are also.

27. "For God has decreed that no one can or will believe or receive the Holy Spirit without that Gospel which is preached or taught by word of mouth" (LW 22:54).